# Jaguar
## A Living Legend

# Jaguar
## A Living Legend

Anders Ditlev Clausager

CHARTWELL
BOOKS, INC.

This edition first published in the USA by Chartwell Books Inc. a Division of Book Sales Inc. 110 Enterprise Avenue Secaucus, New Jersey 07094

ISBN 1-55521-334-0

Printed in Italy

**Photographic Acknowledgments**
All photographs supplied by Neill Bruce with the exception of:
Allsport: 154, 157, 158, 162, 163, 172 tl, tr, c, bl and br, 174, 175 t and b, 178 r and l, 179 tl, tr, c and b, 180 t and b, 181.
Jaguar: 6, 8, 9, 10/11, 12, 16/17, 22/23, 32 t, 40, 41, 44 t, 45, 48, 49, 50, 51 t and b, 64, 65, 77, 78 t and b, 79, 82/83, 86/87, 98/99, 105, 126 t, 130, 135, 143 b, 144, 145, 146 t, 187 t and b, 189, 196.
Peter Roberts/Neill Bruce: 19, 44 bl and br, 61 b.
Quadrant Picture Library: 159, 160/161, 161 inset, 164, 169, 170, 171 l and r.

The author and publishers would like to thank all the staff at Jaguar plc for their help. Neill Bruce would like to thank Nigel Dawes and the Midland Motor Museum.

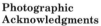

# Contents

Announcing the 1933
SWALLOW
HORNET

•

1932 has given ample evidence of the popularity of Swallow Hornets. Now we are proud to introduce their 1933 successors—even more beautiful—with added refinements — and definite improvements.

Pictured below is the sparkling two-seater priced at . . . £255

SWALLOW COACHBUILDING CO. LTD. FOLESHILL, COVENTRY (Coventry 8027).

SWALLOW HORNET

# INTRODUCTION

Once, the City of Coventry could have been described as the British equivalent of Detroit, the nearest Great Britain came to having a 'Motor Town'. Coventry's prosperity was originally based on the textile and wool trades. With increasing competition from abroad during the 19th century, Coventry turned to alternative forms of light industry — the manufacture of clocks, sewing machines, and bicycles. James Starley, father of the British cycle trade, started up his business in Coventry, and the cycle-making industry flourished in the closing decades of the 19th century. It was therefore no accident that Coventry had a head start in the motor industry. The pool of skilled labour, and the existence of machine shops and other facilities invaluable to a developing industry, combined to attract inventors, businessmen and even a few cranks — all of whom shared the vision of a motorized future.

Chief among them was the notorious promoter H. J. Lawson who started to make motorcars in a disused textile mill by the Coventry canal in 1896. It was his policy to acquire patents and manufacturing rights to foreign cars, and his interests included many eminently forgettable names. But his partnership with F. R. Simms, who held the British rights to the German Daimler engines, resulted in the appearance of the first British Daimler cars. These were the first British cars to be made, and sold, in any quantity. Where many others fell by the wayside, the Daimler company survived and was for many years the spiritual leader of the motor industry in Coventry, if not the entire British industry.

*Opposite page:*
An advertisement for the 1933 Swallow Hornet.

The first four decades of the 20th century were the growth years for the motor industry, and for Coventry. By the 1930s Coventry contributed a substantial proportion of the British motor industry's output. Two of the 'Big Six' companies had their main factories here — Standard and the Rootes Group, both outstanding success stories of the time. There was an incredible variety of small and medium-sized car makers proliferating in and around the city. Anyone shopping for a car in Coventry could pick from small 8 or 10 hp family saloons, to the vast 12-cylinder limousines that Daimler built for Royalty, encompassing every imaginable type of car in between. Even the 1930s depression had less effect in Coventry than, for instance, in the North of England. After a small setback in 1931, car production in Britain continued to grow in an effort to satisfy the ever-increasing demand. By 1939 Coventry still manufactured 14 different makes of motorcar, produced by 11 different companies, and the city also housed any number of component manufacturers and suppliers. While no individual Coventry car maker could hope to challenge the dominant position of giants such as Austin, Morris or Ford in the popular market, between them they offered a seemingly endless variety in the profitable market for medium-sized quality cars. Then as now, two names stood out from the rest — Rover and Jaguar.

With the outbreak of the Second World War, Coventry's motor industry became an important part of Britain's war machine. Polished cellulose and chromium plating gave way to uniformly drab khaki as military vehicles ousted private

cars from the assembly lines. Coventry produced guns, aircraft and all the other paraphernalia of war, and its car makers set up shadow factories to boost wartime production. Inevitably, the city became a prime target for the German bomber command in the Blitz of 1940. More devastation in a limited area was wrought here than anywhere else in the country. Not only did the industry suffer from the effects of high explosives, but the entire city centre was changed irrevocably with the destruction of the ancient cathedral and many other historic buildings. Adolf Hitler added a new verb to the German language — 'Coventriren', meaning to destroy totally. In spite of everything, Coventry's inhabitants had a grim determination and will to survive.

After 1945 there was another boom for the motor industry. Britain was a debtor nation, and rose magnificently to the challenge of exporting goods worldwide. Coventry rebuilt its factories and houses, created a new city centre around a magnificent new cathedral, and saw most of its new cars depart towards export markets. The city and its inhabitants were as motor-minded, prosperous — and as brash — as ever. But gradually, the British motor industry went into decline. Export sales dwindled in the face of competition from Europe and later Japan, and even the home market was invaded by thousands of foreign cars. Many of the small specialist manufacturers relinquished the unequal struggle for survival, and even the big mass producers began to amalgamate and contract. The two biggest car manufacturers in Coventry, Standard and Rootes, were among the first to feel the chill wind of change. Both suffered takeovers in the 1960s. The story of Coventry's motor industry in the last 35 years is a sad one, with once-famous names disappearing for ever.

Many are found in the Museum of British Road Transport in the centre of Coventry. Here, silent but well-polished specimens stand wing to wing in neat rows, lined up as for a roll-call, or waiting perhaps for the final trumpet before bursting into life again. Alvis, Armstrong-Siddeley, Hillman, Humber, Lanchester, Lea-Francis, Riley, Singer, Standard, Sunbeam-Talbot and Triumph are but some of the names from Coventry's past found in this museum, bearing mute testimony to the misfortunes of the British motor industry. Shrine, or a collection of curiosities? It all depends on your point of view.

Coventry today is coming out of another recession. We are told that the recession of the 1970s and 1980s was not as severe as that of 50 years before, yet its effects on Coventry and the motor industry were far more devastating than those of its predecessor. The city still houses three car manufacturers, but of these, the Rover Group merely maintains administrative and other functions in the old Standard-Triumph factory at Canley and along the by-pass; the last car was made here in 1980. On the eastern outskirts, in the wartime Rootes shadow factory at Ryton, now owned by the French Peugeot company, there is quiet confidence that the corner has been turned. This optimism is supported by the growing number of British-built — if French-designed — family hatchbacks and saloons which leave the factory daily. But the new management has turned its back firmly on the troubled and turbulent past of the Rootes group.

The third company is Jaguar, with factories in Browns Lane at Allesley to the north-west of the city, at Radford near the site of Lawson's original 'Motor Mill' of 1896, and with the new showpiece engineering and design centre at Whitley to the east. Here perhaps lies the real hope for a continuation of Coventry's traditions in car manufacture. Here is a company which is in tune with the present and able to face up to the future, without losing sight of the past. Indeed, the traditions of 60 years are vitally important building blocks for Jaguar's future.

Therefore, the motor museum that one finds at Browns Lane is of a different kind. Jaguar's own splendid Jaguar Daimler Heritage Trust collection embraces almost 50 examples of these makes, many of which are displayed to advantage in the company's recently refurbished showroom. The collection is frequently added to with new — or not so new — exhibits, and it is maintained in a spirit which reflects the pride everyone in the company takes in their corporate heritage. This is very much a living collection, with most vehicles in full working order. Sir John Egan himself can usually be seen at the wheel of a veteran Daimler in the annual London to Brighton run, and equally unsurprising are the regular demonstrations of historic racing Jaguars at Silverstone, Le Mans and elsewhere. The collection is a microcosm of the history of Britain's motor industry; even if Jaguar is a relative newcomer, Daimler was there from the start.

These cars bring to life the history of some of Britain's most legendary marques. However if the classic machinery is not sufficient documentation of the company's history, it is reassuring to know that Jaguar also preserve an incomparable collection of records in their archive — a unique

*Opposite page:*
The assembly line at Browns Lane.

source of reference material for the historian. Happily, the company's enlightened approach to public relations ensures that rather than being tucked away in dusty vaults, information is readily available to the researcher, regardless of whether it is merely a question of finding out the original colour of a 50-year-old car, or writing a full-scale business history, even about recent years. In consequence, the history of the company and its products has been better documented than that of almost any other car manufacturer.

'The Legend Grows' is the company's motto, and for once here is a slogan which is perfectly justified. The present and the future of Jaguar

Cars are solidly anchored in an impeccable heritage. Jaguar's traditions are living, in a company full of vitality. Undoubtedly the privatization of Jaguar in 1984 was a turning point in the company's history, as was the introduction of the new XJ6 in 1986. But there have been many such 'cusps' in the past, and a look at Jaguar's history will yield many clues as to how the company may shape its destiny for the future. What follows is the history of a great British company and its products – written in the happy knowledge that it is not a definitive history. Jaguar cars will continue to make history. The legend lives on.

The XJR-S and the XJR-8.

# LANCASHIRE ROOTS
## 1921-1931

The year 1921 was not a very auspicious one for starting a business – least of all in the North of England. A short-lived post-war boom had turned to recession, and in the motor industry in particular many companies were experiencing difficulties. Yet this did not deter two young men in Blackpool who like so many enthusiasts before or since had set their hearts on turning a back-yard hobby into a proper business venture. Their product was motorcycle sidecars.

In this day and age it is only too easy to forget what a fundamental role the motorcycle and sidecar combination once played in British transport, especially in the years before the war. For those who could not afford to buy or run a car – still the vast majority of the population – the motorcycle was a sensible alternative which offered the same convenience and freedom as a car, but was cheaper to purchase and maintain. For the family man of modest means, the 'chair' was a necessity; a girlfriend might, for a time, put up with an uncomfortable pillion seat, but a wife demanded the dignity of a sidecar, and when the children came along, they would need one of those wonderful, typically British saloon sidecars.

These thoughts had not yet occurred to the Blackpool duo, although both were certainly motorcycle enthusiasts. The older was William Walmsley, already married and around 30 years of age with wartime service behind him. He was the son of a wealthy coal merchant from Stockport who had recently retired to the seaside. Walmsley had in fact built his first sidecar in 1920, before the family moved to Blackpool, and a small number of similar sidecars followed, built to the

*Opposite page:*
William Lyons in the very early days.

orders of friends who were impressed with Walmsley's original and unique design – exactly octagonal in section, coachbuilt and covered in polished aluminium.

The Walmsleys' neighbours in Blackpool was the Lyons family. William Lyons *père* was a musician from Ireland who had arrived in Blackpool in the 1890s and had married a local girl; he later built up a business selling musical instruments. They had two children, a daughter and a son also called William, who was born in 1901. William Lyons *fils* left school in 1918, and was briefly apprenticed to Crossley in Manchester, but returned to Blackpool where he became a junior salesman with Brown & Mallalieu, a local garage holding agencies for Rover and Morris. They are still in business, selling Austin Rover cars. In his spare time, the young Lyons was a keen motorcyclist, and it is not surprising that he viewed the activities in the Walmsleys' back garden with the greatest of interest. Soon, William Lyons became a customer for one of Walmsley's sidecars.

It was Lyons' enthusiasm and drive which finally persuaded the other William that they should enter into a partnership to manufacture the sidecars on a larger scale. With support and financial guarantees from their parents, Lyons and Walmsley set up the Swallow Sidecar Company and, by early 1922, had established themselves with a small workforce in premises in Bloomfield Road, Blackpool. The first red letter day in the history of the new company was Lyons' 21st birthday, 4 September 1922. Coming of age, he was now legally accepted as a full partner in the business. Previously, his father had had to sign all documents and cheques.

Gradually, the business grew. In 1923 a Swallow sidecar was for the first time exhibited in the Motorcycle Show, and contact was established with George Brough, the famous motorcycle manufacturer of Nottingham. Brough bought Swallow sidecars, and Lyons and Walmsley, in turn, bought Brough Superior motorcycles – the make which was acknowledged to be the finest of its day, sometimes described as 'the Rolls-Royce of motorcycles'. The Swallow product range was widened; the original 'Zeppelin' Model 1 was joined by other lighter and less luxurious, but also cheaper, models. Model 2 and the long-tailed Model 4 were both pentagonal in section, and there was a more conventionally shaped lightweight model for racing. In 1924, Lyons apparently felt established enough to marry; his chosen bride was Greta Brown, a daughter of a local schoolmaster. Soon after the young couple acquired a car – an early Austin Seven Chummy tourer.

By 1926, the Swallow Sidecar Company had largely outgrown its original premises, even with extra space which had been rented away from Bloomfield Road. If the company was to continue its expansion, and perhaps diversify, which Lyons was already thinking about, new and more suitable premises were a necessity. Then Walmsley senior stepped in and bought a former garage building in Cocker Street, Blackpool. The Swallow company was still small enough that it took only a weekend to complete the move, with the use of a single motor lorry. There was more to it than new premises; the company changed its name, significantly to The Swallow Sidecar and Coachbuilding Company. Initially, Lyons and Walmsley advertised their services in coachpainting, trimming and hood (soft top) work; and among the staff was one Cyril Holland, an experienced coachbuilder who had worked for several companies in the motor industry in the Midlands.

It was Holland's craftsmanship, combined with Lyons' flair, that made it possible to take the next big step – the production of a complete motorcar body. Lyons chose to base this project on the chassis of the Austin Seven, a design he knew well as an owner, and in early 1927 he obtained a new Austin chassis to start work on. Lyons was not the first to conceive the idea of a special-bodied Austin Seven – the pioneer in this field was Gordon England – but Lyons' version of the Austin Seven was probably the most inspired of the many special

bodies on this chassis. He developed a small open two-seater, at first with a hinged hardtop (soon discarded), and with characteristic features such as a cowled radiator, a V-windscreen and a stumpy rounded tail. The first car was demonstrated in May 1927, and soon the Swallow factory was turning out a dozen a week – always assuming that they could get their hands on enough chassis. Lyons also worked briefly on a Morris Cowley-based two-seater but this was a much less distinctively styled machine, and remained a rarity.

It is quite likely that Swallow might have remained a small provincial coachbuilder like so many other firms that eventually disappeared during or after the Second World War, but for the breakthrough in 1927 when the London motor dealer Henlys Ltd placed an order for no fewer than 500 of the smart little Austin Swallows. They also required a saloon version in addition to the two-seater. Lyons accepted the order although he knew his company would be stretched to meet Henlys' demand for 20 cars per week; his partner Walmsley thought him mad. Cyril Holland was put to work developing the saloon body which emerged with a distinctive rounded rear end – giving the car a rather egg-like look – and a smart two-tone colour scheme, divided by a pen nib shape along the bonnet. The inspiration for this was found on an Alvis with a saloon body by Carbodies.

As in 1926, Swallow were outgrowing their premises. But now, two years on, Lyons decided that the time had come for the company to strike out in a different direction. If he had to move to a bigger factory, why not grasp the nettle and move to the Midlands, the heartland of the motor industry where the chassis manufacturers, the component suppliers and the motor trade would be on his doorstep? He explored several possibilities before finally renting part of a disused First World War shell-filling factory on an industrial estate off Holbrook Road, at Foleshill in Coventry. In the autumn of 1928, Swallow moved to Coventry, as did some 30 of the original 50 employees – including Lyons' secretary, Alice Fenton, Swallow's erstwhile salesman, now Lyons' assistant, Arthur Whittaker, and Harry Teather who had joined Swallow at the age of 15. All were to become senior directors of Jaguar Cars in the years to come. Cyril Holland also made the move to Coventry – for him it was more in the nature of a return to his home – but he left Jaguar in 1945, although not before he had made a substantial contribution to the development of the Jaguar style.

*Opposite page:*
A 1929 Austin Seven Swallow saloon.

Settling in at their new address in Coventry — afterwards known as Swallow Road — the company soon expanded the range of special-bodied cars offered. At one time a Swallow saloon body was available on the Italian Fiat 509A chassis; these cars were in fact a batch of obsolete, possibly British-assembled, chassis that the Fiat concessionaire saw no way to dispose of, except by having Swallow elegance and wire wheels transform their somewhat dowdy image. Another short-lived contract was for saloon bodies on the Coventry-built Swift Ten chassis; the first such car was displayed when Swallow exhibited in the Motor Show for the first time in 1929; and a small

number was made until Swift went into receivership in 1931. Sidecars were still a very important part of the business, and very fortunately would remain so until the end of the Second World War.

But more important in the longer term was Swallow's first contact with the Standard Motor Company at Canley on the other side of Coventry. Standard had been one of the many small Coventry car makers from the foundation of the company by Reginald Maudslay (of the engineering family) in 1903. However, in 1929 a certain Captain J.P. Black, formerly a senior director of Hillman which was about to be merged

The larger premises in Cocker Street, Blackpool.

into the Rootes Group, joined Standard as general manager, later becoming managing director. This marked the beginning of the outstanding success story of the British motor industry of the 1930s; under Black's direction, Standard became one of the 'big six' of the industry, with a complete range of popular family cars from 8 to 20hp. The first really successful mass-produced Standard car was the new Nine which had been introduced in 1927, and became the cornerstone of Black's product range. It was also a highly significant car for Swallow for another new Swallow-bodied car in that 1929 Motor Show was the first Standard-Swallow, based on the Standard Nine chassis. This first car had Standard's famous shouldered radiator, but production examples which followed in early 1930 had a special and much more elegant radiator designed by Lyons.

Evidently Black liked what he saw of Lyons' work on the Standard chassis, as soon afterwards he paid him the compliment of adopting a new radiator design for all Standards, clearly derived from that of the Standard-Swallow. In 1931, a further Standard-Swallow joined the product line; the saloon body was of the by now familiar design, but it was mounted on Standard's six-cylinder 15hp Ensign chassis. That same year saw another

six-cylinder Swallow car, the Wolseley Hornet Swallow on a chassis from the famous Morris-owned manufacturer in Birmingham. The Wolseley Hornet pioneered the 'small six' in Britain with its ohc 1,271cc engine when it was launched in 1930, but the standard saloon model was too obviously related to the Morris Minor whose body it shared. Soon a market sprang up for special-bodied Hornets, and Swallow were one of the first coachbuilders to obtain chassis direct from Wolseley. In 1932 Wolseley brought out their tuned sports model, the Hornet Special, which was sold only in chassis form to coach-

builders, among them Swallow, and the Swallow Hornet Special remained in production until August 1933, in two or four-seater form. The two-seater was a particularly eye-catching creation with a boat-tailed body, but both shared helmet type wings and louvred side panels. This Wolseley was the nearest Swallow came to making a sporting car in the early years, and some of its styling features were to influence future products from Swallow Road.

The Austin Seven Swallow was still the best-seller in the Swallow range, but the Standards and the Wolseley were also important models.

*Below:*
A 1931 Austin Seven Swallow saloon, seen here in the Cotswold Motor Museum.

However, during 1931 Lyons decided to further his ambition by making a complete motorcar which would not just be a special-bodied Austin, Standard or Wolseley but which would have a unique identity of its own. In other words, Lyons followed the trail first blazed by Cecil Kimber who had progressed from special-bodied Morrises to MGs some years before. The Jensen brothers would in turn follow the same path. As yet Lyons was not in a position to begin making his own engines or chassis, and at this juncture it may have been a toss up which of the large manufacturers he was going to approach for the supply of these essential components. Luckily Lyons had found a sympathetic co-operator in Standard's Captain Black, and on behalf of Standard Black agreed to supply Lyons not only with their Little Nine chassis, but also with a specially designed six-cylinder chassis which would be exclusive to Swallow.

Henlys were still the most important outlet for Swallow-bodied cars, holding the distribution rights for London and the South of England, and several suggestions for the styling of Lyons' new car came from this direction. A cartoon by F. Gordon Crosby published in *The Autocar* as early as 1929 showed a car of uncanny resemblance to the new coupé on the six-cylinder chassis which was taking shape in Cyril Holland's department of the Swallow factory, with — sometimes conflicting — directions issued by Lyons and Walmsley. An important source of inspiration was the 'long low look' of the American front-wheel drive Cord L.29 car. At the end of July 1931 matters were sufficiently well advanced for *The Autocar* to reveal to its readers that the 'new car which will be put on the market in due course by the Swallow Coachbuilding Company' would be known as the 'SS'. During that summer and autumn, Swallow's advertising contained the by-line, 'Wait! The SS is coming'. There is nothing like a well-orchestrated campaign of teasers to prepare the ground for a new car; something that Sir John Egan of Jaguar Cars Limited surely appreciated in the period before the Jaguar XJ40 was launched. . . .

*Below:*
A 1933 SS1 tourer:
6 cylinders, 2054cc – for
£325 new.

# FORMATIVE YEARS
## 1931-1935

The year 1931 was when the Jaguar tradition was born, despite the fact that the original Swallow company had been formed ten years before and it would be four years before the name Jaguar emerged. But with the SS1, the Swallow company for the first time offered a complete car instead of merely special bodywork. It was with the SS1 that Lyons set out his stall, making cars of a very special kind, and it was the direct ancestor of all SS or Jaguar cars.

What sort of car was this much-talked about sensation of the 1931 Motor Show? A comparable latter-day equivalent might be the Ford Capri, which had an equally great impact when it was announced, and which also set the style for a whole generation of similar machines. Like the Capri, the SS1 was a smartly styled coupé — or, in modern jargon, a 'personal' car. It was a sporting car, yet not a sports car. It was a car that many people bought for the image that went with it — an image that on the other hand deterred those who would later denounce the SS as a 'cad's car'. It was the car with the £1,000 (about $4,000 at the time) look which sold for £310 (about $1,250 at the time). It had an acceptable performance, with a top speed not far short of 75mph (120km/h), but it was not so super-sports as to frighten buyers or insurance companies, and with its traditional sidevalve engine design, it never suffered from the temperamental behaviour often associated with more sophisticated sports car designs. If you owned an MG, a Frazer-Nash, an Alfa Romeo, a Bugatti or a vintage Bentley you would not look twice at the SS; but if you wanted a smartly packaged but *sensible* car at a price not much

*Opposite page:*
A 1935 SS90 Jaguar.

above that of the typical family saloon, then an SS might be the car for you.

Lyons was not an engineer, nor did he as yet employ engineers, so he played safe. The chassis and engines were supplied by Standard; if a mildly modified version of Standard's six-cylinder 16hp 2,054cc engine was not sufficient there was a 20hp 2,552cc alternative available. The chassis was a special design as promised by Black, but the first year's model still had the chassis above the rear axle, and the underslung frame which became an SS Jaguar trademark appeared only on the 1933 model. The whole specification was utterly conventional — not so the bodywork.

An American once defined a classic car as 'an automobile of which at least half the length is hood' (bonnet in English). This description fits the SS1 exactly — that long, low look was taken to an almost ridiculous extreme, with the windscreen well aft of the midpoint of the wheelbase. The car had helmet type wings and was bereft of running boards. The passenger compartment was box-like with no side windows other than those in the doors and although the level of the roofline had been raised above the aesthetic ideal Lyons was striving for, in an effort to provide at least some headroom, the interior was more than a trifle claustrophobic, especially in the (very) occasional rear seat. An extra box for luggage was stuck on the back, looking like the afterthought it was. Centrelock wire wheels, large headlamps and pram-type false hood irons all contributed to the image; but perhaps unexpected was the choice of no fewer than nine two-tone colour schemes as standard.

The same styling was applied to the smaller four-cylinder SS2 companion model which sat on Standard's Little Nine chassis with a 1,005cc engine, selling at £210 (about $850 at the time). Unfortunately a wheelbase of 90in (229cm) as opposed to 112in (284cm) on the six-cylinder car played havoc with the proportions. Nor was the 60mph (97km/h) top speed really quite sufficient for those who liked to think that the SS was a sports car – in consequence the smaller car always played second fiddle, despite its advantages of lower price and annual road tax. Even so, *The Light Car* magazine at least found the SS2 'pretty hot'.

Both cars were in fact very well received by the press and public alike, and Lyons could not possibly be dissatisfied when at the end of the first year, he had managed to sell almost 800 of the new cars – two SS1s to every SS2, so this obviously indicated the way to go in the future. It was therefore the six-cylinder car that received Lyons' attention first; he had never been quite happy with the styling of the 1932 model, and for 1933 he introduced an almost completely restyled SS1. Wheelbase was increased to 119in (302cm), which in combination with a new chassis frame, underslung at the rear, not only helped to improve rear seat accommodation but also further enhanced the car's long and low proportions. Another great improvement were the long, flowing wings, merging into running boards. The price crept up to £325 but Lyons now offered an alternative body style in the shape of an open four-seater tourer. The gratifying result was that sales of the restyled SS1 more than doubled during 1933, while SS2 output remained the same. The new cars were by now so well established that during 1933, Swallow discontinued their other coachbuilding activities although the sidecar business was kept going as before.

For 1934 it was the turn of the SS2 to undergo a similar updating; it emerged with a wheelbase of 104in (264cm) and, again, a new underslung chassis frame. The engine was uprated to 1,343cc and 10hp, with a 12hp 1,608cc alternative. The styling was a carbon copy of the SS1, in coupé or tourer form, while a four-light saloon (in effect, the coupé with rear quarterlights added) was also

*Below:*
One of the later SS1s.

introduced. The SS2 now cost £260, an extra five pounds being asked for the saloon. The 1934 SS1 was less drastically revised, but gained engines of increased capacity — 2,143cc for the 16hp and 2,663cc for the 20hp model. The four-light saloon style was also offered on the larger chassis. The 20hp SS1 was road tested and proved capable of a maximum speed of 77mph (124km/h), and a 1935 SS1 even reached more than 83mph (134km/h) in the hands of *The Autocar*, while the SS2 was still a comparative sluggard, flat out at 63mph (101km/h).

There were no further drastic mechanical changes to either of the SS models for the remainder of their production run, which continued into 1936. But for 1935, SS introduced two additional body styles on the SS1 chassis; neither was made available on the SS2 chassis. First came the SS1 Airline saloon which was typical of the period when so many designers fell victim to the craze of streamlining, yet without a proper understanding of the science of aerodynamics. These cars invariably had a traditional bluff front end and a beautifully smooth rear end. The SS1 Airline was no exception; it looked what it was, an unhappy compromise, and a tail-heavy one at that. But even at a £20 (about $90 at the time) premium over the ordinary saloon, it was surprisingly popular while it lasted, though Lyons himself never liked it. The Airline did have some unique features, such as horizontal bonnet louvres, its own design of dashboard and, oh crowning glory, two side-mounted spare wheels. Presumably there was no room for even one in that shapely tail.

The final SS1 version, and the most expensive at £380 (about $1,575 at the time), was introduced mid-season in March 1935. This was the drophead coupé, a four-seater with a flush-folding hood which was actually hidden away in the luggage compartment when lowered. This was a particularly attractive model, perhaps the most elegant of the entire SS1 range. At the same time as the drophead coupé was introduced, Lyons also unveiled a completely different model, the first SS car that could truly claim the title sports car. This was the SS90, a short chassis open two-seater with the 2,663cc 20hp engine. The wheelbase was quoted as 104in (264cm), suggesting that it could have been based on the SS2 chassis; in fact it used SS1 chassis cut down by hand. The engine was left almost unchanged from the SS1 saloons, with two RAG carburettors and a 7:1 compression ratio. The body featured a sloping tail panel with the spare wheel countersunk, the bonnet had extra louvres on top and the wings were flared. The tail was soon redesigned to a more traditional square-rigged style with a slab tank and a vertical spare wheel. The price was £395 (about $1,600 at the time), and it was claimed that the car would live up to its name with a top speed of some 90mph (145km/h); but the SS90 was hardly given a chance to prove itself, as only some two dozen were made before the model was discontinued in favour of the similar-looking, but much more potent, SS100.

Although by 1935 Lyons could look back over four successful seasons making and selling SS1 and SS2 cars, he was already looking towards new projects. He realized that his next new model would have to have both a new chassis and a new engine; there was obviously a limit to the performance that could be extracted from the fairly tame Standard sidevalve engines. Several ideas were under consideration. A special one-off car was built with an eight-cylinder Studebaker engine in an SS1 chassis (the engine obligingly supplied by Henlys who held agencies for both SS and Studebaker), and another one-off was an SS1 fitted with a Zoller supercharger by Michael McEvoy who, to please Lyons, had special castings made featuring the SS hexagonal symbol. These hexagons featured prominently on many early SS cars, Lyons perhaps imitating Cecil Kimber's use of the octagon as the MG symbol.

In the spring of 1935 Lyons reached a decision. Harry Weslake, the engine design consultant, was asked to produce an overhead valve conversion on the existing Standard six-cylinder engine; and Lyons set up an engineering department at SS, headed by a young man who had previously worked for Humber — William Heynes. Bill Heynes' job was to produce a new chassis design, and generally take charge of the development of the new car, incorporating Weslake's engine and a new saloon body which Lyons and his old assistant Cyril Holland got busy working on.

This was an eventful year for SS in more ways than one. In January, SS Cars went public as SS Cars Limited, with a dual issue of preference and ordinary shares which valued the company at £181,000 (about $750,000 at the time). Hardly comparable with the 1984 share issue — nor is there any evidence that the 1935 share issue created anything like a similar impact, but then at the time the investor had the choice of buying shares in many more different motor businesses than is the case today. The sidecar business was, however, separated out, and was transferred to

an independent company under Lyons' control until he sold this side of the business in 1945.

Also around this time, William Walmsley, the originator of the Swallow sidecar and Lyons' partner since 1921, decided to pull out. For some time there had been differences of opinion between the two partners. Both were full of ideas, but where Lyons was thinking about expanding the business of SS Cars Limited, Walmsley was for ever tinkering with this or that. He was as enthusiastic as ever about both cars and sidecars, but did not have Lyons' business acumen or remarkable foresight, and he was less interested in running the business, in expanding activities or in the public share issue. So Lyons bought Walmsley out, and the two men parted on good terms. In later life Walmsley – among other ventures –dabbled in the caravan business, and he remained a Jaguar customer until his death in 1961.

The event which overshadowed all others for the new SS Cars Limited was the launch of their

new car. This took place at a luncheon for the motor trade at the Mayfair Hotel in London a few weeks before the 1935 Motor Show; this was the famous occasion when Lyons asked his guests to estimate the price of the new car on display, and the average of their guesses worked out in excess of £600 (about $2,500 at the time) – then Lyons revealed that the new car would sell at £385 (about $1,600 at the time). With the new car came a new name – Jaguar. Lyons had asked his advertising agency to draw up a list of suitable animal names, and subsequently picked Jaguar among many other possibilities. The name was registered by Armstrong-Siddeley who had made a Jaguar aero engine in the First World War but they generously gave Lyons permission to use it.

With the coming of the SS Jaguar, the original SS1 and SS2 models were allowed to fade away, although production of the sidevalve engined models continued briefly into the 1936 season, and the original SS1 tourer body was made available on the new Jaguar chassis. The total number produced of the original SS cars was some 6,050, with more than twice as many SS1s as SS2s. During their lifetime, these cars had established the SS company's reputation for producing stylish and luxurious cars, offering a good turn of performance at prices which gave

excellent value for money. As yet, however, the marque had barely established a reputation in sporting circles. The early SS cars were seen mainly in British rallies – a notable SS driver was A.G. Douglas Clease, editor of *The Autocar*, who regularly drove an SS in the RAC Rally – but such awards as the marque gained were most often in the coachwork or concours sections. Teams of SS cars were entered in the International Alpine Trials in 1933 and 1934, and the cars performed well enough although there were several retirements with mechanical problems in the first year; in the following year's rally, the team was placed third in its class. An SS was entered in the Monte Carlo Rally as early as 1933, and the marque's best performances in pre-Jaguar days were in 1934 and again in 1935, when SS1 tourers won their classes in the *Concours de Confort*.

The legacy that the SS models passed on to their Jaguar successors was an unrivalled combination of attractive styling and value for money. These are qualities that are still very much apparent in today's Jaguar cars. In 1935, William Lyons was determined to add other attractions to the list of features of his cars. With the new overhead valve engine, he had a sound foundation on which to build a true high-performance car, and this goal was achieved before World War II broke out.

*Opposite page, top:*
The interior of the SS90 two-seater, only 24 of which were made.

*Below and below opposite:*
The side and rear aspects of the SS90.

# ARRIVAL – THE FIRST JAGUARS
# 1935-1948

The year 1935 was a milestone in Jaguar history. Within less than 12 months, there had been a new company, a new product range and a new name. As we have seen, the first car to bear the Jaguar name continued many of the traditions of the original SS, but added fresh impetus to the image of the marque. It also broke new ground in being the first four-door saloon car that Lyons had offered.

The styling of the SS Jaguar set a theme for the marque that was to endure into the 1960s. As a design it was typical of Lyons' philosophy; it was not startlingly original, as Lyons had undoubtedly been looking at the Bentley 3½-litre which influenced the shape of the bodywork in general, and the new radiator design in particular. Very similar shapes appeared on other British sports saloons of the period: notably the MG SA which was launched at the same time as the SS Jaguar, and the Triumph Dolomite soon after. Nevertheless, Lyons' handling of the overall design theme, as well as his detail work, showed his considerable ability as a stylist, and the end product had a pleasing individuality.

Photographs taken during the development of the Jaguar, as well as many photos taken in subsequent years when other new models were being designed, give an interesting insight into Lyons' methods as a stylist. In Britain in 1935, modelling clay was unknown, and the 'bridge' (a moving gateway and measuring instrument under which a clay model takes shape — it ensures accurate symmetry) had only recently come into use for scale model work in the USA. Lyons eschewed model work and plunged straight

into full-scale development. He used his coachbuilding experience, and had the body shop — or Cyril Holland's department — fashion a full-scale mock up from wood and metal. The mock up was demountable, and alternative pieces were available — for instance different designs of wings — allowing Lyons to play about with different combinations, each of which was photographed for the records, until finally he arrived at a result he was happy with. It is tempting to compare this with a child's Lego/Duplo kit!

The trim and furnishings of the Jaguar were not in any way disappointing. The radiator was reminiscent of Bentley's, with chrome-plated shutters and crowned by a new winged badge which incorporated the old SS logo and hexagonal shape with the new Jaguar name. It was flanked by impressively large headlamps — after the first year, Lucas P.100s were standardized. There were centre-lock wire wheels, and the spare wheel rested in the nearside front wing. Inside all was wood and leather, with a full complement of instruments with white dials set in a black metal panel on the wooden facia. A final typically thoughtful Jaguar touch was a fitted toolkit built into the bootlid.

Under the attractive skin, the new engine was the item most worthy of consideration. The dimensions of the 20hp SS1 unit were unchanged, so capacity was 2,663cc (although the car is invariably referred to as the 2½-litre model). Weslake had made a neat job of the overhead valve conversion; there was surprisingly little change to the bottom end of the engine, but then little was necessary as Standard's six-cylinder

*Opposite page:*
A 1938 SS Jaguar 100
2½-litre open two-seater.

engine carried its crankshaft in seven main bearings and was more than robust enough to cope with the top end alterations. The valvegear was straightforward enough but Weslake's real expertise showed in the cylinder head design, and the new engine developed just over 102bhp at 4,400rpm; an increase of almost 50 per cent compared with the sidevalve unit of the same size! It was sufficient to endow the car with a top speed around 85mph (137km/h). Although the new engine was more of a Jaguar than a Standard design, all Jaguar engines continued to be made by Standard, a situation that persisted until after the Second World War.

Among the ancillaries, it is worth noting that for the first time, Jaguar fitted SU carburettors – two of them, of course – which have since featured on most of the make's carburettor-engined cars. There was also an SU electric fuel

pump, and soon after Jaguar added SU's automatic, thermostatically controlled enrichment device which abolished the manual choke control. The chassis was less radically altered from the SS1; it was a copybook 1930s design with beam axles on semi-elliptic leaf springs front and rear, worm and nut steering and Girling mechanical brakes. Other British quality car makers were already producing designs with independent front suspension, hydraulic brakes or both; but Lyons preferred not to take too big a step at one time, and Jaguar had to wait until 1948 before the chassis design caught up with the state of the art. Summing up, the SS Jaguar 2½-litre was typically British in every aspect of its design; extremely appealing in many ways, but light years behind the best continental opposition (such as the BMW326) in other respects.

*Below and opposite:*
All-round views of a 1938 SS Jaguar 2½-litre drophead coupé.

*Right:*
An SS Jaguar 1½-litre
saloon.

*Right:*
A 1938 SS Jaguar 100.

The 2½-litre saloon was, however, only one of a new Jaguar range. On the same chassis was offered the Jaguar tourer; this had the old SS1 tourer body but could be distinguished from its predecessor by the new Jaguar type radiator. Then there was a four-cylinder Jaguar, on a 108-inch (274cm) wheelbase chassis, but with an identical four-door saloon body; under the bonnet was a modest enough engine, inherited from the SS2 and in fact borrowed from the Standard 12, of 1,608cc capacity and with side valves. With a shorter bonnet, it was not as impressive in terms of styling as the six-cylinder car, but appointments were similar and the 1½-litre saloon retailed at £100 (about $420 at the time) less — £285 (about $1,200 at the time) — and still offered a top speed of 70mph (113km/h).

The fourth and perhaps most impressive member of the Jaguar family was the SS Jaguar 100. This was achieved by the simple formula of taking the new ohv engine and inserting it in the existing chassis and body from the pretty, but arguably underpowered, SS90. Surprisingly little was done to the engine; specifications mentioned larger carburettors and a higher compression ratio, but quoted identical power outputs. But in this much smaller and lighter car, performance was quite spectacular; while the original 2½-litre model never quite lived up to the implied claim of a three-figure top speed, it was found to have a top speed over 94mph (151km/h), and at £395 (about $1,600 at the time), represented unbeatable value in terms of performance among sports cars of the period.

Initially, the sidevalve engined SS cars were continued for the 1936 model year, but the SS2 faded away almost immediately and only small numbers were made of the SS1 until that as well was relegated to the ranks of the has-beens in mid-1936. From then on the Foleshill factory

*Left:*
The interior of the 1938 SS Jaguar 100 2½-litre.

concentrated on turning out ever increasing numbers of Jaguars. The SS1 and SS2 had served the company well but obviously belonged to an earlier period; besides, the SS cars had always been slightly off-beat but the new Jaguars were clearly aimed at a more defined market – the heartland of Britain's specialist car makers which Michael Sedgwick, writing about cars of the 1930s, once summarized delightfully as: 'Betjeman-land . . . the world of tennis and bridge'. The Jaguars were formidable competitors for makes such as MG, Riley and Triumph which were the well-established purveyors of sports cars and sports saloons. Within four years, Riley and Triumph had both gone into receivership, while MG survived allied to the Nuffield Organization. Because Jaguars were essentially sporting cars, they had less of an impact in the non-sporting sector of the quality car market, and makes such as Wolseley, Rover, Humber, Armstrong-Siddeley and the Daimler-Lanchester combine were as yet unaffected by the rising newcomer.

Jaguar could even be considered as a competitor for some of the upper-crust makes – notably Alvis, Bentley and Lagonda; it is perhaps significant that all of these manufacturers moved their top models further up-market, into the 4½-litre bracket and often with four-figure prices, after the appearance of the SS Jaguar. The fact was that a Jaguar offered very similar performance and luxury at half the price; and even if it had not been in Lyons' thoughts to challenge the Bentley and others of that ilk outright, an appreciative public soon began to make the inevitable comparison, which almost always was more advantageous to the Jaguar than to the Bentley. Yet there was a snag; precisely because the Jaguar was so much cheaper, it was derided by some as a flashy car for the *nouveau riche*, and its success among showbusiness people or those in the fashion world earned for it the nickname of 'the Wardour Street Bentley'. Once acquired such an image is difficult to dispel; a generation later, snobs would talk scathingly of 'gin and Jaguar' and think of the marque as a car for cops and robbers.

Such detractors are unlikely to have caused much worry at Swallow Road in 1936 and 1937. The company was fully occupied in making as many cars as possible; selling them was less of a problem. They were undoubtedly aided by the excellent publicity gained by repeat wins in the 1937 and 1938 RAC Rallies, by J.Harrop in an SS100; the saloons mainly showed up in the Concours classes on result sheets, headed by an

overall victory in the *Concours de Confort* in the 1938 Monte Carlo Rally. The marque's early appearances on the race tracks were perhaps more hesitant, although Tommy Wisdom put up some remarkable performances with a much-modified SS100 at Brooklands and Shelsley Walsh. But in general, while the SS100 had the speed potential, it was not always equally sure-footed on the limit, and hence often lost out to its better-behaved arch rival, the Frazer-Nash-BMW 328. Realizing the limitations of the car's handling, Lyons persuaded the entrants of an SS100 in the 1939 TT race to withdraw. He wisely concentrated works support on rally entries where the SS100 could show its mettle as a road car.

The original Jaguars lasted a mere two seasons, and a substantially redesigned range was introduced for 1938. With these cars Lyons took an unusually bold step forward for a relatively small specialist car maker; he introduced a new all-steel saloon body, in a complete changeover from the ash-framed coachbuilt bodies that the company had built up such experience with since 1927. If this does not sound like a very dramatic step, it is worth pointing out that Britain's largest maker of quality cars at that time, Wolseley, only went to all-steel bodies in that same year of 1937, and they bought theirs complete from Fisher & Ludlow. By contrast, while SS contracted out the panelwork and pressings, body assembly was carried out at Swallow Road. The company paid the price for being pioneers; there were tremendous problems getting the all-steel bodies into production, and the 1938 production figures were well down on the previous year's results.

Some subtle re-styling was carried out, and the all-steel Jaguars emerged with an even cleaner line than the original models. The main identification point was that the side-mounted spare had disappeared in a separate compartment under the boot, the windscreen was slightly more inclined, and the leading edge of the front door followed a straight line down to the running board. The door handles were now discreetly incorporated in the chrome trim strip along the waistline. The new body was not all; underneath was a new chassis, designed by Heynes to be rather more rigid than the old SS1-derived frame, and with an extra inch added to the wheelbase which was now exactly 10ft (305cm).

The 2½-litre model was supplemented by a 3½-litre version which was identical in body and chassis but offered 90mph (145km/h) performance at £445 (about $1,800 at the time). Further down

*Opposite page:*
An SS Jaguar 100 3½-litre

the scale, there was a new 1½-litre model with a new engine, although this was still supplied by Standard. The new four-cylinder engine which actually displaced 1,776cc had overhead valves, and pushed the top speed of the car up to a comfortable 75mph (121km/h). This model, too, had the newly-designed chassis, with a wheelbase of 112.5 inches (286cm), and the body was exactly the same as that of the larger cars. This much-revised 1½-litre model sold at £298 (about $1,200 at the time) and the price of the 2½-litre was now £395 (about $1,600 at the time).

All three cars were available with a superbly attractive drophead coupé body as an alternative; this cost £20 (about $90 at that time) more than the saloon models in each case, and represented the best of British styling of the late 1930s. It had of course only two doors, although appreciably wider than the saloon doors. The well-made hood (top) had only the narrowest of pillar-box slit rear

windows, and as there were no quarterlights, rear vision with the hood up was abysmal. The author once had to navigate a post-war export model, with left-hand drive and no external mirrors, through London rush hour traffic, running out of petrol in the process; an experience not lightly forgotten. But it was a marvellous car for the open road on a fine summer's day when you could get that hood out of the way. The introduction of the drophead coupé meant that the last relic from the SS1 years, the Jaguar tourer, was finally swept away.

The last new model for 1938 was fairly obvious, a 3½-litre version of the SS100. This sold for the same price as the 3½-litre saloon, and proved that Jaguar had by now definitely entered the world of high performance; this time the model designation told the truth, as the new car on test recorded a maximum speed of 101mph (163km/h). Other interesting aspects of this remarkable car's

*Above:*
The 1937 1½-litre SS Jaguar, one of the last side-valve models. The spare wheel is carried on the near side.

*Opposite page:*
A 1939 SS Jaguar 1½-litre saloon.

performance were a 0 to 60mph (0 to 97km/h) time of 10.9 seconds, a maximum of 90mph (145km/h) being available in third gear, while in the same gear it took less than six seconds to accelerate from either 30 to 50mph (48 to 80km/h) or 40 to 60mph (64 to 97km/h). These figures were achieved by *The Motor* in 1938 and are curiously comparable to a modern MG Metro except that a 3½-litre engine inevitably has the edge when it comes to in-gear acceleration! The only serious competitors for the SS100 at the time were the afore-mentioned BMW 328 with a top speed around the 100mph (161km/h) mark, costing £695 (about $2,850 at the time) in the UK, and the Railton 'Light Sports' with a 4.2-litre American Hudson straight-eight engine which would reach

no less than 107mph (172km/h) – but at a cost of £878 (about $3,600 at the time), almost twice that of the SS100. On the other side of the coin, the SS100 would gobble a gallon every 20 miles or so, yet this may even today be considered acceptable for a large-capacity sports car.

Wisely, no great changes were made to the SS Jaguar range for the rest of the pre-war period. The firm's best-ever year was 1939 and more than compensated for the miserable 1938 season; total production was over 5,000 cars, more than doubling the previous year's output. Slightly modified 1940 models were introduced at the end of July 1939, and were mainly notable for even better levels of equipment including folding picnic tables in the front seat backs, and what Jaguar

*Opposite page and below:* Views of the SS Jaguar 100 3½-litre which show its powerful appeal.

optimistically called an 'air conditioning plant' in their publicity hype; we would now describe it as a heating and ventilating unit. But even this relatively simple device was a step well in advance of then-current British practice; as late as the 1950s many British family saloons still came without a heater in the standard home market models.

As William Lyons began his career as a stylist and coachbuilder, it is natural that it has invariably been difficult to beat Jaguar at their own game when it comes to coachwork; but there have always been those who tried. The last pre-war season saw a few examples of special bodywork on SS Jaguar chassis. Maltby's offered an unattractive tail-heavy drophead coupé on the 3½-litre chassis for which they asked £575 (about $2,350 at the time) or £110 (about $450) more than Jaguar's own similarly bodied car. It is evident that at least it offered more boot space than the standard car. Much better looking was a razor-edged limousine by Mulliner of Birmingham on the same chassis, built to the order of John Black of Standard who made his wife a present of the car. From certain angles this four-light touring limousine was indistinguishable from a small Rolls-Royce, and its interior appointments including an electrically operated glass division were well up to similar standards. It seems that at least one replica was built, for Black himself, but the outbreak of war prevented further developments.

*Above:*
The SS100 fixed head coupé.

Jaguar contented themselves with a splendid 'teaser' for their 1938 Motor Show stand; a fixed-head coupé on the SS100 chassis, a lovely car which was obviously inspired by the Bugatti Type 57 'Atalante' coupé and none the worse for it. This intriguing one-off happily still exists, and was recently completely restored in Britain after spending many years in the USA. Its styling laid the foundation for the XK120 coupé almost 15 years later. A number of other special bodies were produced on SS Jaguar chassis both pre- and post-war, most of them by continental coach-builders in countries such as Belgium or Switzerland, ranging from reasonably attractive to indescribably vulgar.

During the Second World War, SS Cars Limited turned their hands to a multitude of tasks. While some car manufacturers continued to make small numbers of cars to meet orders from the War Office, or from essential civilian users, or made a variety of military vehicles, the SS Jaguars were suitable neither for war work nor for 'essential' civilian occupations, and in consequence most of the company's war efforts were concentrated in the aeronautical field, with numerous aircraft components being made – including the complete centre sections of Britain's first jet-engined fighter plane, the Gloster Meteor. However, vehicles were turned out as well; almost the last of the original Swallow sidecar line, built to austere WD specifications and a far cry from Walmsley's first Zeppelin. In 1945, Lyons sold the sidecar business to a company which later set up shop at Walsall airport and ultimately, as part of the TI group, was merged with an erstwhile great rival – Watsonian Sidecars of Birmingham; but not before this latter-day Swallow Coachbuilding Company had made a brief and unsuccessful foray into car manufacture, as sponsors of the short-lived Triumph-engined Swallow Doretti sports tourer of the 1950s.

SS Cars Limited did however build a couple of interesting cars during the war; two prototypes of lightweight military general purpose vehicles, the JAP V-twin engined VA designed to be parachuted from an aircraft, and the Ford Ten-engined VB with all-independent suspension. Both showed considerable ingenuity on the part of their designers, the same team charged with producing new Jaguar cars for the post-war period; perhaps the experience gained with independent suspension finally bore fruit with the E-type of 1961! But nothing came of these prototypes; the War Office adopted the American Jeep in place of its Hillman or Morris utility cars, and, after years of design work and deliberation, finally went ahead with the complex Nuffield-designed, but Austin-built and Rolls-Royce-engined, Champ.

When the war ended in 1945, it was more or less back to pre-war business at Swallow Road. However some changes are worth mentioning. In March 1945 the company changed its name from SS Cars Limited to Jaguar Cars Limited; the assumption is that the famous initials had become tarnished but it was only natural that Lyons should wish to regularize the situation by adopting the name of the most successful model for the marque and the company as a whole. Then Lyons had managed to buy the tooling for the six-cylinder engines from Standard, and had the whole production line moved from Canley to Swallow Road, just in time before the mercurial John Black changed his mind. Standard continued to supply the four-cylinder engines for the 1½-litre Jaguar, and indeed fitted the self-same engine to new models of the recently acquired Triumph marque, with which it is said that a piqued Black hoped to offer Lyons competition on his own ground. An important recruit soon after the war to the Jaguar team was a former Daimler apprentice who was appointed service manager – F.R.W. England, so tall that he was inevitably nicknamed 'Lofty'. Later in his career, 'Lofty' England took charge of Jaguar's racing team and eventually became William Lyons' successor.

The post-war cars which appeared in September 1945 were little changed apart from new badges on the radiator and on the rear bumper, where a stylized J replaced the SS hexagon. The range consisted of the three saloon models as before, but the drophead coupé was only available in six-cylinder form when it re-appeared in 1947, and there were no more SS100 sports cars. A major mechanical change was the introduction of a hypoid bevel rear axle on all models – it had appeared briefly on the 1940 1½-litre – and brakes were improved with two leading shoes at the front. One contemporary magazine managed to endow the post-war six-cylinder cars with Girling's hydromechanical brakes but Jaguar were to stick to mechanical actuation until 1948.

There were now two versions of the 1½-litre – a standard model and a more luxurious Special Equipment model. Prices had naturally shot up, and were also subject to the Purchase Tax introduced in 1940; as first announced, Jaguar prices had more than doubled compared with their 1939 level, ranging from £684 (about $2,736 at the time) for the basic 1½-litre to £991 (about $3,964 at the time) for the 3½-litre saloon.

For the first time left-hand drive became available as an option on export models, and from then on exports were to loom large in Jaguar's sales statistics. Naturally there had been a few export sales pre-war, throughout Europe and the Empire, and a few SS1s had even found their way to the USA; but the late 1940s saw the beginning of a general export drive by the British motor industry, spurred on by the Labour government under Clement Attlee who was painfully aware of Britain's new status as a debtor nation and the need to bring in hard foreign currency. Jaguar resumed their contacts with the pre-war dealer network in Europe, and new agents were appointed in countries where the marque had been unknown before the war. Switzerland and Belgium were good markets; for a time Jaguars were even assembled in the old Vanden Plas coachbuilding factory in Brussels to circumvent Belgian import restrictions. Jaguar were now also introduced to the US market in earnest, through dealers such as Hoffman in New York (who was also responsible for bringing Volkswagen and Porsche to the USA) and Hornburg in California. The first shipment went out in early 1947, and a Californian sales drive in 1948 resulted in several sales being made in Hollywood including that of a 3½-litre drophead coupé to Clark Gable, who became a confirmed Jaguar enthusiast.

With petrol rationing still in force, and currency difficulties in the way of travelling abroad, it took time before the international competition scene got going after the war. However the Alpine Rally was held again in 1947, and among the entrants was Jaguar's distributor in Leeds, Ian Appleyard (soon to become William Lyons' son-in-law). He entered his 'new' SS100 in the Alpine (it was one of two SS100s delivered 'new' after the war) and finished third in class. In the following year he improved this to a class win and was awarded an Alpine Cup. He also ran this by now ten-year old car in the 1949 Dutch Tulip Rally, and again came first in his class. But this was almost the end of the active competition career of the SS100; in 1949 there was a new Jaguar sports car to assume its mantle – the XK120.

*Below:*
F.W.R. England, known as 'Lofty', a key figure in Jaguar's history.

# XK – BIRTH OF A LEGEND
## 1948-1950

The year 1948 saw the first post-war British Motor Show held at London's Earls Court, exactly ten years after the last pre-war show. By October 1948, virtually all the important British car manufacturers had introduced their post-war programmes of new models, or were preparing to launch them at Earls Court. The 1948 Motor Show was as full of star attractions as any Motor Show before or since; pride of place went to John Cobb's Railton-Mobil Special which had set a new World Land Speed Record for Britain in the previous year. All around there were new cars, shining examples of Britain's industriousness, ready to be manufactured in their thousands and millions to meet the insatiable demand for new cars from customers at home and abroad.

British would-be car buyers flocking to the show could see, but sometimes not touch and most emphatically not buy, many of the new cars. Export was the order of the day, and the bulk of production of not only luxury and sports cars, but many popular family workhorses, such as the Standard Vanguard, were earmarked for foreign markets. In the home market waiting lists were depressingly long, and those fortunate few who did manage to obtain an early delivery were covenanted not to sell their new cars for a period of two years; this did not prevent a flourishing trade in nearly-new cars at far above list prices, and even the shabbiest and most down-at-heel pre-war models held an artificially inflated value.

Among the new cars on show, the most significant in the family car class was the Morris Minor, although this was not generally recognized at a time when it was thought that medium-to-large sized cars were going to become more important for the British motor industry. Of all the other newcomers, many have now faded into historical obscurity, but one car which, together with the Morris Minor, is still remembered and revered was Jaguar's show stealer – the new XK120 sports model.

In fact Jaguar had replaced their entire range for the occasion of the 1948 Show. The pre-war style saloons and drophead coupés had gone, and in their place stood the Mark V range. The Mark V models are now seen as an interim stage in Jaguar history but at the time they appeared as a worthwhile evolutionary progression. Their styling was subtly modified, with built-in headlamps, rear wheel spats and the extended rear door quarterlight which became such a Jaguar feature. Otherwise the marque's traditional line was unmistakable. Another immediately obvious feature was the adoption of smaller disc wheels. The six-cylinder 2½- and 3½-litre engines were carried over in the new models (the four-cylinder Jaguar disappeared for good when the last of the old style 1½-litre saloons was delivered in 1949), but the chassis was fundamentally redesigned by Heynes and his team. It now featured independent front suspension with torsion bars and fully hydraulic Girling brakes. An interesting change was that Jaguar gave up the traditional underslung chassis and instead took the frame above the rear axle, improving ground clearance and allowing more suspension travel.

The XK120 in effect used a shortened version of the same chassis, with a wheelbase of 102in

*Opposite page:*
The Jaguar XK120 badge.

*Above:*
The Jaguar Mark V saloon.

*Right:*
A 1950 Mark V 3½-litre.

*Below:*
The XK engine, *c* 1950

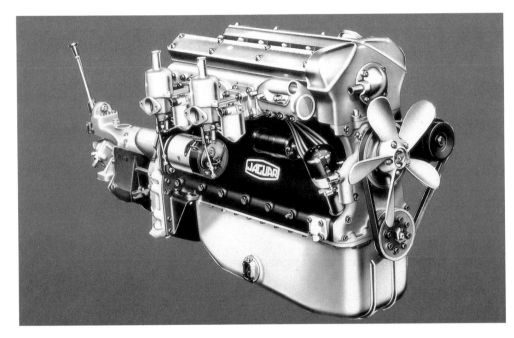

(259cm) as opposed to 120in (305cm) on the Mark V. Its suspension and brakes were similar, and it also rode on disc wheels at first. However the heart of the car was the engine, a brand-new and, by contemporary standards, almost sensational design. It was still a straight six, of 3,442cc, with an 83mm bore fractionally larger than the old push-rod 3½-litre engine, and the 106mm stroke of the 2½-litre version. The bottom end was traditionally robust, with seven main bearings for the crankshaft, but it was the top end which made this engine something out of the ordinary. The inclined valves in near-hemispherical combustion chambers were directly activated by two overhead camshafts, driven by two-stage chains from the crankshaft.

There was of course nothing new in the idea of two overhead camshafts, as the system had been used on racing cars before the First World War, but until 1939 it had always been considered an exotic and expensive form of valve arrangement which was rarely seen on road cars other than Bugattis and Alfa Romeos. The new Jaguar engine, the XK series which gave its name to the car, was the first twin overhead camshaft engine to be manufactured in large numbers at a relatively low price, and it brought this type of engine within reach of far more customers than had previously been the case. In Britain at this time, the only comparable engine was W.O. Bentley's design used in the Lagonda and, soon afterwards, the Aston Martin, and neither of these ever achieved mass-production status in the same way as the Jaguar. There were still only two British engine designs with even a single overhead camshaft: Nuffield's Morris/Wolseley design and that of Singer cars. In Europe, Mercedes-Benz began their range of single ohc six-cylinder engines in1951, while in 1950 Alfa Romeo had introduced their mass produced four-cylinder 1900 model which, like the XK, had twin chain-driven overhead camshafts. The rest of the motor industry was still satisfied with push-rod operated overhead valves, often even with side valves.

The XK engine design had been developed by Jaguar since the war. It is said that the germ of the idea was sown during wartime fire watches at the factory when Lyons would get together with Bill Heynes and two other Jaguar engineers, Wally Hassan and Claude Baily, to discuss the company's post-war plans. Hassan spent his formative years with the original Bentley company in North London; he later worked for ERA, and also for Thomson & Taylor at Brooklands, who among other activities imported Alfa Romeos. He joined Jaguar in 1938 as chief experimental engineer, working under Heynes, and had a considerable influence on both the new post-war chassis with independent front suspension, as well as the XK engine. He later went to Coventry Climax but came back to the Jaguar fold when Jaguar took over this engine manufacturer, in time to take charge of the V12 engine during its development in the 1960s. An equally important member of the team was Baily whose background was with the Morris Engines Branch in Coventry; therefore he had considerable

*Above:*
This 1948 Jaguar 3½-litre drophead coupé was built to a pre-war design.

experience with mass-produced car engines, while Hassan was familiar with the hand-building of racing car engines in a never-ending quest for high performance. The one common element in their background was that both had experience with ohc engines, used almost without exception on the 'W.O.' Bentleys and Alfa Romeos, and also widely used by the Morris-MG-Wolseley companies before 1935.

The new Jaguar engine went through several well-documented prototype stages from 1945 to 1948. It had been the intention to make a 2-litre four-cylinder version as well, and early brochures quoted an XK100 model with this engine of which a prototype had been used in Goldie Gardner's MG record car in 1948 some months before the launch of the production engines. However, the clamour, especially from overseas markets, was for the ultimate high-performance six-cylinder version, so the XK100 faded quietly away, and no Jaguar ever since has had fewer than six cylinders or an engine smaller than 2.4-litres. That the means justified the end became abundantly clear when the production XK120 engine developed some 160bhp at 5,000rpm, an increase of 35bhp over the push-rod engine in the Mark V 3½-litre model; a specially modified XK120 reached 132mph (212km/h) in a demonstration run in Belgium in 1949, and when normal production XK120s became available for independent road tests, they easily achieved 120mph (193km/h) or more.

Lyons basically had wanted the new engine as a power unit for a new large luxury saloon model which would appear two years later, and the sports model was at first intended solely as a kite-flying exercise. The idea was to make a limited

*Opposite page and inset:*
A 1951 Jaguar XK120.

*Left and below right:*
Two XK120s.

*Below left:*
A 1952 XK120 with left-hand drive.

number only, and the XK120 at first had expensive hand-made coachbuilt aluminium bodywork. Only when faced with a huge demand for the new sports car, from the USA in particular, did Jaguar decide to put the XK120 into proper full-scale production, with steel bodywork, and these cars began to appear in quantity in early 1950. There was very little in the way of external difference that would assist the casual observer to distinguish an alloy-bodied XK120 roadster from a later steel-bodied car. In terms of styling, the original XK120 roadster was perhaps Lyons' masterpiece; although he had again drawn inspiration from other sources – such as the Le Mans-winning Bugatti Type 57 'tanks' and the Mille Miglia BMW 328 from 1940 – the XK120 was still a highly individual design. Apart from relatively insignificant cars such as a handful of BMW-inspired Frazer-Nashes and the unsuccessful aerodynamic HRG, the XK120 was the first full-width bodied sports car in Britain, breaking with the traditional sports car shape typified by MG or Morgan. Inevitably the XK120 had its imitators, and its influence was seen in the styling of the entire next generation of British sports cars, from the Jowett Jupiter to the MGA.

The XK120 was introduced at a home market price of £988 (about $3,952 at the time) basic, or £1,263 (about $5,052 at the time) including Purchase Tax. As usual, Jaguar managed to offer an unbeatable package in terms of value and performance for money, and the car also

continued the company's tradition of attractive styling. This time the added ingredient was the sophistication of the engine design. The XK120 was not yet the perfect Jaguar; although the chassis design was new, it had been conceived mainly with a 90-100mph (145-161km/h) saloon car in mind, and the power of the XK engine in the lightweight sports car was arguably too much for it. When the XKs began to appear on race tracks they often lost on corners what they had gained on the straights; the steering was Burman's recirculating ball system (to which Jaguar remained strangely faithful for a long time) and was not the most endearing aspect of the car; and, above all, the XK120 was horribly under-braked.

Admittedly, Jaguar were always careful to make the point that the XK120 (like the SS100) was a fast roadster, not a racing car. Nevertheless, works cars – usually the original alloy-bodied version – soon began to be seen in racing as well as rallying. The famous 132mph (212km/h) run took place in June 1949, the car used was a very early white XK120 which was subsequently registered HKV500, and this then became one of the three works cars entered for the Production Car Race at Silverstone in August 1949. Leslie Johnson was the driver of HKV500 and he scored the first victory for the new model, with team-mate Peter Walker in second place. In 1950 the works cars went abroad, and Johnson was placed fifth in the Italian Mille Miglia road race. The XK120 also entered the rally scene; Ian Appleyard (whom we have already encountered at the wheel of an SS100) was allocated another of the early alloy-bodied cars, registered NUB 120, and on his first appearance in this car in the 1950 International Alpine Rally, was awarded another *Coupe des Alpes* to add to his fast-growing collection of trophies.

Jaguar repeated the win in the One-Hour Production Car Race at Silverstone in August 1950 – this was the occasion when Tazio Nuvolari nearly drove one of the works XK120s, HKV 500 by then painted red in honour of Italy's most famous racing driver, but was prevented from doing so due to failing health. In the following month a young driver who was rapidly making a name for himself took an XK120 to victory in the Tourist Trophy race at Dundrod near Belfast; he was Stirling Moss, and this was the first time he raced for Jaguar. Meanwhile in the USA another famous name appeared at the top of results lists – Phil Hill who scored many of his early successes in an XK120.

*Below:*
Ian Appleyard's winning XK120 in the International Alpine Rallies.

Equally important was Jaguar's first appearance in the 24-hour race at Le Mans in June 1950. A team of three XK120s was entered; technically these were private cars but the factory gave extensive support both in preparing the cars and in organizing the team. The cars were little modified from standard and were not truly competitive against such cars as the almost-GP-racers entered by Talbot which eventually took first and second places; nevertheless, the Leslie Johnson/ Bert Hadley car hung on to third place until its clutch expired with three hours to go. The two other cars, entrusted to Nick Haines/Peter Clark and Peter Whitehead/John Marshall, finished in 12th and 15th places. As a first outing, it had certainly been sufficiently encouraging for Jaguar to begin entertaining the idea of actually winning at Le Mans.

All in all, 1950 was not a bad year for Jaguar. In that autumn's Motor Show, another new model was introduced – the car that Lyons had always intended to go with the XK engine: the Mark VII saloon. This created as much of a stir as the XK120 had done two years previously. Where the Mark V had been an essentially traditional car, the Mark VII was completely up-to-date with its full-width bodywork. Lyons had combined elements from both the Mark V, with its characteristic window shapes, and from the XK120 whose wing treatment and profile were echoed in the Mark VII. At the front, a traditional upright Jaguar radiator maintained dignity without looking out of place. The Mark VII was justifiably considered to be one of the most handsome saloon cars at the time, although subsequently it came to appear rather dated – but then the basic shape was retained in production for no less than 11 years. It is still instructive to compare a Mark VII with, say, a Humber Super Snipe of 1951, as one of few other contemporary British saloon cars of similar size.

The Mark VII was by far the biggest car that Jaguar had made until then. It inherited the chassis, with a wheelbase of 10ft (305cm), from the Mark V; but modern styling, and the need to provide more boot space, meant that it ended up being over 16ft (488cm) long and more than 6ft (183cm) wide. It also weighed a not inconsiderable 33cwt (1,677kg). The engine was of course the same as in the XK120. That this luxurious full five-seater saloon could be offered for £1,275 (about $3,570 at the time) including Purchase Tax was just another Jaguar miracle, although when the model began to appear in any quantity on the home market in early 1952, a small increase in

the ex-works price and a considerable increase in the rate of Purchase Tax had pushed the UK retail price up to £1,694 (about $4,743 at the time). At this time the model was road tested by both *The Autocar* and *The Motor,* and both magazines recorded top speeds comfortably over the 100mph (161km/h) mark. It was the first Jaguar saloon to achieve this kind of performance; but what was almost as impressive as the performance figures, was the way in which they were achieved. The Mark VII was no uncomfortable, cramped and harsh 'sports saloon' where civilized amenities had been sacrificed for the sake of speed – it was by contrast extremely fully equipped, comfortable almost to limousine standards and also immensely dignified. Undoubtedly many buyers were attracted to it because of its looks and performance, but there were certainly those who bought it for its other qualities. Among the satisfied Mark VII owners Jaguar could soon count Royalty – HM Queen Elizabeth the Queen Mother took delivery of a Mark VII in 1955, by which time HM Queen Ingrid of Denmark had already had her Mark VII for some years. In both cases, links between Jaguar and the two Royal houses were forged which last to this day.

The most important commercial success was achieved by the Mark VII in the USA. It was one thing selling an out-and-out sports car such as the XK120 to the American public – selling a large saloon was a far more remarkable achievement. British saloon cars had certainly been sold in

*Below:*
The Mark VII saloon.

America before, Jaguars among them, but apart from these and the Riley 2½-litre most British saloons exported to the USA had been small family cars such as the Austin A40 or the Morris Minor, which both enjoyed a brief vogue, perhaps mainly because of their 'novelty' value in an era when the average American car was a six-seater with a six or eight cylinder engine of three to four litres, and still growing. The Mark VII seemed to be so close in size and specification to American cars that many people believed it could never succeed in the USA, especially not at over $4,000 which represented a hefty premium over the better-quality domestic cars such as Buick or Chrysler which cost around $2,500; even a Cadillac could be bought for little more than $3,000. Of course the Jaguar never achieved US sales on the scale of any domestic make, but a considerable proportion of the almost 13,000 Mark VIIs exported in the first four years of the

model's life went to the USA. During the same period, fewer than 8,000 cars were released in the home market.

The advent of the Mark VII spelled the end of the Mark V and the old push-rod engine with its heritage going back to the 1935; however Mark V production was continued well into 1951, most of these later cars being sold in the home market while the Mark VII was still for export only. The end of Mark V production meant that Jaguar – for the time being – offered only one engine size, the 3.4-litre XK, and two models, the XK120 roadster and the Mark VII saloon. There was no drophead coupé version of the Mark VII as there had been of the Mark V, and all soft top Jaguars ever since have had only two seats. An additional model did see the light of day in the spring of 1951, a fixed-head coupé version of the XK120 with styling features that linked the car both with the 1938 Motor Show special, the SS100 coupé, and

*Below:*
The XK120 coupé which had a memorable high speed endurance run at Montlhèry in 1952.

with the Mark VII. The XK120 coupé was equally as attractive as the original roadster, and possessed an identical performance. It was inevitably only available for export at first but eventually reached the home market at the same price as the Mark VII, or slightly more than the XK roadster. It never figured as much in motor sport as the open model, but an XK120 coupé did win an Alpine Cup in the 1953 Alpine Rally, and a memorable exploit was the continuous high-speed endurance run of seven days and nights at Montlhèry in 1952, when a works coupé, registered LWK 707, averaged over 100mph (161km/h) for the week.

Meanwhile the XK120 roadster continued its competition career. In 1951, Stirling Moss was the driver who brought Jaguar the third consecutive victory in the Silverstone Production Car Race, and Ian Appleyard and NUB 120 added further laurels: winning the Tulip and RAC Rallies, as well as another Alpine Cup – Appleyard's third. The XK120 was rapidly becoming *the* rally car and also won Europe's most demanding rally, the Liège-Rome-Liège, where Johnny Claes and Jacky Ickx (senior) drove good old HKV 500. As will become obvious, after 1951 the XK120 became to some extent superseded in sports car racing although it was still capable of winning events for a few more years; but after Jaguar began to build proper racing cars, most XK120 successes were scored in road rallies. NUB 120 served Ian Appleyard well, as the 1952 Alpine Rally earned him a fourth Alpine Cup, the third in this car, and he thus became the first man ever to win the Alpine Gold Cup for three consecutive un-penalized runs. Appleyard repeated his RAC Rally win in 1953, and in a new car, another XK120 registered RUB 120, won his fifth Alpine Cup the same year. Through much of his rallying career he was accompanied by Mrs Appleyard, née Lyons, as co-driver and navigator. Occasion-ally, they would venture out in a Mark VII saloon, and in this car they were rewarded with a second place in the 1952 Tulip Rally, and another second place in the 1953 Monte Carlo Rally.

The mid-winter run to the Mediterranean was fast becoming a happy hunting ground for the big Jaguar saloons. An intrepid Irishman, Cecil Vard, had sprung to fame by coming third in his Mark V in the 1951 Monte Carlo Rally, while in the following year two of the new Mark VIIs in the hands of French drivers finished fourth and sixth. 1953 was a particularly good year for Jaguar; in addition to the Appleyards' second place, Cecil Vard and the Mark V were back for a fifth place,

and other Mark VIIs finished in eighth, 11th and 15th places. But at the end of 1953, Ian Appleyard virtually retired from active participation in motor sport, to concentrate his efforts in the family business of selling Jaguar cars. He did make two appearances later on, in the 1955 Monte Carlo Rally and the 1956 RAC Rally – both of course in Jaguars – and in the latter event was awarded second place. However, the legend remains as one of the most successful partnerships between man and machine in the history of international rallying.

*Above:*
Another Alpine Rally XK120.

*Below:*
The Appleyard Mark VII saloon which came second in the 1953 Monte Carlo Rally.

# C-TYPE – SUCCESS, FIRST TIME!
## 1951-1953

The year 1951 marked the beginning of the Jaguar legend. The outstanding reception awarded to the XK120 and its sporting successes notwithstanding, it was the emergence of the Mark VII saloon which put Jaguar on top of the commercially more important saloon car market; while in motor sport, it was Jaguar's decision to build a true racing car as a contender for Le Mans which would finally and irrevocably put the Jaguar name on the roll of honour.

It was a year full of activity, not least as the company began a gradual move from the old factory at Foleshill. Since 1928, the floor space had been increased more than ten-fold, but Lyons could not obtain permission for further buildings on the site, and space was rapidly becoming a problem with ever-expanding production of both saloon and sports cars. Although the Mark VII saloon bodies were supplied by Pressed Steel, as we have seen engine manufacture had been accommodated in-house since the war, and annual production was now around 6,000 cars. The problem was solved by Jaguar taking over a wartime Daimler shadow factory in Browns Lane, at Allesley to the northwest of Coventry. Agreement was reached at the end of 1950, but with the need to maintain production throughout, the move took place in stages and it was not until almost two years later that Jaguar were finally installed in their new home – which, with further extensions, has served as the headquarters of the company ever since, although Browns Lane is today only one of three Jaguar factories. Initially, the Browns Lane factory was leased by Jaguar, but in 1959 it was bought outright from the Ministry of Supply. The Swallow Road premises were sold to Dunlop for wheel manufacture.

*Opposite page:*
The 1953 Jaguar C-type.

The idea of building a Jaguar racing car had been prompted by Walter Hassan as early as 1949, when, in a famous memo to Lyons, he pointed out the shortcomings of the XK120 production model compared with special competition cars such as the Healey Silverstone and the Frazer-Nash Le Mans, and advocated that Jaguar should build a special competition model 'which would sell at some increased price'. It is hard to say whether the idea of success in motor racing or the idea of the additional business appealed more to Lyons! The demonstration of the XK120's capabilities, as well as its shortcomings, in the 1950 Le Mans race was an additional spur, and in October 1950 Lyons gave the go-ahead for the development of the XK120C, where C would mean competition. That a team of three cars was actually ready for the Le Mans race in June 1951 was quite an achievement, even by Jaguar standards.

It is absolutely clear that most of Jaguar's efforts in racing, then and later, were aimed at this one event. Lyons sanctioned the racing programme with an eye to the publicity that would result from success; and he was well aware that Le Mans was by far the most important and prestigious sports car race in the calendar, apart from having a special significance for British enthusiasts who looked back to the 1920s when the Bentleys had dominated the Sarthe circuit. Ever since, Le Mans had become the race where British entries usually outnumbered the rest, even if Britain had won Le Mans only once since the last Bentley victory in 1930, with the Lagonda in 1935. Almost equally important, Le Mans was the European race which attracted most interest in the USA, and the publicity resulting from a Le Mans win would be of major importance to the marketing and sales of Jaguar cars in this crucial market.

Because of its unique organization, Le Mans was – and is – the most demanding of all sports car races. It is run over a specially closed section of public highway, including the immensely long Mulsanne straight which permits very high speeds. But speed is not enough; stamina is of equal importance in a 24-hour race during which a car, even at the beginning of the 1950s, was likely to cover more than 2,000 miles. One of the specific reasons for arranging a 24-hour race at the inception of the Le Mans race in 1923 was to test the electrical equipment of the cars, and obviously this can still be a major contribution towards success or failure. In general, the regulations of the race were designed to encourage reliability and endurance in the competing cars, which originally were expected to be near-production type touring sports cars.

When Jaguar began to design a competition car, they started with the considerable advantage of one of the best engines in the business. Although originally intended as a saloon car engine, the XK engine had proved capable of being developed to a very high level of performance, yet it was also sufficiently robust and reliable for a 24-hour race. But almost everything else was changed radically on the C-type. For a start, the box-section frame of the XK120 was scrapped, a tubular space frame being evolved to take its place. While the front suspension was similar to that of other Jaguars, the rear axle was somewhat more positively located and springing was by transverse torsion bars rather than longitudinal semi-elliptic springs. Initially of course, the C-type had drum brakes, with full hydraulic actuation by Lockheed. The steering was, for the first time on a Jaguar, by rack and pinion. The new chassis was clothed in a sleek aluminium body, designed by Jaguar's aerodynamicist Malcolm Sayer to retain a clear family resemblance to the XK120, yet with a much smaller frontal area. The weight of the complete car was around 20cwt (1,016kg), a worthwhile saving from the 26cwt (1,321kg) of an XK120 roadster; the wheelbase had been shortened by 6in (15cm) to exactly 8ft (244cm), and the car was more than a foot (30cm) shorter overall. As befitted a true racing car of the day, the C-type ran on centrelock wire wheels, which were as yet not offered on the XK120, even as an option.

By increasing the compression ratio and making various other suitable modifications, the engine power was increased to 200 or 210bhp, depending on whether the compression ratio was 8 or 9:1. Harry Weslake was again called in to advise Jaguar on how to get the best performance from their engine. The result was highly satisfactory;

a production C-type with the 8:1 compression ratio and a 3.3:1 final drive was tested by *The Motor* in 1952 and proved to have a top speed of some 144mph (232km/h), and the works racing C-types were certainly quicker than that. The initial testing of the first C-type took place at the MIRA proving ground at Lindley and also at Silverstone; remarkably few problems were experienced, and in June the first three C-types (the only three which were, as yet, in existence!) were shipped over to Le Mans for the practice sessions in advance of the race itself.

The Jaguar drivers were Peter Walker/Peter Whitehead, Stirling Moss/Jack Fairman and Leslie Johnson/Clemente Biondetti; a fourth Jaguar, an XK120, was privately entered by Bob Lawrie and Ivan Waller. The race began well for Jaguar and the three C-types were soon in the lead, headed by the Moss/Fairman car. In the process, Stirling Moss set a new lap record. Misfortunes soon overtook his car, as well as that of

*Left:*
The Walker/Whitehead C-type which won the 1951 Le Mans.

Johnson and Biondetti; both retired before the half-way mark. That left only one C-type in the race, but the two Peters, Walker and Whitehead, more than saved the day for Jaguar and for Britain; they won handsomely at a record average speed of more than 93mph (150km/h), bringing the Le Mans laurels to Britain for the first time in 16 years. Nor must it be forgotten that the

*Below:*
Peter Walker (in white) the winner (with Peter Whitehead) of the 1951 Le Mans.

Lawrie/Waller XK120 also finished the race, in 11th place, a most honourable result for a true production sports car. Jaguar had beaten the best cars fielded by France, Italy and the USA, and had also seen off British challengers such as Aston Martin, Allard, Healey and Frazer-Nash.

That a brand-new racing car should not only compete but actually win such a difficult race on its first outing, was a cause for the greatest satisfaction at Jaguar and indeed throughout Britain. At long last here was a British car to assume the mantle of the Bentley; it was obviously the start of a new era for Britain in international motor sport. The sensational debut of the C-type was set in relief by the disappointing showing in the same year of the BRM V16 Formula One car, the British contender for Grand Prix racing that so much effort had been put into and of which so much had been hoped. It would be another few years before Britain began to dominate the Grand Prix circuits, but in the meantime the dark green Jaguars kept the Union Jack flying as far as sports car racing was concerned.

The second appearance of the C-type was at the Dundrod TT in September 1951, and this turned into a Jaguar procession; the three Le Mans cars were entered, with Stirling Moss, Peter Walker and Leslie Johnson driving, Tony Rolt being called in to share the Johnson car. All three finished, in that order; Moss's win compensating him for the problems that had doomed his Le Mans effort to failure. And apart from Moss winning two races at the Goodwood International Meeting in the single C-type entered, that was it – the 1951 racing season. Four entries and four victories; not a bad record for a first season's showing for a new model of which there were still only the three cars in existence.

By contrast 1952 was an unhappy year for Jaguar. The year opened ominously with the announcement of another formidable challenger in sports car racing, the Mercedes-Benz 300 SL. This was as yet a prototype, whereas the C-type Jaguar had now gone into limited production and was reaching selected customers in Britain and abroad at a price of £2,327 ($6,516 at the time) each, including UK Purchase Tax. Henceforth private entrants would contribute as much, if not more, than the works team to Jaguar's honours list; foremost among the privateers was the new Ecurie Ecosse team with its distinctive dark blue cars. The Scottish team's first C-type was driven by Ian Stewart. C-types were also reaching American drivers, but at the time of the first Sebring 12-hour race in March 1952 this had yet to happen, though an XK120 still took second place.

One of the first events in the British calendar was the meeting on Easter Monday at Goodwood where private XK120s came first and second in the sports car race; but historically, more important was the first appearance of a works C-type with Dunlop disc brakes, driven into fourth place by Stirling Moss. The same car was then shipped out to Italy for the Mille Miglia at the beginning of May; Jaguar had entered XK120s in the classic road race in 1950 and 1951, with a fifth place to Leslie Johnson in the first year, otherwise accidents or mechanical failures had forced the cars into retirement. Now Moss would try his luck again, with Jaguar test driver Norman Dewis acting as navigator. They were well-positioned when the steering gear was damaged in a very minor collision with a rock, and a Jaguar was again out of the race. Later in the same month Moss won both the saloon and the sports car events at the Silverstone Production Car Races, in a Mark VII and a C-type respectively. By now, June and Le Mans were fast approaching, and some feverish development was taking place in the workshops of Jaguar's racing department.

The new Mercedes-Benz had shown such speed potential in its early outings that Jaguar were seriously worried, and in an attempt to improve the performance of the C-type, the gifted stylist and aerodynamicist Malcolm Sayer had undertaken wind tunnel experiments with C-type scale models, trying to find a more wind-cheating shape. The Le Mans C-types emerged with a longer and lower nose, which necessitated a smaller radiator with a remote header tank mounted on the bulkhead behind the engine, and the radiator grille was also much smaller. The tail was lengthened to a sharp point. It was the new front end which proved the Jaguars' undoing; the practice sessions showed their penchant for overheating, and although larger header tanks were hurriedly substituted before the race itself, none of the three works cars lasted for more than four hours – the Rolt/Hamilton car was the last to retire, with a blown head gasket. At the end of the day, the race was a walk-over for the Mercedes-Benz team, though only after the veteran French driver Levegh had led for the first 23 hours in an epic solo effort in his Talbot.

This was the only occasion when these strangely shaped C-types were seen in public, and at the Reims sports car race later on in the same month the classic C-type shape was back. In the absence of Mercedes-Benz and Ferrari works teams, Stirling Moss gave Jaguar a well-deserved victory, and this was another historic occasion — for the first time a motor race had been won by a car with disc brakes. The remainder of the season brought some satisfaction for Jaguar in the shape of wins in various minor events; Peter Walker began to storm up hills such as Shelsley Walsh and Prescott in a most determined manner, while in the USA Phil Hill who had got his hands on one of the first C-types to arrive in the American continent, won the Elkhart Lake Race in September. At home, the works cars were entered for the nine-hour race at Goodwood in September, but this produced two retirements and only a fifth place for the surviving car of Moss and Walker.

On the production front there was relative calm for the time being, and the only new models during 1952 were special equipment versions of the XK120 with higher compression ratios and various other engine modifications, together with centrelock wire wheels as standard, all for an extra £115. The entire Jaguar operation was by now well established in the company's new home at Browns Lane, and early 1953 saw two interesting additions to the existing range. The first was a Mark VII saloon equipped with fully automatic transmission, a two speed Borg-Warner box controlled by a selector on the steering column; initially production was reserved for the export markets, and this model only became available in the UK in 1955. The other was a drophead coupé version of the XK120, offering wind-up windows in the place of loose sidescreens and a snugger hood than that of the roadster.

After the *débâcle* of 1952, Jaguar's works team prepared carefully for the 1953 season. A new

A 1954 XK120 drophead coupé.

*Opposite page, above and left:*
A 1954 XK120 drophead
coupé with 'Duncan
Hamilton' wheel spats.

*Opposite page and above:*
Details of the 1954 XK120 drophead coupé.

*Left:*
A 1954 XK120 fixed head coupé.

*Left:*
A 1954 XK120 drophead
coupé and (*opposite page*)
further details of this
magnificent example.

team manager had been appointed, Mortimer Morris-Goodall, ostensibly to allow 'Lofty' England to concentrate on his duties in the service department but of course 'Lofty' could not keep out of the Jaguar pit at the major races. In fact 1953 was the first year for FIA's new sports car championship, and the first race counting towards this was the 12-hour at Sebring in March. The works cars were absent but American privateers in C-types kept the Jaguar flag flying by coming third, fourth and fifth. The first outing for the works team was the Mille Miglia in April; Moss drove a proper works car while Tony Rolt borrowed Tommy Wisdom's C-type. Both were more or less production specification C-types but were fitted with disc brakes. In addition Leslie Johnson ran his own C-type fitted with a five-speed overdrive gearbox, and there were three other privately owned C-types in the race. But all three British driven C-types were soon out of the running – Moss's rear axle failed, Johnson's fuel tank split and Rolt ran a big end bearing. Only a French-owned C-type finished, while an Italian driver in a Mark VII was second in the touring car class. This was the last time a works Jaguar was entered in the Italian road race, which had brought Jaguar little luck and fewer laurels.

Before Le Mans in June, Jaguar unveiled a new prototype racing car which has since become universally known as the 'C/D type'. This was based on the C-type as far as the chassis and engine were concerned but was clothed in a new body which was very clearly the forerunner of the D-type which would follow in 1954. The C/D-type was never raced but was extensively tested, both at the Jabbeke motorway and at various circuits.

In April, Jaguar went on another pilgrimage to the Jabbeke motorway in Belgium, with three cars – an XK120 fitted with undershield and an aeroscreen which, in the hands of Norman Dewis, reached almost 142mph (229km/h); a Mark VII saloon which surprised everybody with a maximum speed of over 121mph (195km/h); and a C-type with the production type engine, which was run twice, with the 1952 Le Mans type bonnet and with the normal bonnet. As it turned out there was no great difference in the speeds measured; the car's best run was at 148.435mph (238.882km/h).

At the *Daily Express* meeting at Silverstone in May, Stirling Moss upheld the tradition by winning the touring car race in a Jaguar Mark VII; he was not so lucky in the sports car race at the same event, as he crashed his C-type in practice and in the race itself had to be content with seventh place, while Peter Walker and Graham Whitehead were fifth and sixth respectively in their C-types, and Hawthorn's Ferrari won. There was less hope for the Targa Florio, but Tommy Wisdom entered the C-type that Moss had run in the Mille Miglia; he finished the course honourably for a 16th place.

The proper 1953 C-types were only unveiled at Le Mans. The three works cars were 2cwt (100kg) lighter than before, thanks to light alloy radiators, the use of smaller diameter frame tubes and lightweight bodies. They were naturally fitted with Dunlop disc brakes on all four wheels, while the engines had new cylinder heads and three Weber carburettors, pushing power output up to around 220bhp. The developed 'Mark II' C-type was timed on the Mulsanne straight at 151.9mph (244.5km/h). The drivers were Tony Rolt and Duncan Hamilton, Stirling Moss and

*Opposite and above:*
Le Mans 1953 – the high
point of the C-type's career.

Peter Walker, and in the 'reserve' car, Peter Whitehead and Ian Stewart. In addition there was a Belgian-entered production C-type with two SU carburettors and drum brakes. The main competition was expected to come from Ferrari, especially the 4½-litre car driven by Ascari and Villoresi, the Alfa Romeo Disco Volante 3-litre cars and the American Cunninghams.

Stirling Moss took the lead early in the race but dropped back with fuel feed problems. Thanks to the disc brakes, the Jaguars had a distinct advantage and could set a pace it was hard for the Italian cars to follow; gradually most of the Alfa and Ferrari team cars retired, and by midnight the Rolt/Hamilton C-type was comfortably in the lead. The Whitehead/Stewart car was fourth, and the Moss/Walker car had climbed back into fifth place. Ascari and Villoresi were second, with the fastest Cunningham in third place; and with the retirement of the Ferrari, only the American car spoiled the Jaguar calvacade. Rolt and Hamilton cruised home to a fine victory, with the Moss/Walker car second; the Cunningham stuck to third place, but Whitehead and Stewart came fourth, and the Belgian C-type finished ninth. For the first time the winner's average was over 100mph – 105.841mph (170.334km/h) to be exact. This race was the high point of the C-type's career, and the most convincing victory ever for Jaguar's works team.

A number of less important events followed. In the week after his Le Mans victory Duncan Hamilton wrapped his own C-type round a lamp post while taking part in a sports car race at Oporto in Portugal, putting himself in hospital.

*Overleaf:*
Two shots of the 1953
C-type.

Stirling Moss took a works C-type (though not a lightweight model) to the Isle of Man for the BRDC Empire Trophy race, finishing second to an Aston Martin DB3S, with Ecurie Ecosse C-types coming fourth and fifth. At Reims in July, Moss and Whitehead won the 12-hour sports car race held prior to the Grand Prix. The next round of the sports car championship was the 24-hour race held at Spa in Belgium at the end of July; this was, however, a poorly-supported affair, and the works Jaguars stayed away, allowing the Hawthorn and Farina Ferrari victory over two Ecurie Ecosse C-types; on the same day Stirling Moss came second in his Le Mans car in the Lisbon sports car Grand Prix. Two Le Mans cars, together with the works reserve car, were entered for the nine-hour race at Goodwood which was not a championship event, but Moss/Walker and Rolt/Hamilton both retired with lubrication problems, leaving Ian Stewart and Peter Whitehead to finish third behind two Aston Martins. The Ecurie Ecosse cars dutifully finished fourth and fifth.

In the first Nürburgring 620-mile (1,000km) race, Ian Stewart and Roy Salvadori took a C-type to second place, gaining valuable championship points for Jaguar but again having to give way to a Ferrari. The Dundrod TT followed in September, with two private C-types entered in addition to all three works lightweight cars, but the works cars all suffered gearbox problems and only the Moss/Walker car lasted the whole race – or nearly so. The car broke down just before the finish but Moss pushed it across the line to finish fourth. The last championship race of the season was the Carrera Panamericana in Mexico but Jaguar stayed away, and this event was a memorable victory for the Lancia works team. The overall result for the championship was Ferrari first, Jaguar second; the Jaguars had only won once, at Le Mans, but to Jaguar (or, for that matter, to the world at large) this was the one important race to win.

In the autumn, Jaguar went to Belgium for another high-speed test at Jabbeke; this was the famous occasion when a specially streamlined XK120, with full undershield and a perspex bubble over the cockpit, was driven by Norman Dewis at a resounding 172.412mph (277.47km/h). This was an indication of what was to come; another pointer to the future was that Jaguar sold the three works lightweight C-types to Ecurie Ecosse, and the last production C-type was delivered to its customer. Something was coming for 1954; it remained to be seen what.

*Left:*
One of the three 1953 lightweight C-types sold to Ecurie Ecosse.

# WORLD BEATERS ON ROAD AND TRACK
# 1953-1955

Jaguar had an excellent year in 1954. They had won Le Mans for the second time in the previous year. The company had, for the first time, produced more than 10,000 cars in a 12-month period and the accounts revealed that the after-tax profit was close to £200,000. There was a new and exciting racing car, as well as several interesting production cars, under development.

The year began modestly enough with the announcement that a Laycock-de-Normanville overdrive would be available on the Mark VII so that customers had the choice of three different transmissions – manual, manual with overdrive or automatic. As it turned out, there was little difference in terms of performance and fuel consumption between a standard Mark VII and an overdrive-equipped car. Since then Jaguar believed in offering customers the choice between the three options – until the 1970s when manual boxes were discontinued on some models, and five-speed gearboxes made separate overdrives redundant. The Mark VII continued to distinguish itself in the Monte Carlo Rally; old-timer Vard changed from his faithful Mark V to a works Mark VII and came eighth while Adams was sixth in a sister car, and another Mark VII took a prize in the *Concours de Confort*.

The Jaguar works team was temporarily absent from the racing scene, busily developing its new cars, so it was left to Ecurie Ecosse to uphold the honours. One of the more unlikely events was a Formule Libre race at Ibsley where an Ecurie Ecosse C-type finished second after a BRM V 16 Grand Prix Car! The existence of a new Jaguar racing car was revealed to the public at the beginning of May, at the time of the pre-race test session at Le Mans; but to the disappointment of enthusiasts at the time, the new car was not ready

for the International Trophy meeting at Silverstone. Here Jaguar gained the customary victory with a Mark VII in the touring car race, driven – unusually – by Ian Appleyard, but Peter Walker's C-type was outclassed by the Ferraris in the sports car race, and he had to be content with third place.

When the new competition model was first seen in public, the bodywork undoubtedly appeared as its most impressive feature; partly because of its clear resemblance to the experimental C/D type of 1953, and partly because Jaguar did not immediately release a full technical description. The new car was not even referred to as the D-type at first; initially this was only a handy internal reference for the new racing car and was only adopted officially after the prototype had been made. Where the C/D-type had been based on a C-type spaceframe chassis, the D-type was a true monocoque made from magnesium alloy. The monocoque formed the centre section of the car with the cockpit; attached to it was a substantial front subframe which carried the engine and front suspension, while the rear axle and suspension were attached to the rear bulkhead of the main monocoque. The steering and suspension followed C-type principles, brakes were Dunlop discs all round, but the traditional wire wheels of the C-type were replaced by centrelock disc wheels of light alloy.

The major change to the engine was the adoption of dry-sump lubrication which lowered engine height in the interest of a smaller frontal area. Furthermore the engine was installed at a slight angle from the vertical, and an off-centre bulge in the bonnet fitted tightly over the cam covers. The lubrication system included two oil pumps, a front-mounted oil cooler and a hefty oil

*Opposite page:*
The radiator grille of a 1956 XK140 fixed head coupé.

*Overleaf, main picture and left inset:*
A 1955 D-type, short nose.

*Overleaf, right inset:*
A 1955 D-type, long nose.

tank behind the left front wheel. As on the later C-types, three twin-choke Weber carburettors were used, and with a 9:1 compression ratio, power output was in the region of 250bhp at 6,000rpm. The clutch was a dry triple-plate type, and there was a new gearbox with synchromesh on all forward ratios.

The bodywork bore witness to Malcolm Sayer's aerodynamic expertise. The headlamps were faired in behind perspex covers, as was the auxiliary driving lamp seen on the early works cars. The radiator air inlet was a typical Jaguar oval but was now horizontal rather than vertical. As on the C-type, the bonnet comprised the entire front end which was hinged to swing forward. The pronounced oval section of the monocoque dictated the basic shape of the car. The driver had a faired-in headrest which on many cars sported the optional tailfin. A hinged flap in the headrest concealed the fuel filler; the flexible aircraft-type fuel tanks held 37 gallons and took up most of the space available in the tail, except for a very minimal boot which housed the spare wheel, accessible through a trap door at the back. The car was naturally somewhat short on comfort, especially for anyone brave enough to ride in the rather symbolic passenger seat. The driver was comfortable enough, provided he was not too big or bulky. With a wheelbase of 7ft 6in (229cm), an overall length of 12ft 10in (391cm) and a scuttle height of 2ft 7½in (80cm), the D-type was a lot smaller and lower than the C-type; at 17cwt (864kg) it was also 3cwt (152kg) lighter.

The pre-Le Mans test runs revealed that the D-type had a top speed of at least 169mph (272km/h) on the Mulsanne straight, and was capable of lapping the circuit at over 115mph (185km/h). These figures were encouraging as being better than any car in the 1953 race. The 1954 Le Mans saw a particularly wide and interesting field of cars. While Alfa Romeo and Mercedes-Benz were absent, Ferrari and Maserati from Italy, Cunningham from the USA, Talbot and Gordini from France and Aston Martin were all contenders in addition to the Jaguars. Unlike the C-type three years before, the D-type was not destined to win on its first outing though it came very close to doing so. Stirling Moss set the pace and was timed at Mulsanne at over 172mph (277km/h), but the D-type he shared with Peter Walker was later forced out of the race with brake failure. The car driven by Peter Whitehead and Ken Wharton also retired, with gearbox and cylinder head trouble. All the three works D-types suffered from fuel feed problems which led to misfiring, but the Duncan Hamilton/Tony Rolt car at least stood the distance. While the opposition had been decimated as well, the Ferrari of Gonzalez and Trintignant was still ahead and despite lapping regularly at 117mph (188km/h), Hamilton failed to catch the Italian car by three miles. A Belgian C-type finished fourth, in the farewell appearance of this model on the Sarthe circuit. At least Jaguar's second place was most honourable in view of the fact that the D-type gave away some 1½ litres on capacity to the Ferrari, and it was also the closest second placing at Le Mans until Ford's 'photo-finish' in 1966.

In the following month, the D-type got its first win in the 12-hour race at Reims; Whitehead/ Wharton and Rolt/Hamilton were first and second in two of the works cars, while the Moss/Walker car was put out by transmission trouble though the Belgian C-type of Laurent/Swaters followed the works cars home again, this time in third place. Next on the agenda came the Tourist Trophy at Dundrod in September; Jaguar entered three cars. As a matter of interest, in an effort to beat the handicap formula used at the TT and which favoured the smaller-engined cars (the winner was a diminutive two-cylinder DB Panhard), Jaguar ran two D-types with cylinder dimensions similar to those of the new compact 2.4-litre saloon car which was due for launch in the following year. In one of the small-engined D-types, Whitehead and Wharton finished fifth; the Moss/Walker car in a repeat of the 1953 race broke down just before the finish but Moss coaxed it across the line for an 18th place. The 3.4-litre car of Rolt and Hamilton had retired. There were no further races for the works team during 1954.

At the Motor Show that autumn, Jaguar demonstrated their willingness to pass on at least some of the fruits of their racing experience to customers. As yet there was no disc-braked road

*Opposite top:*
1955 D-type, short nose.

*Opposite bottom:*
1955 D-type, long nose.

*Below:*
The XK140.

car but the XK engine was improved with a high lift camshaft which helped to increase the power output to 190bhp. The new engine was fitted in a slightly-modified Mark VII, now known as the Mark VIIM, while the XK120 was replaced by the XK140. This was immediately identifiable by its stouter bumpers and bigger radiator grille with only seven bars. The XK140 featured another racing-inspired improvement, the rack-and-pinion steering gear from the C and D-types, and overdrive was now available as an optional extra. The bodystyles were the same as those on the XK120 but the coupé had an altered roofline which enabled two small children (or one consenting adult) to be carried on occasional seats in the back. The basic open two seater now cost £1,598 ($4,474 at the time); the fixed-head coupé cost £1,616 ($4,525 at the time) – the same as the

Mark VIIM – and the drophead coupé was priced at £1,644 ($4,603 at the time). It may be mentioned that when production D-types became available in 1955, they sold at £3,878 ($10,858 at the time) each.

In fact three D-types were supplied to outside customers in the spring of 1955, two to Ecurie Ecosse, one to the Belgian Ecurie National Belge team, and some of the 1954 works cars were also being sold to private owners as Jaguar was preparing a new team of cars for the 1955 season. One of these cars was acquired by Briggs Cunningham who had almost stopped building his own sports cars and instead began a long involvement with Jaguar. He entered it for the 12-hour race at Sebring in March 1955, with Mike Hawthorn and Phil Walters driving and they scored the first important win for a D-type in this

*Opposite page:*
A 1956 XK140 fixed head coupé.

*Below:*
An Ecurie Ecosse D-type.

*Below:*
In the D-type, Ivor Bueb (*top*) and Mike Hawthorn (*bottom*).

racing season. One of the new Ecurie Ecosse D-types won the Ulster Trophy race held at Dundrod in May. Jaguar's works team again reserved their efforts for Le Mans; among the races they gave a miss was Mille Miglia which this year was won by Stirling Moss, with Dennis Jenkinson navigating, in the new Mercedes-Benz 300SLR on its racing debut. One appointment that was kept by Jaguar was the by now traditional entry in the Monte Carlo Rally in January; a team of three Mark VIIs was entered, driven by Vard,

Appleyard and Adams. The best place was eighth for Adams but all three cars finished more or less intact and they were awarded the Faroux Team Prize.

Le Mans was eagerly awaited by the motor racing enthusiasts who looked forward to the battle of the giants between Jaguar and Mercedes-Benz. Nor could the entries from Ferrari, Maserati or Aston Martin be overlooked; Cunningham had one of his own cars in addition to the 1954 D-type. The works D-types for the first

time featured the modified 'long-nose' bonnet, while engine output was up to 285bhp; there were also several other modifications, including a gearbox oil pump and an extended subframe. Moss having gone to the rival German team, the Jaguar drivers were Mike Hawthorn/Ivor Bueb, Tony Rolt/Duncan Hamilton and Don Beauman/Norman Dewis. The opening stages of the race fully lived up to expectations, with Hawthorn in the Jaguar and Fangio in the Mercedes gradually pulling away from all other contenders – the

German car in front, but the British car always close behind. Then tragedy struck soon after 6pm (1800 hours) – Levegh's Mercedes ran out of control and crashed into the grandstand opposite the pits. The driver and more than 80 spectators were killed in motor racing's greatest single disaster. Although the race continued, later in the night the two remaining Mercedes-Benz cars were withdrawn; this left Hawthorn and Bueb in undisputed control of the situation. Don Beauman parked his D-type in a sandbank from where it

*Below:*
Mike Hawthorn in the D-type at the 1955 Le Mans.

could not be dislodged, and the Rolt/Hamilton car was put out with gearbox problems, compounded by a leaking fuel tank. Every single Ferrari and Maserati retired, so did the lone Cunningham, and this gave a comfortable victory to the Hawthorn/Bueb D-type. An Aston Martin DB3S was second, and the Belgian D-type driven by Claes and Swaters was third. The next three places were filled by 1,500cc Porsches. It is still argued who would have won if the Mercedes had not been withdrawn but it must be pointed out that the average speed of Hawthorn and Bueb was

a new record at 107.067mph (172.307km/h), and Hawthorn also set a new lap record at over 122mph (196.3km/h). But it was a bitter victory, and personal tragedy also struck the Jaguar team when William Lyons' only son, John, who, at the age of 25 had only just completed National Service after an apprenticeship with Leyland, was killed in a road accident on the way to Le Mans when the Mark VII in which he was travelling was in head-on collision with an army truck.

In the wake of the Le Mans tragedy, the French Grand Prix and its attendant sports car race at

A 1955 D-type, short nose.

Reims were cancelled. Instead Jaguar sent a works car to the British GP meeting at Aintree where Hawthorn could only achieve a fifth place behind the Aston Martin team, while Ninian Sanderson in an Ecurie Ecosse D-type was sixth. It was left to Ecurie Ecosse to uphold honours in the Goodwood 9-hour race in August, where Sanderson and Desmond Titterington came second, again beaten by an Aston Martin. Come September and the TT, the Dundrod circuit was to become the scene of the second — and final — confrontation between Jaguar and Mercedes-Benz. Led by Stirling Moss, the German cars scored a resounding 1-2-3 victory; but not before Hawthorn and Titterington in the single works-entered D-type had given them a good run for their money, only to have the D-type's engine blow up on the last but one lap. As usual, this was the end of the season for Jaguar's works team; they let Mercedes run away with the Targa Florio and the sports car championship, after which the Stuttgart firm promptly withdrew from motor racing. Jaguar stayed in for the time being, although it was left more and more to private owners, notably of course the Ecurie Ecosse, to keep the flag flying.

If Jaguar were becoming less interested in racing, there were good reasons. The company had now reached the primary objective — winning at Le Mans — three times. Certainly there would be a Jaguar works team for the 1956 season, and there were still a number of remarkable victories to come in the future, but nevertheless 1955 was a turning point in the history of the company — the 'high noon' of Jaguar's racing career, and important also in the history of Jaguar production cars. Unveiled in September 1955, just before the Motor Show, was an entirely new model, the result of three years' work and an expenditure of more than £1,000,000 in development and tooling costs, the true forerunner of all modern Jaguar saloons: the 2.4-litre model.

The most important aspect of the new car was that for the first time on a Jaguar, the separate chassis had been discarded in favour of unitary body construction. Seen from the 1980s this does not seem a bigger step than Jaguar's introduction of all-steel bodywork in 1937. But in 1955, while all the big six mass producers in Britain had gone over to unitary construction (led by Vauxhall in 1937, although Standard and Austin had only discontinued their last family saloons with a separate chassis in 1954-55), Jaguar was one of the first small specialist manufacturers to take this step. True, Jowett and Singer had both employed unitary structures for their post-war saloon models, but both had come to grief over the Javelin and the SM1500 respectively — if for different reasons. Daimler was toying with a small unitary construction Lanchester saloon but was ultimately frightened by the tooling cost. Rover only went to unitary construction with the 3-litre model in 1958, and Armstrong Siddeley never got as far as that. Jaguar went to the Pressed Steel Company at Cowley — by this time the only independent large-scale steel body manufacturer in Britain, as Briggs had been swallowed by Ford, and Fisher & Ludlow by BMC. PSC had a wealth of expertise with unitary construction methods, and were already connected with Jaguar as they supplied the bodyshells for the Mark VII Saloon.

It must also be considered that the 2.4-litre was probably the first true sports saloon in the modern sense of the word, and set a fashion that many other manufacturers would follow in the next ten years. Compared with the Mark VII, it was a compact car being about 15ft (457cm) long overall, yet comfortable for four or five passengers with luggage. It was quick by contemporary standards, with a top speed just over 100mph (161km/h) and a 0 to 60mph (0 to 96km/h) acceleration time around 15 seconds. It was reasonably economical — overdrive-equipped cars returned 18 to 23mpg on road tests. It was well equipped to the point of being luxurious, even in the rare standard model, and the normally seen 'special equipment' version still cost only £1,299 ($3,637 at the time) in the UK. Above all, it was a superbly attractive car, with a modernized and softened version of the typical Jaguar styling, having a clear family resemblance to both the XK140 and the Mark VII.

A survey of cars then available in Britain shows that not many could match the new Jaguar on the combination of price, looks and performance. Daimler's Conquest Century saloon — never as quick as the Jaguar — cost £1,661 ($4,651 at the time) and even a price reduction in 1956 could only just bring it under the £1,500 mark ($4,200 at the time). Armstrong Siddeley showed two new compact saloon cars in 1955, sharing a rather ugly bodyshell; the 234 was the obvious Jaguar competitor but at first cost £1,510 ($4,228 at the time), soon reduced by £100 ($280 at the time). It did not quite reach a 100mph (161km/h) top speed, and was saddled with an unfashionably large four-cylinder engine. The unenthusiastic reception of this car probably contributed to Armstrong Siddeley's decision to stop making cars a few years later. Another 2.4-litre big four, and of venerable pre-war design at that, was offered in the Riley Pathfinder; this was the one that came closest to the Jaguar on performance as well as in looks, and backed by BMC resources it was actually cheaper at £1,241 ($3,475 at the time). But the Pathfinder suffered from dubious handling, it went against the prevailing trend towards six-cylinder engines, and scarcely appealed even to aficionados of the traditional Rileys. Rover strictly speaking did not challenge the 2.4-litre but their twin-carburettor, overdrive-equipped 105S model of 1956 was an admirable car in its own right which gave surprisingly little away to the Jaguar on performance, although it was some £150 ($420 at the time) dearer. However the day of a true sports saloon from Solihull was not yet at hand. None of these cars caused Jaguar to worry unduly, and of even less concern were the tarted-up go-faster family saloons of the Standard Vanguard Sportsman/Austin A105 ilk, soon followed by Vauxhall Crestas and Ford Zodiacs — six-seater family barges which offered some performance potential to such customers who were not enthusiastic enough to resent soggy handling and equally soggy steering-column gearchanges. Some such cars ended up costing almost as much as the cheapest Jaguar anyway.

Apart from its lithe new body, the 2.4-litre bristled with interesting features. The engine followed well-tried XK practice, but had a much shorter stroke; the dimensions of 83×76.5mm were the same as those of the special TT D-type, the only version of the XK engine which was actually oversquare. Capacity was 2,483cc so strictly speaking Jaguar ought to have called it the 2.5-litre; possibly this would have led to confusion with the pre-1950 Jaguar saloons. While Jaguars normally adhered firmly to SU carburettors, the 2.4-litre had twin Solexes, an unusual choice which persisted for many years and which must have been made on grounds of cost. Steering was still by recirculating ball, and the front suspension was by unequal length wishbones and coil springs. The rear axle was located in a manner not unlike that of the C and D-types, with radius arms and a Panhard rod, but rather than torsion bars, Jaguar now employed semi-elliptic leaf springs, mounted completely in front of the axle as cantilever springs — perhaps in an effort to bring suspension stresses into the main part of the body; certainly the rear end of the bodyshell was quite simple in design. Brakes were Lockheed hydraulic with vacuum servo assistance, as yet operating in drums.

The main floor of the bodyshell was reinforced by two integral box-section rails which at the front were extended to carry the engine and front suspension, with additional stiffening to the bulkhead; at the back, these vestigial chassis rails terminated in spring hangers underneath the rear seat pan. These open box sections where the rear springs were mounted were parts where in old age many cars of this type would suffer from the dreaded corrosion; in fact the compact Jaguars have acquired something of a reputation of being prone to rust, as have most of their contemporaries with unitary bodywork, but the whole structure was commendably strong and weight, at 25cwt (1,270kg), was not excessive for a car of this size. The interior was in true Jaguar tradition, with a four-spoke steering wheel and a full set of instruments scattered across the centre part of the walnut fascia — symmetry was

*Left:*
The 1955 2.4-litre saloon.

full-scale model to the production car. This time Lyons went completely away from the traditional wing line still seen on the Mark VII, yet no one could call the 2.4-litre slab-sided, so well were its proportions handled. Characteristic of the car was the way in which the plan view tapered, most noticeably towards the rear, working happily with the falling curve of the boot lid to give the car something akin to a teardrop shape. The front resembled the XK140, with the same vertical oval grille, and for the first time Jaguar employed a one-piece curved windscreen. The rather thick screen and door pillars gave the car a nice, chunky look; the doors were of the one piece type, rather than the half-doors with chromed channel window frames seen on other Jaguar saloons since the Mark V. Traditional for Jaguar were the spats fitted over the rear wheels, but for the first time since 1948, wire wheels were offered as an option on a saloon model. Spats were omitted on cars with wire wheels.

Although it is quite likely that the 2.4 was built down to a price, there was very little evidence that this was the case as far as refinement, performance and equipment were concerned, and the car was exceptionally well received both in Europe and in the USA. One American road tester described it as 'one of the most satisfying small sedans around' – small perhaps by American standards or even when compared with the Mark VII, but to most Europeans it was a medium/large car. Its closest European equivalent was perhaps the Mercedes-Benz 220a, launched in 1954 with a boxy unitary construction body which was larger and roomier than the Jaguar but weighed about the same. The Mercedes had a 2.2-litre single ohc six-cylinder engine originally developing 85bhp which was sufficient to give this car a performance not far short of the 2.4-litre Jaguar's. We may compare prices in the Swiss market where, in 1956, the basic 2.4-litre and the Mercedes-Benz 220a cost exactly the same – Swiss Fr 16,900. However it is a fact that the 'Ponton' generation of the 220 reached a production total of over 116,000 cars in the 1954-60 period, while it took Jaguar 14 years to make their total of 145,000 cars of all types using the basic 2.4-litre body design. Still, this was an impressive figure by Browns Lane standards, and more than anything else demonstrates how well Lyons had judged the market when he launched that first 2.4-litre model.

more important than ergonomics in 1955. The cut-price standard model was somewhat spartan, lacking among other items a rev counter and a heater, but the special equipment model (which was soon standardized as most customers preferred it) was generously fitted out. An overdrive was optional, and in 1957 automatic transmission was added to the options list; it was controlled by a lever poking out from the centre of the lower fascia rail, which at least meant it was not necessary to switch its position on the left-hand drive cars! Manual cars of course wore the gearlevers on the floor, while the overdrive control was a tiny toggle switch on the upper fascia rail, just by the driver's right hand.

The styling of the original 2.4-litre car was definitely another Lyons success. The factory photos of the development mock-ups document that very few changes took place from the first

# RETREAT FROM RACING
# 1956-1958

The year 1956 began on a happy note for William Lyons who, in the New Year's Honours List ,was created a Knight Bachelor, a fitting recognition of his contribution to the industry, and to British prestige in motor sport. A few months later, this honour was followed up by a Royal visit to the Jaguar factory where HM The Queen admired the Le Mans-winning D-type, and HRH The Duke of Edinburgh was particularly interested in the work of the drawing office.

The Monte Carlo Rally was another happy event for Jaguar. Ronald Adams, Frank Bigger and Derek Johnson took a well-used works Mark VII saloon to first place overall, a well deserved victory which had long eluded the marque. This was the swan-song for the big Jaguar in rallying, but a new generation of compact saloons was ready to continue the Jaguar tradition. Another swan-song was the final appearance of Ian Appleyard in the RAC Rally in March 1956; he entered an XK140 fixed-head coupé, and was awarded second place overall in the general classification. The same event saw the competition debut of the 2.4-litre which in the hands of Bill Bleakley won its class and was fourth overall. The new model also made its first appearance in a race in the spring of 1956, when Paul Frère won his class in the Spa Production Touring Car Race in May; his car was much modified with a C-type cylinder head, and was claimed to have a top speed of 125mph (201km/h).

In the first major race of the season, the 12-hour at Sebring, Briggs Cunningham sponsored a team of four D-types which were fitted with new fuel injection engines, primarily developed with an eye to the new fuel consumption rules introduced for Le Mans. In this guise the 3.4-litre XK engines developed some 300bhp. However the entire team retired with brake problems, said to be caused by the hot weather of Florida in March. The 1956 racing calendar was upset by the decision to delay Le Mans until August, to allow time for extensive alterations to be carried out at the circuit after the lessons of the 1955 tragedy; therefore Jaguar's next important race was at Reims in July, where the factory and Ecurie Ecosse entered two D-types each. These four cars finished in the first four places, the winners being Hamilton and Bueb in a fuel-injected works car, Hawthorn and Frère in the other works car (which had Weber carburettors) were second, while Titterington/ Fairman and Flockhart/Sanderson of Ecurie Ecosse followed them home.

At Le Mans, the organizers had thrown in a few new regulations to make life difficult especially for the big-engined cars. The fuel capacity was restricted to 29 gallons on which 34 laps had to be covered before the first fuel stop was permitted. There was also an early (and rather silly) attempt at enforcing touring-type specification which dictated that cars had to have full-width windscreens. The Jaguar works team consisted of the three D-types, all with the Lucas fuel injection, entrusted to Mike Hawthorn/Ivor Bueb, Paul Frère/ Desmond Titterington and Jack Fairman/Ken Wharton. Ecurie Ecosse had a single,carburettor-engined D type in the hands of Ron Flockhart and Ninian Sanderson, there was a Belgian D-type, and privateers Peter Bolton and Bob Walshaw entered an XK140 fixed head coupé Special Equipment model. The main opposition came from Aston Martin, Ferrari, Gordini and a brace of Maserati-engined Talbots — all, be it noted, with engines of less than 3 litres capacity. The Jaguars were understandably the hot favourites.

*Opposite page:*
The 1957 XK-SS under the bonnet.

*Right:*
The Mark VIII saloon.

All the more galling therefore that a silly accident on the second lap should put two of the works D-types out of the race. The track was slippery from recent rain, and approaching the Esses, Paul Frère braked too hard, went into a skid and hit the barrier. Jack Fairman who followed close behind managed to avoid Frère's car but in doing so, was hit by a Ferrari. All three cars were damaged and retired. Afterwards, Frère sportingly accepted the blame in public for this unhappy incident. Meanwhile, the Hawthorn/Bueb car had trouble with the fuel feed which it took a long time to trace to a cracked pipe; this put the surviving works Jaguar right at the bottom of the lap chart, but once the fault had been traced, Hawthorn and Bueb began the long climb back. The Ecurie Ecosse D-type had now gone into second place behind the Moss/Collins Aston Martin, and for the rest of the race these two cars conducted their own private battle, with the only surviving Ferrari a lap behind in third place. On Sunday afternoon, it was the Scottish D-type which received the chequered flag, bringing Jaguar a fourth Le Mans victory, and the first for Ecurie Ecosse. The Aston and Ferrari

*Below:*
The Jaguar XK140 badge.

were second and third, while the Belgian D-type came fourth and Hawthorn/Bueb finished in sixth place after a magnificent effort. The XK140 put up a remarkable performance and was in 11th place when disqualified for having refuelled a lap too early — a simple mistake which, it seems, was owing to lack of organization in the pit-work.

Then in October 1956 it was announced that Jaguar were retiring from racing. The official reason was that the factory did not wish to incur the expense of developing another new competition model which would become necessary with further changes in race regulations. By now, Jaguar had achieved what they wanted, and by retiring from racing and closing down the competition department, full attention could be given to developing and making new road cars in ever-increasing numbers. Each new Jaguar now carried a badge on its bootlid proclaiming the four Le Mans wins; the company could rest on its laurels with no little satisfaction. The works racing cars were sold to Ecurie Ecosse, and for the time being small scale production of the D-type continued.

An indication of where Jaguar was heading for

a hood and a luggage rack on the tail; the car was even fitted with bumpers. But in fact all XK-SS cars — and they only made 16 of them — were converted from D-types held in stock, finished or half-finished cars. No really reliable performance figures were ever published but it was estimated that a road equipped XK-SS with suitable gearing would have a top speed of at least 144mph (232km/h) and *The Autocar* measured acceleration from 0 to 100mph (0 to 160km/h) in 14.4 seconds. Most of the cars were sold in North America, the price being variously quoted as $6,900 or $5,600.

Whether the XK-SS was merely Jaguar's way of shifting unwanted D-type stock or whether it was the intention to make more XK-SS cars on a series production basis we shall never know; in the evening of 12 February 1957 fire broke out in the factory at Browns Lane, and when the next morning dawned it was seen that a quarter of the works had been destroyed before the blaze had been stopped. The affected areas were mainly the final assembly lines, and the despatch bay; almost 300 finished or near-finished cars were destroyed, including five D-types which were scheduled for

the future was given by the range announced for 1957. The XK140 was now available with automatic transmission, and there was a new model in the shape of the Mark VIII which was a development of the Mark VIIM. The Mark VIII featured a C-type cylinder head and larger carburettors which increased power output to 210bhp; it was also rather more luxuriously equipped. Externally, it was distinguished by a new radiator grille, a curved one-piece windscreen, a chrome trim strip which divided colours on two-tone cars (this form of colour scheme being in itself an innovation for Jaguar), and slightly cutaway rear wheel spats. It replaced the Mark VIIM in production although the older model remained in the new season's catalogue.

In 1957 the Suez crisis triggered off petrol rationing, which caused the Monte Carlo Rally to be cancelled. Amid the gloom, Jaguar announced a new sports car in the unusual month of January. This was the fabled XK-SS which was in effect a road-going version of the D-type, with a re-designed cockpit which, although still spartan, gave slightly better accommodation for two people. There was also an ordinary windscreen,

*Overleaf:*
Four views of the Jaguar XK-SS (1957).

*Below:*
The badge of the XK-SS.

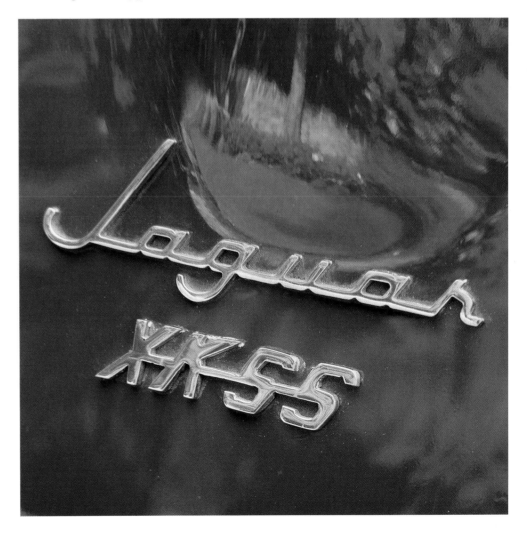

conversion to XK-SSs. All the D-type/XK-SS tooling was lost, putting an end to further developments of this exciting line.

Remarkably, a few days after the fire a shortened assembly line was started up again; maximum effort was put into clearing the affected areas of the factory, and all the damaged cars or parts were ruthlessly scrapped. While rebuilding work was going on at Browns Lane, Dunlop helped out for a time by giving Jaguar accommodation in the old factory at Swallow Road. But within a matter of months, Jaguar were back to normal, and 1957 set another record for production with almost 13,000 cars delivered in the year ending 1 August. Almost two-thirds of these were saloons, reflecting the continued popularity of the 'executive' Mark VIII and the growing demand for the compact saloon cars of which there were now two.

The 3.4-litre saloon was launched almost in the week after the fire, a happy coincidence which demonstrated that Jaguar were undaunted by misfortune. It was a simple enough recipe – take one 2.4-litre saloon and insert a 3.4-litre 210bhp

engine. In fact it took a bit of engineering shoe-horning to get this rather taller power unit under the bonnet, and there was a larger radiator and a larger clutch, as well as a stronger rear axle. The overdrive and automatic gearbox options were offered from the start of production. Surprisingly little had been done in the chassis department, and the drum brakes – which initially were the only type offered on the 3.4-litre – came in for a good deal of criticism in road test reports. Quite simply, they were insufficient for a 28½cwt (1,448kg) car with a top speed of 120mph (193km/h). In the autumn of 1957, Jaguar took heed and offered four-wheel Dunlop disc brakes as an option on both the compact saloons, and from then on most customers specified these. Externally there was little to distinguish the 3.4 from a 2.4; a slightly wider radiator grille was soon standardized also on the smaller-capacity car, so there were only the badges, cutaway rear wheel spats and the twin exhaust pipes to tell you which model it was that had just overtaken you.

Some months before the advent of the disc-braked saloons, Jaguar had introduced their first true production touring model so equipped. Admittedly other manufacturers had brought out road cars with disc brakes before Jaguar; the Jensen 541 fitted them on all four wheels from the autumn of 1956 and at the same time the Triumph TR3 had discs at the front, while the rare Austin-Healey 100S of 1955 also used four-wheel discs. Most significant from a mass-production point of view was the Citroën DS19 of October 1955, and the decision to use discs only on the front wheels was justified at least on this front-wheel drive car. Nevertheless, Jaguar were the true pioneers of disc brakes – it will be remembered that the C-type raced with them in 1952 – and the XK150 of May 1957 was thus the result of some five years of careful experiments and development carried out in co-operation between Jaguar and Dunlop. In fact there was a standard model of the XK150 available with drum brakes and disc wheels, but almost all the production cars were 'Special Equipment' models featuring wire wheels and disc brakes.

The XK150 replaced the XK140; the body styling was updated, although to this author at least the new car was nowhere as elegant as the original XK120 had been. Somehow the XK150 contrived to look both fatter and sleeker – but then that is how you would expect a successful cat to look! The wing lines were modified and smoothed out, there was a new and wider radiator

*Right, below and opposite page:*
A 1959 XK150S coupé.

grille and the bonnet was also widened. The hefty bumpers were carried over from the XK140, and when fitted with wire wheels the XK150 did not carry rear wheel spats – though that had also applied to the XK120 and 140 models. The windscreen was now of the curved one-piece type. At first only fixed head or drophead coupé models were offered, although a two-seater roadster was introduced belatedly in 1958 and was almost exclusively sold in the American market. The standard engine developed 190bhp but the Special Equipment version had the 210bhp unit similar to the 3.4-litre saloon engine. As before, overdrive and automatic transmission were options. A year after the introduction of the XK150, the XK150S became available with what was known as the 'Gold Top' engine although this owed more to Harry Weslake than to the Milk Marketing Board. The revised cylinder head with three 2in SU carburettors and twin exhausts pushed the gross power output up to 250bhp at 5,500rpm.

Even after the factory's withdrawal, the name Jaguar was still to be reckoned with in racing. In the 1957 Sebring race, a Cunningham-entered D-type ran with a new engine size of 87×106mm for 3,781cc. Hawthorn and Bueb brought it into third place. This engine was a factory development which was scheduled to find its way into production in the near future. Nearer home, Ecurie Ecosse ventured out with two D-types for the last Mille Miglia but this was to prove no happier than previous Jaguar efforts in this race; both cars retired. Nor did much luck favour the Scottish team at Spa or the Nürburgring, as on both occasions they were beaten by the works Aston Martins.

The Astons were also entered for Le Mans, together with an impressive line-up of new machinery from Ferrari and Maserati – the latter marque's entries included the Costin-designed aerodynamic coupé driven by Stirling Moss and Harry Schell – and both Italian contenders had 4-litre engines developing at least 400bhp. Ecurie Ecosse had a 3.8 litre fuel-injected D-type driven by Flockhart and Bueb, and Duncan Hamilton had a similar car, co-driven by Masten Gregory. The Scottish team's second car was a 3.4-litre carburettor car assigned to Sanderson and Lawrence. In addition there were production D-types entered by Belgian and French teams. The rules demanded full-width windscreens of at least 15cm (6in) in height, measured vertically, and a hood which had to 'effectively protect all the available seats' which at Le Mans meant a

minimum of two. The intention was to reduce maximum speeds, which were indeed down by 10mph compared with the previous year, although the final results were again new records for distance and average speed.

It was a very good race. Mike Hawthorn in the most potent Ferrari set a new lap record which was unbroken for five years; he also led the race from the start but soon gave way to Jean Béhra in the biggest Maserati. But when both cars retired with mechanical failures – as did most of the Italian entries – Flockhart and Bueb slipped into the lead and never looked back. At the half-way mark, most of the Italian opposition and even three of four Aston Martins had been eliminated from the running, and there were four Jaguars in the first four places on the scoreboard; only the Hamilton/Gregory car was trailing slightly. By mid-morning, the four leaders had sorted themselves out in the order they would eventually finish – Flockhart and Bueb first, Sanderson and Lawrence in the second Ecurie Ecosse car in second place, followed by the French and Belgian D-types respectively. Then there was a single Ferrari interloper, but Duncan Hamilton's D-type was sixth having made worthy progress in the second half of the race. Jaguar's fifth and (until 1988) final Le Mans victory, honourably scored by Ecurie Ecosse, was by far the most impressive – five cars started, five finished, in the first four and sixth places. Le Mans had not seen anything like it since the comparable performance of the Bentleys in 1929.

There was nothing really that could follow this act and perhaps for that reason Ecurie Ecosse stayed away from the sports car race at Reims, notwithstanding the successes achieved by Jaguars on this track in the past. There was in fact little further activity for the remainder of 1957, with the exception of that oddity of an event, the so-called 'Monzanapolis' arranged on the high-speed Monza track in Italy where American Indianapolis 500 single-seater racing cars were pitted against three Ecurie Ecosse Jaguars. As expected the D-types were outclassed – they could not match the winning American's average speed of 160mph (257km/h) – but they ran like clock-work to finish in fourth, fifth and sixth places, and created a stir among the Americans who had not imagined that 'cheap production sports cars' would acquit themselves so well against the expensive specialized Indianapolis machines. A similar event was held in 1958, and for this David Murray of Ecurie Ecosse collaborated with Brian Lister (whose Jaguar engined sports cars had put

up many a creditable performance in racing) to produce an extraordinary Jaguar-engined single-seater for which 200mph (322km/h) was claimed. Alas, Jack Fairman broke a camshaft in this car and ultimately finished eleventh, bracketed by the two proper D-types entered which came ninth and twelfth.

For 1958 in general, a capacity limit of three litres was imposed on sports car racing so Jaguar made a special 2,986cc version of the XK engine which was fitted to the Ecurie Ecosse D-types. This had the standard 83mm bore but a shorter stroke of 92mm; it developed some 254bhp at 7,000rpm, using Weber carburettors and a compression ratio of 10:1. One of the Ecurie Ecosse cars, driven by Fairman and Lawrence, finished seventh at the Nürburgring in May. The 1958 Le Mans was wet and nasty; it rained for 15 of the 24 hours. There were five D-types in the race. Both the Ecurie Ecosse cars suffered piston failures in the early stages of the race, and a privately-owned D-type crashed soon after. With the road and weather conditions, accidents prevailed, and there was, sadly, one fatality – the French driver 'Mary' (Jean-Marie Brussin) whose D-type came to grief on a muddy stretch by the Dunlop bridge. The only remaining D-type was that of Duncan Hamilton and Ivor Bueb who valiantly held on to second place, until Hamilton overturned the car at Arnage when trying to avoid another competitor in the rain. The final winners were Olivier Gendebien and Phil Hill in a Ferrari.

Was the D-type being outclassed? It would seem so; inevitably Jaguar's withdrawal from racing meant that less effort was being put into keeping the car truly competitive against new designs from Aston Martin or Ferrari, despite the support given by the company not only to Ecurie Ecosse but also to the Lister-Jaguars. Ironically it was the Lister, or other Jaguar engined-machines such as the Tojeiro-Jaguar, the Cooper-Jaguar and the HWM-Jaguar which now featured more and more in racing. In a gesture almost symbolic of the new era, Ecurie Ecosse ran a Lister and a Tojeiro in the 1958 TT; and in that autumn they put their D-types up for sale; retaining only one car – for old times' sake? – which was seen at Le Mans for another two years. But 1958 was the last big onslaught of Jaguars at Le Mans. Though there would be a brief renaissance for the marque at their favourite venue when E-types ran in the GT class in the early 1960s, this was followed by a hiatus of 20 years before the big cat once again returned to prowl its customary habitat.

*Opposite page, top:*
A 1959 XK150S.

*Opposite page, centre and bottom:*
A 1957 XK150.

*Left:*
Elegant details of the XK150.

# EXPANSION AND DIVERSIFICATION
## 1958-1960

Although 1958 might have seen the virtual abdication of Jaguar from sports car racing, examples of the marque were still being rallied and also began to feature in saloon car racing which really got off the ground in Britain when a new championship was instituted in that year. The Mark VII had already proved itself in touring car and production car races in the early 1950s but its successors, the Mark VIII and, later, the Mark IX, were rarely seen on the track; by contrast the new generation of compact saloons appeared everywhere.

The 3.4-litre was a readymade racer and made its debut at Silverstone in the *Daily Express* meeting in September 1957, where Mike Hawthorn, Duncan Hamilton and Ivor Bueb came first, second and third in their new 3.4s – and let it be added that these were early drum-braked models. When the 1958 championship got under way, the most consistent 3.4 driver was Tommy Sopwith, although Sir Gawaine Baillie, Duncan Hamilton and, on one famous occasion, Mike Hawthorn also won races. Hawthorn's win was at Silverstone in May; it is amusing now to look at pictures of his 3.4 litre saloon complete with standard wire wheels, bumpers and a badge bar which sported the badge of the recently-formed Jaguar Drivers Club! At the end of the season Sopwith was just pipped at the post of the championship by the Austin A105 driver Jack Sears; although for the next few years it was Jaguars which would dominate saloon car racing. It took a little longer for the new car to find its feet in rallying; despite a record number of 30 Jaguars entered in the 1958 Monte Carlo, the highest placing achieved was 24th. However, the Morley brothers, Donald and Erle, who later leapt to fame in the Austin-Healey 3000, won their

*Opposite page:*
The 1958 Jaguar Mark IX saloon.

class with a 3.4-litre in the 1958 Tulip Rally. But tragedy struck in the Tour de France; Peter Whitehead, winner of the 1951 Le Mans, was killed when he crashed the 3.4-litre he shared with his half brother Graham.

The only new Jaguar launched in the autumn was the Mark IX, a further development of the Mark VII/VIII theme, and externally barely distinguishable from the latter, but important as being the first Jaguar which used the 3.8-litre engine in production (the engine size first seen in the 1957 racing season). It was also the first model which had four-wheel disc brakes as *standard*; it will be remembered that these were still officially 'optional' on both the XK 150 and the small saloons! The Mark IX engine developed 220bhp; other interesting aspects of its specification were the vacuum-assisted braking system, and another first on a Jaguar – power-assisted steering. The manual transmission model still gave you a fiver's change out of £2,000 ($5,600 at the time), while the bigger engine gave a useful boost to performance with a top speed now around 114mph (183km/h), almost 10mph (16km/h) more than the previous model.

At the end of the 1958-59 financial year, Jaguar passed two significant milestones: the number of cars produced was now over 20,000 for the 12-month period, and during that time profits had exceeded one million pounds – in fact, at £1,385,000 ($3,878,000 at the time) the profits had more than doubled from 1957-58. The excellent financial results obtained throughout the years when Jaguar were an independent company – right up to 1967, in fact – were in no small measure due to Sir William Lyons' careful husbanding of resources. There was never any money spent unless it was absolutely necessary,

*Previous pages left:*
The Mark IX saloon,
introduced in 1958.

*Previous pages above and
below right:*
Detailed views of the
Mark IX.

and overheads were always kept down to a minimum — even if Browns Lane at times presented a scruffy aspect! No one in the industry or the motoring press ever quite understood how Sir William managed to keep his cars so reasonably priced, but part of the secret was that Jaguar were effectively mass-producers compared with companies such as Daimler or Armstrong Siddeley. Of the quality car makers at the time, only Rover achieved production figures comparable with Jaguar's. No wonder that between them the two companies dominated the quality car market. Sir William was therefore able to take full advantage of the economies of scale when buying components or materials. At the end of each year a substantial proportion of the profits would be ploughed back into the business, and Sir William's policy in paying dividends was somewhat conservative — he himself held the absolute majority of shares in Jaguar anyway. Nevertheless the value of Jaguar shares as recorded by the stock exchange more than trebled during the 1950s — something from which today's Jaguar shareholders may take heart — and there was never any problem in raising additional capital; several new share issues were successfully completed.

Further new models were introduced during 1959. The 3.8-litre engine was installed in the XK 150 models which were now available with a bewildering array of four different engines: 3.4, 3.4 S, 3.8 and 3.8S! In the triple-carburettor S form the 3.8 litre engine was rated at 265bhp (in common with all other Jaguar bhp figures at the time, the gross output was quoted) with a 9 to 1 compression ratio. The S models were only available in manual gearbox form with overdrive as standard, while all three types of transmission were offered in the 'cooking' XK150s. The 3.8S model also featured a limited slip differential. This was the fastest Jaguar production road car before the advent of the E-type; in 1960 John Bolster of *Autosport* recorded a top speed of 136mph (219km/h). In the previous year, *The Motor* had tested a similar car with the 3.4 engine which reached a maximum of 132mph (212km/h). The UK price of the 3.8S model was £2,175 ($6,090 at the time) at the end of 1959; this made it the most expensive Jaguar at the time, and it may be remembered that a basic Mini cost just under £500 ($1,400 at the time) in the same year.

However impressive this final version of the XK range may have been, the other new range of Jaguars was rather more important. The small saloon car range was very considerably revised and emerged as the Mark II — the original 2.4 and

*Right:*
The 1959 Jaguar XK150S,
with a 1971 E-type V-12.

3.4 models were never called the 'Mark I' but this piece of retrospective nomenclature is now often used. The Mark II models had subtly restyled bodywork, with a deeper front screen and a larger wrap-around rear window, while the side windows were also increased in size as the one-piece doors gave way to half doors with chromed channel window frames. The radiator grille was slightly altered, and all the Mark II models featured the cutaway rear wheel spats first seen on the 3.4-litre. This was the most successful restyling job ever done on an existing bodyshell; Sir William had a tendency to get it right first time, but later updates of his shapes were often less attractive than the originals. The XK150 or XK140 never matched the XK120 for purity of line, and the Mark VIII/IX shape was rather fussy and over-adorned compared with that of the Mark VII. But while the original 2.4/3.4-litre design had been a good-looking car, the Mark II was equally attractive. Inside was a completely new design of fascia, with the speedometer and rev counter set in front of the driver and the auxiliary instruments and switches grouped on a centre panel; this set the pattern for Jaguar dashboards throughout the 1960s and beyond. Another new idea was a centre console which accommodated the radio and a useful cubby-hole.

Mechanically the Mark II models were not subject to so many changes but disc brakes were now standard and power-assisted steering became available as an optional extra. The 2.4-litre engine still used two Solex carburettors but had an improved cylinder head design and now developed 120bhp. The 3.4-litre engine was more or less unchanged, but there was an additional model in the shape of the 3.8-litre which was fitted with the 220bhp engine from the Mark IX. This was the most convincing sports saloon from Jaguar yet; with manual gearbox and overdrive, its top speed was 125mph (201km/h). Without extras, the car cost £1,779 in the home market, while an American customer would pay $4,795 for the overdrive-equipped model; the 3.8 was the only Mark II normally sold in the USA, in either overdrive or automatic form. The Mark II models retained their popularity throughout a long production run which lasted until 1967, and the 3.8 was always the favourite of the range — with 'cops' as well as 'robbers'. Many police forces took to the car for patrolling Britain's new motorways, while a 3.8 featured as a get-away car in the Great Train Robbery. Now it is the most sought-after classic Jaguar saloon. Many enthusiasts still mourn the passing of a 'small' Jaguar from the

*Above right:*
The badge of the Jaguar
Mark II 3.8 saloon.

*Above, right and opposite
page:*
Three views of the 1962
Jaguar Mark II 3.8-litre.

range, and hope that some day Jaguar will bring back a compact sports saloon.

On the sporting side, 1959 brought some excellent results for the Jaguar saloons. The year opened well with three 3.4-litre saloons winning the Charles Faroux Team Trophy in the Monte Carlo Rally; two of the cars were placed eighth and ninth overall, and in addition George Parkes/ Arthur Senior/Geoff Howarth won their class. Parkes and Senior just missed winning an Alpine Cup when they took the same car on the Alpine Rally, while Parkes was placed fifth in class in the RAC Rally. But the two outstanding victories of 1959 went to the Morley brothers together with Barry Hercock who came first in the Tulip Rally, and Nano de Silva Ramos/Jean Estager who won the touring car category in the Tour de France. In saloon car racing, the 3.4-litre continued to dominate events; in eight meetings during 1959, this model scored seven firsts, four seconds and two thirds. The leading drivers were Roy Salvadori in John Coombs' car, and Sir Gawaine Baillie and Ivor Bueb from the aptly named Equipe Endeavour. Sadly, two fatal accidents marred Jaguar's year.

Mike Hawthorn was killed in January when his 3.4-litre road car overturned on the Guildford bypass, and, later in the year, Ivor Bueb met his death at the wheel of a Cooper Formula Two car which he was driving in a French race. Hawthorn and Bueb had shared the winning Jaguar at Le Mans in 1955, and Bueb had won again in 1957, while Hawthorn had become the World Champion Formula One driver in a Ferrari in 1958. More than 30 years after his death, you can still hear people arguing whether Hawthorn or Stirling Moss was the most outstanding driver of their generation; both contributed immensely to British prestige in the world of motor racing.

Ecurie Ecosse took their last remaining D-type to Le Mans in 1959, this time fitted with their own 3-litre version of the XK engine. But Innes Ireland and Masten Gregory had little luck – they were in second place when engine trouble forced them to retire. The same car reappeared at Le Mans in 1960, now driven by Ron Flockhart and Bruce Halford; to conform with new regulations it was fitted with a windscreen no less than 25cm (10in) tall and a rather symbolic boot. That year

Mike Hawthorn at the 1956 Le Mans.

it got as high as fourth place before breaking its crankshaft, and with this farewell appearance the D-type largely faded from the race tracks. But there was another Jaguar at Le Mans in 1960, a much more interesting car. This was the E2A prototype, which for the first time gave the public a glimpse of Jaguar's eagerly awaited new sports car which had been under development since 1957 and would go into production in 1961. Briggs Cunningham had persuaded the factory to release E2A for him to enter at Le Mans, where the car ran in the American racing colours of blue and white, driven by Dan Gurney and Walt Hansgen. The car never threatened the Ferraris seriously, and after being damaged in a minor collision it retired with a blown head gasket. As it appeared in 1960, E2A looked like a cross between the D-type and the production E-type – the light alloy bodywork had E-type proportions but was riveted together like the D-type, the centrelock wheels and the tailfin were pure D-type but the deep windscreen required by regulations gave it a definite E-type look. Underneath was a fuel-injected 3-litre XK engine, while the monocoque-type construction and independent rear suspension were largely typical of the forthcoming E-type. The car was later raced in the USA but eventually came back to the UK as part of Guy Griffiths' collection of Jaguars and other racing cars at Chipping Campden.

Most of the saloon car racing drivers changed over to the new Mark II 3.8-litre model when it became available, but although the Jaguars continued to dominate their class, the saloon car championship still eluded the marque – in fact a Jaguar never did win the British saloon car championship. The outstanding result of the season was the *Daily Express* Trophy meeting at Silverstone in May where Jaguar scored a traditional victory – the 3.8s were first, second and third, Roy Salvadori winning at 87.55mph (141km/h) which would have been a quite respectable figure even for a sports car, with Stirling Moss and Graham Hill in second and third places. At the British Grand Prix meeting in July, Colin Chapman of Lotus took a turn at the wheel of John Coombs' 3.8 (normally driven by Salvadori)

The Jaguar E2A prototype, first seen by the public at Le Mans in 1960.

and won his race, again with other 3.8s in second and third places.

Making up for his disappointment in 1959, George Parkes returned to the Alpine Rally together with Geoff Howarth in a 3.8-litre Mark II in 1960; this time they came fifth overall and for their efforts, received one of the six Alpine Cups awarded. Another cup went to the Frenchmen Jose Behra and Rene Richard who in a similar car were placed third overall, and also won their class. Next, Parkes and Howarth notched up a class win in the Tulip Rally, one of three class wins for Jaguars in the 1960 Tulip. It was, however, the French team of Bernard Consten and Jack Renel, who scored the best result for Jaguar in the 1960 rally season. They won the touring car category in the Tour de France outright, and what is more, they repeated this three times in the following three years. The RAC Rally had moved to November at the end of the season, and 1960 was the last year before the special stages of the rally moved into the forests which would not suit Jaguars quite so well as the old-style road rally had done. Jack Sears and Willy Cave gave Jaguar a final fling in the RAC by winning their class and coming fourth overall in their 3.8-litre.

On the business side, a most important step forward for Jaguar came with the announcement in May 1960 that Jaguar were to take over Daimler from the BSA group. The main reason for this was that Daimler possessed a large and rather under-utilized factory complex at Radford on the northern side of Coventry, not far from the original Motor Mill on the Coventry Canal where F. R. Simms and H. J. Lawson first began to manufacture cars in 1897, under licence from the German Daimler company. Daimler was therefore one of the oldest and most hallowed names in the British motor industry, and had gained further respect by becoming the favourite car of Royalty; King Edward VII was the first British sovereign to own a car, and he chose a Daimler. For years after, Daimlers were the natural choice for Royal transport, both as state cars and as private cars.

The BSA group had bought the Daimler company in 1910; soon after the company introduced the Knight sleeve-valve engine which became a Daimler hall mark for the next 20 years. In 1930 BSA also bought the Lanchester company, another of the industry's pioneers as Frederick Lanchester had run his first car in 1896. These early Lanchesters were noted for their individualistic engineering but during the

1920s the company had offered a range of luxury cars equal to Rolls-Royce and one of their customers was HRH The Duke of York, later King George VI. But Lanchester got into financial difficulties during the depression and after the company was merged with Daimler the original Lanchester factory in Birmingham was closed; subsequent Lanchesters came from the Daimler factory in Coventry and were in effect smaller badge-engineered versions of Daimler cars.

From the 1930s onwards both marques adopted a pre-selector gearbox with a fluid flywheel automatic clutch, and an often bewildering range of models was offered, from a 1.4-litre Lanchester Ten to the vast V12-engined Daimler Double-Sixes which were eventually replaced by a series of only slightly less gargantuan straight-eights. After the war, Daimler and Lanchester came under the influence of the BSA chairman Sir Bernard Docker and his famous wife, Lady Norah; they were responsible for a series of flamboyant special-bodied cars, the Docker Daimlers, which, with gold-plated fittings or zebra-skin upholstery, were guaranteed to enliven the dullest Earls Court Motor Show. However, the Daimler company tried to compete with Rolls-Royce, Jaguar and Rover, all at the same time, but without ever really having one truly successful model. Sir Bernard was finally ousted in a boardroom revolution, and as part of the subsequent cut-back in company activities a promising prototype of a new small car, the unitary-construction 1.6-litre Lanchester Sprite with Hobbs automatic transmission, was shelved in 1956, and with it the Lanchester name disappeared.

Daimler's chief engineer at the end of the 1950s was Edward Turner who is remembered by motorcycle enthusiasts as the designer of the Ariel Square Four and the original Triumph parallel twin. He developed two new V8 engines, of 2.5 and 4.6-litres capacity respectively; both were of advanced light-alloy construction and although only a single camshaft in the centre of the V was used, they featured hemispherical combustion chambers and valves in V-form. The smaller engine made its debut at the beginning of 1959 in the SP250 sports car which was a remarkable break with Daimler tradition. It was unfortunately not a perfect car; the glass fibre bodywork was awkwardly styled, and the chassis was an inferior copy of the Triumph TR3. However the engine was praised by all for the turbine-smooth way in which it delivered its power, right up to the 121mph (195km/h) top

speed. The larger V8 was being readied for production at the time of the Jaguar takeover, and appeared before the 1960 Motor Show in the Majestic Major, an additional model to the existing saloon and limousine range, although its six-cylinder stablemates were soon discontinued.

The negotiations between Sir William Lyons and BSA's chairman, Jack Sangster, who as a young man designed the Rover Eight of 1919 (his family had founded the Ariel motorcycle firm and he rose to his position at BSA through the motorcycle industry) were completely amicable, and at the end of the day Sir William paid £3,400,000 (about $9,520,000 at the time) – out of cash in hand – for the Daimler and Lanchester rights and names, the business and goodwill, and the Radford factory. Part of the deal was the Daimler commercial vehicle business which primarily meant buses but also included armoured fighting vehicles; this brought Jaguar into a completely new sphere of activities, while the Daimler car programme supplemented Jaguar's existing models nicely. The SP 250 was a cheaper and smaller sports car than Jaguar's own XK 150 range, and the big Majestic Major models (which were in the £2,500 to £3,000/$7,000 to $8,400 bracket) were a useful supplement to the Mark IX at the top end of the luxury limousine market.

The intention, carried out within a few years, was to streamline production facilities so that all car assembly would be carried out at Browns Lane, and Radford would be turned over to machining and assembly of engines and gearboxes. The additional factory space virtually doubled Jaguar's capacity, and put an end to the company's problems in this respect. It was not possible to extend the Browns Lane factory any further, and Sir William Lyons wisely did not wish to set up a satellite factory outside Coventry; this was the era when car manufacturers were encouraged to build new factories in the development areas, and both BMC and Rootes moved to Scotland while Standard-Triumph, Ford and Vauxhall set up on Merseyside; even Rover opened a plant at Cardiff. How right Sir William's instinct was has been proved in later years when the Triumph plant at Speke, the BMC-Leyland truck factory at Bathgate and the Hillman Imp factory at Linwood have all been closed down. What was not foreseen in the early 1960s was that Daimlers would eventually lose their own engineering identity and largely end up as badge-engineered Jaguars; but at least Jaguar have dutifully kept the proud name alive on a range of cars that are a credit to the Daimler tradition.

The purchase of Daimler was, although the most important, only the first in a series of moves by Sir William Lyons to widen the field of operations for his company. In 1961, he bought Guy Motors, truck manufacturers of Wolverhampton, from the receiver for a modest £800,000 ($2,240,000 at the time); the 'assets' included the rights to long-gone companies such as Sunbeam and B.U.T. trolleybuses. Under Jaguar's ownership Guy was turned around and a new range of Big J trucks was introduced in 1964. By that time Sir William had made a further acquisition, the Coventry Climax engineering business which was bought from the Lee family in 1963. Coventry Climax had supplied engines to small specialist car manufacturers (and some quite large ones, too) since the years before the First World War, but their main business was now in fire pumps and forklift trucks, although they had gained more publicity from supplying engines to sports and racing car manufacturers such as Cooper and Lotus; four World Championships in Formula One have come the way of Climax-engined cars. It was also a Coventry Climax engine design which was adopted by Rootes for the Hillman Imp small car in 1963. With the acquisition of Coventry Climax, an old employee returned to the Jaguar fold, none other than Wally Hassan who had been instrumental in the design of the XK engine and now came back to help with the next generation of Jaguar engines.

Of all the acquisitions from this expansionist period in Jaguar's history, it is only Daimler which remains linked with the company today. After the Leyland merger in 1968, Guy was transferred to the Leyland Truck and Bus Division. Guy trucks at least kept their identity until the marque went out of production; the Fallings Park plant was kept busy on other Leyland products until finally closed down in the purges during Sir Michael Edwardes' tenure of BL. It was also during this time that Coventry Climax, then a part of BL's Special Products Division, was sold to the company with the other great name in forklift trucks, Conveyancer. After having gone into receivership in 1986, Coventry Climax were bought by the Swedish Kalmar group. While the manufacture of Daimler armoured cars was continued by Jaguar for some time – the final Ferret model had an XK engine – the Daimler bus activities also passed into the Leyland melting pot, and from there to oblivion.

*Opposite page:*
A 1965 Daimler Majestic Major hearse, an example of Daimler versatility.

# ACHIEVEMENT WITHOUT PARALLEL
## 1961-1967

The year 1961 was Jaguar's *annus mirabilis*. It was the year when the fruits of the company's investment in motor racing were harvested; it was the year of the E-type which made its debut to an incredulous international audience at the Geneva Motor Show in March. The impact of an all-British supercar capable of a top speed of 150mph (241km/h) was, to put it mildly, considerable − and it was not lessened when it was announced that this outstanding engineering masterpiece would sell for £2,098 (around $5,875).

The E-type had been under development since 1957. The concept of the car, including its styling, was derived from the D-type, and the D-type construction method was also employed; basically the body was a monocoque from the scuttle aft, and in front of this there was a subframe carrying engine and front suspension, covered by a one-piece forward-hinging bonnet. One important innovation was incorporated in the E-type − the independent rear suspension with inboard-mounted disc brakes. Two rather different proto-E-types were built; E2A was intended purely as a sports-racing car to replace the D-type at Le Mans where, as we have seen, it made a belated appearance in 1960. E1A was on the other hand the direct progenitor of the true E-type as it was intended as a road car replacing the XK150. It was fitted with a 2.4-litre engine and, like E2A, had an aluminium body.

During 1958-59 the E-type assumed its final shape, in the open two-seater form originally envisaged; the fixed head coupé came later. With hindsight, it is tempting to describe the coupé model as a hatchback, as the rear window opened

*Opposite page:*
A 1965 Jaguar 3.8 S-type

sideways to give access to the luggage platform behind the seats, of which there were only two. For production cars, a change was made to steel bodywork; the bodyshell was welded up from a comparatively large number of small panels with joints lead-filled afterwards. This was a legitimate way of keeping down tooling costs but inevitably increased the labour content per car; that Jaguar chose this method of body construction was perhaps an indication that they seriously underestimated the potential production life of the E-type, just as they had with the XK120 in 1948.

The front suspension with wishbones and torsion bars was familiar to any Jaguar enthusiast, but the new rear suspension was different. Geometrically the rear suspension formed a parallelogram, of which the upper side was the drive shaft with two universal joints, while the lower side was a tubular link; at the outer end the two links were joined by a cast aluminium wheel carrier. The lower link was forked at both ends, being pivoted to the wheel carrier, and at the inner end it was pivoted to the subframe which carried the entire rear suspension, final drive and inboard-mounted brakes in a self-contained unit. Longitudinal location was provided by a pair of trailing arms attached to the lower links. On either side were two coil springs and telescopic shock absorbers to look after suspension and damping, with the assistance of an anti-roll bar.

The remainder of the specification held fewer surprises; Dunlop disc brakes were fitted all round, with vacuum servo assistance and a front/rear split hydraulic circuit, while steering

*Above:*
These views of a 1962 S1
3.8 E-type show the lines of
the open two-seater form
originally envisaged for the
car.

*Right:*
A 1963 Jaguar S1 3.8
E-type coupé

was by rack and pinion. The engine was the 3.8-litre XK with three SU carburettors and a 9 to 1 compression ratio, with a quoted gross power output of 265bhp at 5,500rpm; the same as in the final XK 150 3.8-litre S model. A then novel feature was the thermostatically controlled electric radiator cooling fan. The gearbox was also carried over from the XK150 but was now made by Jaguar themselves instead of, as previously, the Moss company; the four-speeder was as yet innocent of synchromesh on the bottom ratio, and an automatic alternative was not available.

There was not a great deal of room in the interior and the fit of the bucket seats was on the snug side, although in fact they did not offer a great deal of support and one was likely to slide around on the leather upholstery. The dashboard layout was borrowed from the Mark II saloon with rev counter and speedometer straight ahead, and auxiliary gauges above a row of switches in the centre of the panel. In the best sports car tradition, the heating and ventilation arrangements were on the primitive side. The habitability and ergonomics of the E-type were those aspects most frequently criticized in the early road tests and continued to be the least desirable aspects of the car throughout its lifetime.

Otherwise, every magazine editor or staff writer

who could lay hands on an E-type was full of praise for the new Jaguar. Both *The Autocar* and *The Motor* (whose testers tried the coupé and the open car respectively) recorded top speeds around the 149-150mph (240-241km/h) mark; from a standing start, 60mph (97km/h) was reached in 7 seconds and 100mph (161km/h) came up after 16 seconds — while one was still in third gear. The price one had to pay for performance of this order was a fuel consumption of 18mpg; but who would call this unreasonable? Performance apart, it was the sheer refinement and tractability of the E-type which attracted notice; here was a car that was as suitable for a Le Mans entry as it was for high-street shopping, always assuming one could find somewhere to stow the parcels. It fell to Henry N. Manney III and *Car* magazine to coin the most famous description of the E-type as 'the greatest crumpet catcher known to man'.

Despite its obvious attractions undoubtedly there were those who were disappointed with the E-type — those who had hoped for a true successor to the D-type which could bring the Jaguar name back to prominence on the race tracks. Of course the E-type was raced — it even won, in the hands of Graham Hill, on its first outing at Oulton Park in April 1961 — but it was a road sports car, and no lightweight at that. To keep a foot in the door

*Above:*
A lightweight 1963 E-type, twelve of which were made in that year.

of the GT sports car class, Jaguar supported John Coombs whose early E-type (which originally had the famous BUY 1 registration mark!) was extensively modified with thinner-gauge steel for the monocoque, an aluminium bonnet and Weber carburettors. The development work on this car led directly to the true lightweight E-type competition model of which some 12 were made during 1963. These cars had all-aluminium bodywork, the cylinder block and crankcase being also of aluminium, and the engines had dry-sump lubrication and fuel injection. A five-speed ZF

gearbox was fitted. Weight was reduced from the standard steel roadster's 24cwt (1,219kg) to little over 18cwt (914kg). Six cars were sold to British drivers, including of course John Coombs; four went to the USA of which Briggs Cunningham had three, one went to Australia and the final car was sold to Peter Lindner and Peter Nöcker in West Germany.

Cunningham had already taken an E-type – a lightened coupé – to Le Mans in 1962 where he and Roy Salvadori were rewarded with a fourth place, while Peter Sargent and Peter Lumsden in a part-aluminium roadster fitted with a hardtop and a D-type engine had come fifth; a third E-type, the coupé of Charles and Coundly, had retired early in the race. The lightweight E-type's competition debut came at Sebring in March 1963 where two of Cunningham's cars came seventh and eighth behind a string of Ferraris. The cars were also making their mark on British circuits in the hands of drivers such as Roy Salvadori, and Graham Hill who drove John Coombs' light-weight to victory in the *Daily Express* meeting at Silverstone in May. In the Nürburgring 1,000 km (620 miles) race, Lindner took an early lead with the German lightweight car but subsequently retired, as did Sargent/Lumsden in a sister car. For Le Mans, it was Cunningham who again upheld the tradition by entering three E-types; Richards and Grossmann finished ninth but the two other cars in the team both retired. There were other appearances later in the season but the Jaguars were finding it increasingly difficult to keep up with Italian opposition in the shape of the Ferrari 250 GTO.

In 1964 a young Formula 3 driver called Jackie Stewart drove Coombs' lightweight car on a number of occasions when he was not at the wheel of one of Ken Tyrrell's BMC-Coopers. Little luck attended the Jaguars this year; at Le Mans, both the lightweight cars entered retired, and this was the last appearance of the Big Cat at the Sarthe Circuit for 20 years. Later in the year, Peter Lindner was killed while driving his E-type in the 1,000km (620 miles) race at Montlhèry. At the end of the 1964 season, Jaguar stopped their support for semi-private entrants such as John Coombs and Briggs Cunningham; after that, E-types in Britain were primarily seen in club level racing, while in the USA there were still many successes to come for the E-type in SCCA production sports car racing in the 1964-66 period.

Going back to 1961, when the Motor Show came around in October Jaguar had not only the E-type on their stand but also another new model, the Mark X saloon which replaced the Mark IX. The new model followed the E-type's lead in adopting independent rear suspension, while at the front a coil and wishbone layout similar to that of the small saloons was employed. Also similar to the Mark II was the use of unitary construction bodywork; Jaguar had now said goodbye to the separate chassis. Much of the strength of the body came from generously-dimensioned sills; they were so deep and wide they created some obstruction to entry and exit, especially as the seats were very low in the car.

Mark X power came from the three-carburettor 3.8-litre engine, and the usual transmission options were available. Power-assisted steering

*Above left:*
The driver's view: the 1961 Jaguar S1 'flat floor' 3.8 E-type.

*Above right:*
The Jaguar S1 'flat floor' 3.8 E-type.

*Above:*
A 1966 Jaguar Mark X, now with the 4.2 engine.

was now standard, and the dual-circuit vacuum-assisted all-disc brake system followed the general lines of that on the E-type. However the major innovation of the Mark X was its styling; the front end leaned aggressively forward and sported double headlamps flanking a smaller and squarer version of the Mark IX grille. The bonnet was wider and flatter than before, and the wing line was a continuous curve from headlamp to tail-lamp; the rear wings had a pronounced separate shape without quite being tailfins. The windscreen was of the wrap-around type, and the traditional elongated rear quarterlight was still in evidence. The most prominent feature of the car was the bulging section of the body; the overall effect was to give the Mark X a rather cigar-shaped look. It was a very large car, too – almost 17ft (518cm) long and more than 6ft (183cm) wide, it rode on a 10ft (305cm) wheelbase, but at 4ft 6½in (138cm) was no less than 8½in (22cm) lower than the Mark IX.

At the time, the styling of the Mark X was considered a great improvement over its predecessor, and it was obviously very much in tune with contemporary styling developments although it retained the essential Jaguar character. In later years the shape dated quite quickly, and it is now perhaps the least admired of the Jaguar saloon range. Its sheer vastness has probably contributed to this! An important feature of the car was the roomy and well-appointed interior, with a massive transmission tunnel topped by a centre console in front. It was laid out as a five-seater, but with 50in (127cm) across the interior obviously a generous five-seater. Rear seat

passengers were especially well looked after with picnic tables, armrests and their own heater outlets. It was perhaps not surprising that Jaguar soon offered a Mark X limousine with a glass partition between the front and rear compartments! This version also had a radio and clock for the rear compartment, a cocktail cabinet and reading lamps, while electrically operated windows were optional on both models.

The Mark X was a lot of car for the money at just under £2,400 ($6,720 at the time) including tax in 1961; and despite its dimensions and the not inconsiderable weight of 37cwt (1,880kg), the Mark X had excellent performance too. Top speed was around 120mph (193km/h) – about on par with the 3.4-litre engined Mark II, and a good 5mph (8km/h) more than a Mark IX. It could reach 60mph (97km/h) from standing start in less than 11 seconds, and it took 33 seconds to get to 100mph (161km/h). Fuel consumption was a rather daunting 14 to 16mpg, disappointing when compared with the old Mark VII which would usually return 20+mpg. The Mark X was a supremely comfortable car to travel in, and road manners were surprisingly good for a car of this size although the amount of roll on corners, while not in absolute terms excessive, underlined the fact that this was more of a limousine than a sports car.

Not that Jaguar needed another sports saloon at the time; the popularity of the Mark II models was undiminished. The 3.8-litre continued to win in touring car races during 1961, Tommy Sopwith's Equipe Endeavour being most successful with team drivers Graham Hill and

Mike Parkes taking turns to win. Sir Gawaine Baillie and Peter Jopp won their class in the Alpine Rally, while Bernard Consten and Jack Renel repeated their win in the Tour de France. In Germany, Peter Lindner and Peter Nöcker (whom we have already mentioned as the owners of a lightweight E-type) had also taken to racing Jaguar saloons; they won the Nürburgring six-hour race and Lindner scored sufficient class wins in GT and touring car races to win the German championship.

For 1962, a small number of 3.8-litre saloons were specially prepared by Jaguar for their French and German distributors; four cars went to France for the use of Bernard Consten and others in rallying, and three cars went to Peter Lindner's growing stable, which was rewarded with a 1-2-3 win in the six-hour touring car race at the Nürburgring in June 1963 while Lindner and co-driver Walter came first in the more strenuous 12-hour race at the same venue in the following month. Another 1-2-3 win came in that year's Tour de France where Consten and Renel, the usual winners, were followed home by two other 3.8s. In Britain, Graham Hill was now driving John Coombs' 3.8-litre saloon as well as the lightweight E-type and he notched up most of the saloon car race wins, but Roy Salvadori, also in a Coombs car, accounted for two historical results: a second place after a Chevrolet at Brands Hatch in May – the first time that a Jaguar had been trounced in the big car class – and soon afterwards, a most satisfying victory over that same Chevrolet at Crystal Palace. In October 1962, Lindner and Nöcker brought their 3.8 to England for a six-hour race for Group 2 saloons at Brands Hatch; they achieved a very creditable second place having covered 167 laps as against the 171 of the winners, Mike Parkes and Jimmy Blumer, whose mount was also a 3.8.

However the days when the compact Jaguars dominated saloon-car racing were fast drawing to a close. A short-lived fashion for large American saloons such as the Chevrolets or the Ford Galaxies was followed in British racing by the determined onslaught of newcomers such as the Ford Lotus-Cortina and the BMC Mini-Coopers; much smaller and more agile cars which in the right circumstances soon turned out to be as fast as the Jaguars. In fact 1963 was the last good year for the small Jaguar saloons even if a 1-2-3 win in the Brands Hatch six-hour race was spoiled by the disqualification of Salmon and Sutcliffe following post-race scrutineering which made Salvadori and Hulme the winners, followed again by Lindner and Nöcker. The two German drivers had already scored an important win on their home ground by beating Böhringer's Mercedes-Benz 300SE in the Nürburgring six-hour race in June, and Nöcker went on to become the first European touring car champion, driving Lindner's Jaguar. Consten and Renel scored their fourth and final victory in the Tour de France, but this was the last important win for a Jaguar Mark II saloon in international motor sport. Before Jaguar bowed out of competitive motoring altogether, an impressive demonstration had been staged at the Italian Monza track in March 1963; the Castrol Oil Company and Jaguar had a shot at emulating the famous 100mph (161km/h) for a week-long run of the XK120 coupé in 1952. The chosen vehicle was a 3.8-litre saloon; regrettably the heavily-laden car began by breaking its rear axle due to the pounding from the bumpy surface, and the team had to start the run all over again. This meant that there was only time to complete four days, but average speed for this period was 106.6mph (171.6km/h) – enough to set a number of new class records.

On the production side, 1962's most important new model had been not a Jaguar but a Daimler. Reputedly following representations from Daimler dealers, Jaguar took a Mark II bodyshell and installed the 2½-litre Daimler V8 engine in it, the result being the Daimler 2½-litre saloon which was only distinguishable externally from its Jaguar counterparts by its 'D' badges and

*Below:*
A 1969 Daimler V8-250, perhaps the most satisfying version of the Mark II bodyshell.

*Left:*
The traditional interior of
the 3.4 S-type.

discreet fluting to the radiator grille and number-plate light housing. The engine was both lighter and more powerful than the 2.4-litre XK engine and the result was a 110mph (177km/h) car which handled better than the Jaguar, and was priced in between the 2.4-litre and 3.4-litre models. The Daimler was at first offered only with automatic transmission but the lightly revised 1967-69 model which was called the V8-250 was offered with Jaguar's all-synchromesh gearbox with overdrive as an alternative. To many people the small Daimler was and is the most satisfying version of the basic Mark II theme, offering sufficient performance allied to almost uncanny refinement and silence. Easy high-speed cruising with scarcely a whisper from that turbine-smooth V8 was a great part of its attraction.

From 1963 onwards, arguably Jaguar's product planning became somewhat confused. In the 1963 Motor Show there was a new Jaguar saloon; not as might have been expected a replacement for the Mark II but an additional model. The rationale behind the S-type was to fill the gap between the compacts and the Mark X, and in terms of pricing the S-type worked out around £200 ($560 at the time) more than the Mark II models with equivalent engines. The S-type was

offered with either the 3.4 or the 3.8-litre twin-carburettor engines; its front end was almost identical to the Mark II's but the rear end followed the styling of the Mark X. The most important mechanical change compared to the Mark II was the adoption of independent rear suspension, similar to that of the Mark X. The interior of the new model was also similar to the Mark X's in the design of the dashboard and the seats, although there was of course no more room than in the Mark II. The S-type was slightly longer, heavier and therefore slower than equivalent Mark II models but it offered improved handling and was more refined. It remained quite popular during its five-year production run.

In 1964 came a more important long-term development — the appearance of a new version of the XK engine. By boring the 3.8-litre engine out to 92mm, capacity was increased to 4,235cc and although bhp remained unchanged at 265, there was a useful increase in maximum torque from 260 to 283lb/ft, still delivered at 4,000rpm. The new engine was equipped with an alternator instead of a dynamo, and it was accompanied by a new all-synchromesh gearbox. The 4.2-litre engine was introduced in the Mark X saloon which was virtually unchanged in most other

*Far left:*
The Jaguar 3.8 S-type —
popular during its
five-year run.

respects, save for an improved heating system and the option of full air conditioning; and it also went into the E-type which at the same time benefited from a revised interior, most importantly with much-improved seats.

There were no great changes to the existing range of Jaguar cars throughout 1965 although it was commonly known that the company was working on a two plus two version of the E-type which it had originally been hoped to have on the Motor Show stand in October 1965; but the launch of the new model was delayed until March 1966. At a glance the new car looked exactly like the original E-type fixed head coupé but when the two cars were placed side by side, it was revealed that the two plus two had an extra 9in (23cm) in the wheelbase — shown up by the much wider door — and that 2in (5cm) had been added to the height of the car. The rear floorplan was extensively redesigned to accommodate extra seating in the back, and the rear seat had a folding squab permitting extra luggage space if you were travelling alone or two-up. The other main external recognition point was the higher and more upright windscreen. Interior appointments were uprated but the provision of a lockable glovebox would have seemed more relevant on the open E-type than on the new coupé! For the first time, an E-type was available with automatic transmission as the two plus two was offered with a Borg-Warner box. It was only possible to install

this in the long-wheelbase model where there was more space available, so the open E-type and the short-wheelbase two-seater coupé (which continued in production) stuck to manual transmission only.

A further new model announcement was made in 1966 when Jaguar gave birth to twins at Motor Show time. With the Jaguar 420 and the Daimler Sovereign, Jaguar succumbed to blatant badge-engineering; no Daimler V8 for the Sovereign as both cars had the 4.2-litre XK engine. The new cars were based on the S-type but the front end was now also restyled on Mark X lines, with a squarer radiator grille and four headlamps. In these cars the 4.2-litre engine 'made do' with two SU carburettors instead of the three fitted to the Mark X and the E-type so power output was slightly down at 254bhp; in practice the 420 turned out to have a performance on par with the rather heavier Mark X. At the same time, the 4.2-litre Mark X was re-named the 420G — where the G might have stood for Grand, or even Gross? The new-style nomenclature which aped Mercedes-Benz spread further down the range in 1967 when the Mark II 2.4-litre and 3.4-litre models became the 240 and 340, while the 3.8-litre model was discontinued. The 240 and 340 were identifiable by new slimmer bumpers and different hubcaps; and to reduce cost, equipment was not as comprehensive as before — fog lamps had disappeared and standard trim was Ambla rather than leather. On the credit side, the 240 was fitted with two SU carburettors and power was increased from 120 to 133bhp. The price of the cheapest Jaguar was a still remarkable £1,365 ($3,276 at the time) and even the 340 model cost only £1,442 ($3,461 at the time) – less than a Ford Zodiac Executive or a Vauxhall Viscount and comparable with the £1,418 ($3,403 at the time) tentatively asked for Austin's ill-fated new 3-litre.

Even the prolific new model programme that Jaguar undertook in the 1960s, which only found its culmination with the introduction of the XJ6 in 1968, was overshadowed by the turn of events which now overtook the Jaguar company. In 1966, Sir William Lyons was 65 years of age and had seen enormous changes in the British motor industry during his 45-year career. Instead of a multitude of small independent companies fiercely competing against each other, the trend was now towards large corporations with the remaining small independents either being taken over or being squeezed out of business. There was also the growing influence of the multi-national companies; Ford was the second-largest car manufacturer in Britain, GM owned Vauxhall, and Chrysler had begun its takeover of the Rootes Group. Among British companies, the Leyland truck maker had absorbed the tottering Standard-Triumph group in 1961 and rejuvenated the Triumph marque; Rover had taken over the small Alvis company and would in turn also become part of the Leyland group. Singer had long been part of Rootes, Jaguar themselves had bought Daimler and several companies had gone out of business altogether – Armstrong Siddeley, Jowett and Lea-Francis. It seemed that the days of the small independent car makers were coming to an end.

Another factor which influenced Sir William was that in 1965 the Pressed Steel Company which supplied Jaguar bodies had merged with their main customer, BMC. Pressed Steel was the last of the independent large-scale car body manufacturers in Britain as, more than ten years previously, BMC had bought Fisher & Ludlow and Briggs had been taken over by Ford. In the circumstances it seemed sensible to safeguard Jaguar's future by entering into an alliance with one of the the 'big five' car makers; of these, Ford, Vauxhall and Rootes were presumably excluded as prospective partners owing to their American ownership, and that the choice fell on BMC was mainly due to the question of securing Jaguar's

body supply. While Lyons had held tentative talks with Sir William Black and Donald Stokes of Leyland in 1965, the stumbling-block had been that Lyons was unwilling to give up his personal control of Jaguar even though he was offered the job of running all of Leyland's car business which would include Triumph.

In 1966, Lyons was approached by Sir George Harriman, BMC's chairman and managing director. Harriman made the proverbial offer that Lyons could not refuse; he was willing to buy the Jaguar company (in which Lyons held 260,000 of 480,000 voting shares) but with an assurance that Jaguar would remain autonomous under Lyons' executive control. Agreement was reached in July and the merger was made public at the end of the month. A new holding company, British Motor Holdings or BMH, was set up as the owner of both BMC and Jaguar, each with their subsidiary companies. The merger had few practical effects for either BMC or Jaguar, but steps were taken towards joint purchasing of supplies and some use of common components, and in many export markets BMC (or an existing BMC agent) took over the Jaguar franchise from long-established and experienced Jaguar importers. This happened in the USA in particular.

It may not have been known to Lyons that even before he concluded his deal with BMC, BMC had already been talking to Leyland about the possibility of the two companies merging, although nothing had come from these discussions originally begun in 1964. However by 1966-67 there was growing pressure from government to effect a merger between the only two remaining all-British car and truck makers; Harold Wilson's Labour government, with Tony Benn as Minister for Technology, did not relish seeing Rootes being gobbled up by Chrysler. The rapidly worsening financial position of BMC which was losing market share to Ford and was heading for a loss in 1967, appeared to underline the need for a merger with Leyland whose record of success in both the car and commercial vehicle fields under Donald Stokes was impressive. With prompting from the Industrial Reorganization Corporation, and thus from the government itself – at times Harold Wilson personally became involved in the discussions between Leyland and BMC – merger talks got under way in the second half of 1967. On 17 January 1968, it was announced that BMC and Leyland were to merge as the British Leyland Motor Corporation. What would be the position of Jaguar in this new conglomerate?

# XJ – PINNACLE OF EXCELLENCE
# 1968-1975

Thus 1968 began on a fateful note for Jaguar. Within the short space of 18 months, the company had changed from being the proudest independent car maker in Britain to becoming a small subsidiary of an automotive giant, the second largest European car maker after Volkswagen.

Sir William Lyons did not at the time openly oppose the BMC-Leyland merger; in the circumstances he probably felt that it would have been a waste of time – that the merger was a foregone conclusion, dictated by the government and by personal ambitions. So Lyons was left to fight a rearguard action to preserve Jaguar as an autonomous entity; he did this by first supporting the BMC faction within British Leyland, and when this position became untenable after the disastrous BMC financial results for 1967-68 provided an opportunity for a change of BMC chairman, Lyons extracted a promise from Stokes directly that Jaguar would not be interfered with, and that Lyons should continue to exercise control over Jaguar as executive chairman. Stokes was mindful of the prestige embodied in the Jaguar name and the personal standing of Sir William, and agreed readily enough; and it is a fact that of all the British Leyland companies, over the next 16 years Jaguar was much less interfered with by the Leyland board, or by the government, than almost any other subsidiary company.

Lyons even became vice-chairman of British Leyland and worked closely with Stokes as chairman – there is no doubt that Lyons' immense experience in the quality car business was of the greatest benefit to the new corporation in those early days when it still seemed that British Leyland had everything going for it. As far as the car-buying public was concerned, a Jaguar remained a Jaguar; although the process of

tidying up the dealer network – begun in the overseas markets after the BMC-Jaguar merger in 1966 – was now accelerated and spread to the home market. Many of the important Jaguar distributors already held franchises for other Leyland products anyway – such as Henlys for Rover, or Appleyard for Morris – and on the whole the unification of the Jaguar and British Leyland dealer networks was fairly sensible.

Purely by coincidence the first new British Leyland model came from the Jaguar stable, although it was badged as a Daimler. This was the DS420 limousine launched in 1968. By this time the previous large Daimler saloon/limousine model, the Majestic Major with Daimler's own 4.6-litre V8 engine, was dying on its feet; so was BMC's top-hatted Vanden Plas Princess limousine. The new model replaced both. Some thought had been given to continued manufacture of the Daimler engine – when experimentally installed in a Mark X, the big V8 had endowed this car with an almost embarrassingly good performance – but the complication and cost of building a unique engine in small numbers dictated the use of the 4.2-litre XK engine in the new limousine. The car was based on a lengthened floorpan from the Jaguar 420G, and also had the suspension and braking systems from the largest Jaguar but the new wheelbase of 11ft 9in (358cm) endowed it with accommodation for up to nine people on three rows of seats. It was by far the largest unitary body structure ever made in Britain.

The production process was quite complicated as the floor pressings came from Pressed Steel but the complete bodyshell was assembled by Motor Panels in Coventry and then sent to Vanden Plas in London for painting and trimming; Vanden

*Opposite page:*
Launched in 1971, the Series 3 E-type had the new V-12 engine.

Plas accepted this work in lieu of the similar work they had carried out on the Princess limousine, and within the Leyland hierarchy Jaguar eventually assumed responsiblity for the erstwhile Austin subsidiary, Vanden Plas. They continued to do so until 1979 when Vanden Plas' Kingsbury factory was closed down, and limousine production was transferred to Browns Lane. The styling of the DS 420 was typically dignified and, to those with long memories, evoked certain Hooper-bodied Daimlers of the 1950s; its furnishings and trimmings were subject to customer requirement and varied from almost spartan on the average hire-car to the sumptuous on limousines or even landaulettes supplied to heads of state. With remarkably few revisions, the DS 420 continues in production to this day, and has almost cornered a niche of the market which includes undertakers; it is frequently encountered with hearse bodywork, and for this purpose it is still available in 'chassis' form; it is probably the last car in Britain for which a chassis-only price is quoted.

A far more important new model was announced in September 1968 – the Jaguar XJ6. It was increasingly obvious that the entire Jaguar saloon range which consisted of four different bodyshells (240/340, S-type, 420/Sovereign and 420 G) and used four different sizes of the XK engine design – not to mention the Daimler V8 – was in need of both updating and rationalization. Since 1964, a new Jaguar saloon had been under development. The most important aspect of the new car was the all-new bodyshell which set a new standard for Jaguar elegance and, while retaining the well-defined Jaguar characteristics, brought the styling of the marque thoroughly up-to-date. Perhaps the most remarkable proof of how successful Lyons' styling was for the XJ6 is the fact that with a minimum of alteration the basic shape survived for more than 20 years, as a truly classic and timeless design. Equally important was the way in which the new body was engineered; Jaguar's number one priority was refinement and silence, and the engineering team under the direction of Bob Knight made enormous progress in insulating any noise, vibration or harshness which might penetrate to the interior of the car. Both front and rear suspension – in layout little changed from the previous all-independent Jaguar models – were mounted on separate subframes which in turn were rubber-mounted to the bodyshell. The front subframe also took most of the weight of the engine.

While Jaguar's all-new V12 engine (of which more later) was already under development during the gestation period of the XJ6, it was not possible to have it ready for the 1968 launch of the new model, although from the start the XJ was designed to accept the V12. So the XJ6 appeared with the well-tried 4.2-litre engine in twin-carburettor, 245bhp form. Jaguar offered an alternative in the shape of a new 'small' XK engine, the 2,791cc unit of 83 x 86mm bore and stroke. The 2.8-litre size was chosen as being suitable for a number of European markets which imposed annual car tax based on engine size. The 2.8-litre was never as popular as the bigger model, and although top speed was down by only 7mph (11km/h) and acceleration figures were still very respectable, a gain of 2mpg on fuel consumption figures was barely worthwhile in pre-fuel crisis days. Besides, the small engine turned out to be prone to piston failure in operation. The 2.8-litre lingered on in the catalogue until 1974 and, towards the end, was sold exclusively abroad.

When the magazines got their hands on the XJ6, they loved it. The car was by far the most refined and comfortable Jaguar ever made; its road holding and handling, in part thanks to Dunlop radial tyres and anti-dive geometry for the front suspension, was without peer. In terms of performance, the manual transmission 4.2 would see off any previous Jaguar saloon with the exception of a hard-driven 3.8-litre Mark II; top speed was around 124mph (200km/h), acceleration from 0 to 60mph (0 to 97km/h) took just under 9 seconds and 0 to 100mph (0 to 161km/h) took 24 seconds. When the car was driven hard, fuel consumption was at the rate of 15mpg. Such slight criticisms as were made concerned the scarcely adequate legroom in the back – fine for a sports saloon, less fine for an executive limousine – the old-fashioned ergonomics as Jaguar stuck firmly to their now traditional dashboard layout, the inefficiencies of the ventilation system and the perhaps over-light power steering (standard on the 4.2). Nevertheless, the XJ6 was proclaimed to be a British world-beater. With the XJ6 model, Jaguar had emerged as one of the world' leading luxury car manufacturers. Their product was in most respects superior to anything Mercedes-Benz or BMW could offer; no American luxury car could compare with the Jaguar's unique blend of driveability and comfort; and for the first time favourable comparisons were being drawn between the Jaguar and the Rolls-Royce. Accolades soon came the way of the XJ6; although it was not Car Of The Year – 1968's winner was the Peugeot 504 – the Jaguar received another 'car of the year' award from the British *Car* magazine.

Jaguar's only problem was that they just could not make enough XJ6s to keep up with demand. Very soon there were lengthy waiting lists; with some preference being given to deliveries to the USA and other export markets, at times home market buyers were quoted two-year delivery and even abroad the shortage was acute. Once, outside British Leyland's headquarters in London, Lord Stokes had to run the gauntlet of a demonstration of disgruntled would-be XJ6 buyers – from, of all places, Switzerland – who could not obtain delivery. The situation was eased when, during 1969-70, Jaguar finally cleared up the production programme; the last remnants of the old saloon car range such as the 240, the 420 G and the two Daimler models – V8-250 and Sovereign – disappeared. The only saloon made from then on was the XJ6, although from the autumn of 1969 the XJ6 range also included a new Daimler Sovereign. Apart from the fluted radiator and inclusion of overdrive as standard on the manual-transmission model, it was exactly like the Jaguars and was also offered with both engine sizes.

Around the same time as the XJ6 went into production, Jaguar revised the E-type which in the 1968 Motor Show appeared as the Series 2 model. The changes made to the E-type were largely dictated by new US regulations; for instance, the removal of the headlamp perspex covers which had already happened a year earlier on the so-called 'Series 1½' E-type. New on the Series 2 were full-width bumpers as opposed to quarter bumpers, bigger sidelamps and tail-lamps both repositioned below the bumpers, and safety-dictated retouches to the interior such as rocker switches. The air intake was larger to cope with the demands of air conditioning, an option only offered on LHD cars, primarily for North America; also intended mainly for American customers was the optional power steering. On the two plus two there was a new windscreen with the bottom edge pulled forward for greater rake which significantly improved the car's looks. Regrettably US emission standards now meant that cars for this market had less powerful de-toxed engines which were fitted with two Zenith-Stromberg CD carburettors. In this form the engine was rated at 171bhp so top speed was down to approximately 125mph (201km/h), with a much lower final drive ratio than home-market cars which still managed comfortably above 140mph

The distinctive badge of the Series 2 E-type.

(225km/h); but no E-types were really ever quite as fast as the original Series 1 models!

With the XJ range, including the sisters-under-the-skin Daimler versions, fully established in production, Jaguar's total output for 1970 nudged 30,000 cars of which almost three-quarters were XJ-type saloons; this meant an average of 420 XJs per week, every week. Behind the scenes at Browns Lane, they were preparing to spring another surprise on a startled world. On 29 March 1971, almost ten years to the day of the debut of the original E-type, the E-type Series 3 was launched; under its bonnet was the new Jaguar V12 engine. Only after the introduction of the new E-type was the remarkable saga of the V12 engine's development unfolded, and the existence of the XJ13 racing car revealed. Jaguar's engineers had begun to design a V12 engine as far back as the 1950s; originally this powerplant had been intended to keep Jaguar competitive in motor racing, and as first designed the V12 had four overhead camshafts and with bore and stroke firmly oversquare at 87 by 70mm, capacity was

*Right:*
A 'cutaway' V12 engine.

*Far right and below:*
A 1971 V-12 E-type.

*Above and opposite page:*
The Series 3 E-type was the
first recipient of the V-12
engine. This 1971 roadster
has manual transmission
(*below, right*) and optional
wire wheels. The blatant
V12 badge was not optional.

just under 5 litres. The original racing V12 was fitted with Lucas mechanical fuel injection and had a compression ratio of 10.4 to 1; it developed no less than 502bhp at 7,600rpm.

It seems that the engine design was settled before much thought was given to what kind of car the V12 should go into. Bearing in mind the rapid switch from front to mid-engined cars which had taken place in sports-car racing in the early 1960s, it was not surprising that Jaguar should choose to build a mid-engined car as the vehicle for a possible return to racing. The XJ13 took shape in 1964–66; it was constructed as an all-aluminium monocoque, with a Malcolm Sayer-designed shape which was clearly a direct descendant of the D and E-types. Many of the chassis parts were borrowed from the E-type, and a five-speed ZF gearbox was fitted. The finished car was tested in 1967 when it put in the famous all-time record lap of MIRA's proving ground at

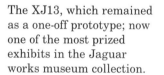

The XJ13, which remained as a one-off prototype; now one of the most prized exhibits in the Jaguar works museum collection.

161.6mph (260km/h) and proved capable of some 175mph (282km/h). Undoubtedly, with further development the XJ13 could have been made a competitive Le Mans challenger – at least if it had been ready before 1968 when new regulations limited sports car prototypes to 3,000cc. One rather questions whether Jaguar would have built 25 XJ13s for homologation as Porsche did with their 12 cylinder 5-litre car, the 917; and would the XJ13 ever have matched the 200+mph (322km/h) top speed of the German car?

Arguably the XJ13 came a couple of years too late to make an impact in sportscar racing; the car was also built at a time when Jaguar had their hands full developing the XJ6 model and could ill afford the time and money to start a new racing car project from scratch. So the XJ13 remained a one-off prototype; it was perhaps better so than if the car had been raced and had lost. It was badly crashed at MIRA in 1971 when being filmed prior

to the launch of the V12 E-type but luckily the original body formers had been preserved and the car was meticulously rebuilt over the next two years. It is now one of the most prized exhibits in Jaguar's works museum at Browns Lane.

But after the XJ13 had been abandoned, Jaguar's engine design team led by Claude Bailey, Walter Hassan and Harry Mundy, turned their attention to developing the V12 into a suitable power unit for road cars, primarily of course with an eye to installation in the XJ saloon; but as mentioned above, the new engine could not be ready for the launch of the XJ6 in 1968. It was then decided, in a repeat of the sequence of events leading to the debut of the XK engine in a sports car in 1948, to introduce the V12 in the E-type first. Compared with the proposed racing engine, the production V12 was much 'softer'; it employed only two overhead camshafts, one per bank, and had flat-faced cylinder heads with the combustion chambers in the pistons – the Heron head also found on the Rover 2000. The bore was increased to 90mm for a capacity of 5,343cc. As originally installed in the E-type the V12 was equipped with four Zenith-Stromberg carburettors and developed 272bhp at 5,800rpm; the power output figure was now quoted in net or DIN bhp so it was strictly speaking not comparable with the 265 gross bhp figure quoted for the 4.2-litre XK engine. Another interesting statistic was that, thanks to its all-alloy construction, the V12 was only 80lb (36kg) heavier than the XK engine.

Of course V12 engines were not unknown. Packard made the first series production V12 back in 1916; between the wars V12s had a vogue in America and even penetrated well down in the marketplace with the Auburn and the Lincoln Zephyr. In Britain, Daimler, Rolls-Royce and Lagonda all made V12 engines before 1939. However, after 1945 only Lincoln continued to make a V12 and even they stopped in 1948; afterwards V12 engines became almost exclusively associated with Ferraris until their monopoly was challenged by Lamborghini in the 1960s. Naturally there have been a few more 12-cylinder engines in racing cars, both in V-form and flat-12s such as the Porsche. But whereas both the Italian supercars were only in small-scale production, the Jaguar V12 was from the outset conceived with what must be called mass production in mind; by 1987 the total number of V12 engines made by Jaguar was over 100,000, and the design had become the most popular V12 engine in history.

The Series 3 E-type which became the first recipient of V12 was also revised in other respects. The short-wheelbase coupé was dropped, and the roadster was now built on the longer wheelbase from the two plus two. There was an even bigger front air intake fitted with a cross hatch grille reminiscent of the XJ6 and with an additional air scoop below. Well-ventilated pressed steel disc wheels were now fitted as standard with wire wheels on the option list. From the rear the new model could be identified by four exhaust pipes and some rather blatant Jaguar V12 badges. The use of the longer wheelbase on the open car meant that this, too, became available with Borg-Warner automatic transmission as an alternative to the manual box. Manual cars had a bigger clutch to cope with the torque from the V12; a manual E-type was just possible even if the car now weighed around 29cwt(1,473kg). Although no figures are available it is likely that more V12 E-types were made with automatic transmission than with manual. One enthusiast who dared to question Harry Mundy about the use of automatic transmission on a sports car was told bluntly that he, the enquirer, would not be able to change gear faster than the Borg-Warner box anyway, and comparative acceleration figures for automatic and manual E-types tend to confirm this. Less forgivable was the standard fitment of Jaguar's usual light power steering. A six-cylinder Series 3 E-type was quoted but only a few such cars were built.

V12 road tests proved that the car's acceleration was the equal of the Series 1 3.8-litre model, but the best top speed figure achieved in an independent road test was 146mph (235km/h) and the US specification cars were a good 10mph (16km/h) slower than this. Fuel consumption was around 15mpg. While in many respects the E-type was becoming somewhat old-fashioned, notably in the matter of cockpit accommodation and layout, the V12 engine won universal praise for its quietness, smoothness and sheer power. It is however a measure of how standards of road behaviour had risen in ten years – not least due to Jaguar's own XJ6, of course – that there were some comments about the superb engine being fitted to an outdated chassis. Nevertheless, the V12 E-type was equally impressive as a grand touring express and as an out and out sports car. The V12 even gave the E-type a final fling in motor racing; Jaguar's American importer, now British Leyland Inc, supported the Group 44 and Huffaker teams in the Sports Car Club of America championships in the 1974 and 1975 seasons, and in the latter year Bob

Tullius of Group 44 won the championship by a clear margin.

In 1972, Sir Williams Lyons, who had celebrated his 70th birthday the previous year, retired from his post as chairman and managing director of Jaguar; he was appointed honorary president of the company and continued to take an active interest in the proceedings at Browns Lane. In his retirement year, Jaguar could celebrate the 50th anniversary of the foundation of the original Swallow Sidecar Company which among other festivities was marked by a special exhibition in the Herbert Art Gallery in Coventry. Lyons' successor was 'Lofty' England, the one-time service manager who had also masterminded Jaguar's racing career. However his tenure was to be a short one; in the autumn of 1973, England – then 62 – took a step towards his own retirement by becoming non-executive chairman of Jaguar, and after a few more months he retired completely to live in Austria. Lord Stokes appointed Geoffrey Robinson – who had previously managed BL's Italian subsidiary, the Innocenti company – as managing director and chief executive of Jaguar, at the head of a seven-strong management board, among whose members chief engineer Bob Knight was the only Jaguar employee of long standing.

It was while England was boss at Jaguar that the long-awaited 12-cylinder saloon appeared – the always-intended XJ12. The marriage of the XJ body and chassis with the V12 engine had a happier result than had been achieved with the Series 3 E-type. The absence of noise and vibration from the V12 engine complemented the fine chassis engineering which had gone into the XJ design; and with very little extra weight to carry, the XJ12 performed quite remarkably better than the XJ6. Top speed was in the region of 140mph (225km/h), which made the XJ12 not only the fastest Jaguar saloon so far but also quite likely the fastest four-door saloon car made anywhere in the world until that time. Even with the massive 6.3-litre V8 engine in the 300 saloon, Mercedes-Benz could not match the Jaguar's performance. The XJ12 saloon engine had four carburettors similar to the E-type engine, but unlike the sports model the saloon was only offered with automatic transmission. Externally the car was identifiable by a vertical-bar grille with a V12 badge and the ventilated wheels used on the E-type. Very few modifications to the chassis specification had been necessary; the most important improvement was the ventilated front disc brakes which were later standardized on the XJ6 as well. Launched at a price of £3,726 (around $8,942 at the time) the XJ12 was in every way a remarkable motor car.

Shortly after the inevitable Daimler version appeared, reviving a famous Daimler name – the Double Six. The old Daimler apprentice 'Lofty' England may well have remembered the Daimler Double Six which he drove into second place in the first RAC Rally in 1932! A few months after the debut of the XJ12, criticisms of the lack of rear seat legroom in the XJ models were silenced when in the 1972 Motor Show, Jaguar introduced a range of long-wheelbase models on which an extra four inches had been added to the benefit of rear seat passengers, visible externally in the longer rear doors. Long-wheelbase versions of the XJ12, XJ6 4.2 and Sovereign 4.2 models were offered, while the long-wheelbase Double Six went one better as it became the Double Six Vanden Plas model with special luxury trim, including separate rear seats. The longer wheelbase was standardized on all 12-cylinder four-door cars when the Series 2 versions came out in 1973, although a short-wheelbase XJ6 four-door model survived into 1974.

It is necessary to make the point about four-door cars because when the updated Series 2 XJ range appeared in the autumn of 1973, the biggest news concerned a two-door pillarless coupé version which was to become available in four different models – as either a Jaguar or a Daimler, with either the 4.2-litre XK engine or with the V12. While the two-door cars were announced and displayed in the 1973 Motor Show, it was stated that they would not be available until the following spring; in fact, they did not emerge in quantity until early 1975, due to problems with the sealing between the door-glass and the quarterlight. With its longer door and vinyl-covered roof in addition to the pillarless side glass area, the two-door model, officially known as the XJC, was distinctive as well as pretty; but was always a limited production model and only just over 10,000 two-door cars were made from 1975 to 1977. The excuse for discontinuing the model was that, as by then it was the only XJ model to retain the original short wheelbase, it had become uneconomic to manufacture.

In general terms, all Series 2 XJ models had a raised front bumper to comply with new American bumper-height legislation; this meant that sidelamps were repositioned below the bumper, and radiator grilles were shallower. The XJ6 and XJ12 now shared a common cross-hatch grille, and the ventilated wheels were also found

*Opposite page:*
A 1972 V-12 E-type roadster. The bigger front air intake and additional air scoop can be seen.

on all models. Inside the new cars, the most apparent change was a new dashboard which proved that Jaguar had taken notice of the critical remarks about the cars' ergonomics: all the instruments were now grouped in front of the driver, and there were new and much improved controls for the lights and wipers. The old water-valve heater also gave way to a far superior air-blending one. A very small number of 2.8-litre engined Series 2 cars were made for certain European export markets, but the model was finally discontinued in early 1974. Series 2 nomenclature was later revised; in 1975 the XJ6 became the XJ 4.2 and the XJ12 was now known as the XJ 5.3, but the old style names remained in popular usage and were brought back by Jaguar for the Series 3 models four years later.

The year 1975 brought some important alterations and additions to the Jaguar saloon range. On the 12-cylinder models, carburettors were replaced by Lucas/Bendix/Bosch electronic fuel injection which made it easier for Jaguar to meet tightening American exhaust emission standards, and incidentally also improved power output to 285bhp. Fuel consumption was somewhat better at 13-14mpg compared with the rather daunting 11-12mpg which had been the norm for a carburettored V12, and top speed was up to 147mph (237km/h). A more appropriate 'economy' model was the XJ 3.4 which brought back the classic 3,442cc XK engine in revised form. This had a more sensible fuel consumption of 20mpg although inevitably top speed was down to 115mph (185km/h) – little different from the 2.8-litre car. The 3.4-litre engine was also offered in the Daimler Sovereign but this model was discontinued in 1977; the 3.4-litre Jaguar survived in production as the 'bargain' model of the range although on average it accounted for less than 15 per cent of six-cylinder XJ production. There was no two-door 3.4-litre car, nor any Vanden Plas or Jaguar Sovereign luxury versions with this engine size. A final new saloon model during 1975 was a Vanden Plas version of the Daimler Sovereign 4.2 which matched the corresponding Double Six model for luxury.

In 1974, the E-type finally went out of production; the last 50 cars which came off the line (all roadsters as the coupé had been discontinued in the previous year) were painted black, with one exception. The last but one was British Racing Green to special order from the Jaguar collector Robert Danny. The very last car, registered HDU 555N, was kept for Jaguar's own collection. For the first time since 1948, there was no open sports car in the Jaguar range. Was the marque going to become solely a luxury car manufacturer from now on, or would the E-type be replaced? Before that question could find an answer, Jaguar were once again overtaken by outside events, and this time the implications for the company were far more serious.

*Left:*
A 1975 XJ6 4.2 coupé.

*Left:*
The very last of the E-types, which is now in Jaguar's own collection.

# THE LEYLAND YEARS
# 1975-1983

In 1975 Jaguar became 'Leylandized'. It will be remembered that, back in 1968, Sir William Lyons had wrested a guarantee from Lord Stokes that Jaguar would be allowed to continue to operate independently; but Lyons had retired in 1972, and in the same year Jaguar Cars Limited had ceased to exist as an independent company, and was swallowed up by British Leyland UK Limited. While Jaguar still operated largely independently under its own chief executive, events elsewhere were fast overtaking the Browns Lane operation. When, in 1974, British Leyland as a whole made its first big loss, the Labour government commissioned the report from Sir Don Ryder which led to the virtual nationalization of the company in the following year, and also to far-reaching changes in its organization and operating methods.

The fact that Jaguar had not made a loss, and indeed under Geoffrey Robinson had produced a record number of cars in 1974 – 35,882 to be exact – mattered little. As far as Ryder was concerned, the answer to Leyland's troubles lay in grouping all the car making subsidiaries together in one more closely-knit company; the result was Leyland Cars, which combined Austin-Morris, Rover-Triumph and Jaguar. Browns Lane suffered the indignity of becoming 'Leyland Cars Large Car Plant'. The whole management structure was also revised following the Ryder report; casualty number one was Lord Stokes who was replaced by a non-executive chairman (Sir Ronald Edwards, and, on his death, Sir Richard Dobson) while Alex Park became chief executive director. As far as the new Leyland Cars company

*Opposite page:*
A Lister special XJ-S 5.7.

was concerned, Derek Whittaker became chief executive, while the post of chief executive for Jaguar was deleted. Geoffrey Robinson resigned at the ripe old age of 36 and began a new career in politics; in a by-election soon after, he was elected Labour MP for Coventry North-West, the Jaguar constituency.

So who exactly was running Jaguar? An 'operating committee' was set up but Browns Lane plant director Peter Craig actually did the day-to-day work, until his death in early 1977. One other figure emerged – chief engineer Bob Knight, a Jaguar man through and through, who now found that his engineering department was one of few remaining bastions of Jaguar independence. Bob Knight made a point of reporting directly to Derek Whittaker and in 1978 was given the title of managing director of Jaguar Cars. But by that time, Leyland had undergone another shake-up; late in 1977, Michael Edwardes had arrived from Chloride to assume the posts of chairman *and* chief executive, and he soon began a 'rolling re-organization' of the corporation. This meant that for quite some time, no one in British Leyland could be absolutely sure from day to day where their place in the system was!

Michael Edwardes realized the folly of trying to label everything as Leyland and one of his remedies was to allow the re-emergence of the respected old marque names. As a first step, Leyland Cars was split in two; Austin-Morris under Ray Horrocks and a new amalgamation, Jaguar-Rover-Triumph under William Pratt Thompson whose operation also included Daimler, Vanden Plas and (less logically) MG.

Pratt Thompson took up residence at BrownsLane but the JRT phase lasted less than two years. In 1980, Rover, Triumph and MG joined Austin-Morris in BL's new Light Medium Cars Division – soon re-named Austin Rover Group – under Harold Musgrove. This left Jaguar (including Daimler and in theory Vanden Plas, although after the 1979 closure of the Kingsbury plant this was little more than a name) once again on their own. In April 1980, a new full-time executive chairman was appointed to run what would soon become Jaguar Cars Limited; reputedly the choice of Sir Michael Edwardes himself, the appointee was John Egan. In the same year Bob Knight retired and was replaced by James Randle as Product Engineering Director.

Although John Egan was born in Lancashire, he had grown up in Coventry, the son of a car dealer, and he might be described as a local lad who made good. After an early career with Shell and GM's AC-Delco company, he joined British Leyland where he helped make a success of the Unipart parts subsidiary. From 1976 to 1980 he was an executive of the parts operation of the Massey-Ferguson tractor company whose factory in Banner Lane at Tile Hill outside Coventry had been built by the Standard Motor Company as a war-time shadow factory. Egan was just 40 when he was approached with the offer to take over Jaguar; after some time to think it over, he accepted out of a deep sense of commitment to the motor industry, and to Coventry. One of Egan's first actions after his appointment was to make it clear that he was personally committed to Jaguar's future. More than anything else this was a much-needed boost for morale in the company; and Jaguar were in disarray by early 1980.

The five years that had elapsed under the Ryder plan had seen Jaguar production nose-dive from 1974's record level of 36,000 cars to less than 14,000 in 1979. A number of factors had conspired to make Jaguars less popular in world markets; ever-increasing oil prices obviously did not help, and American sales had suffered from the pound's rise against the dollar since 1977. Worse was the undeniable fact that Jaguar cars were getting a reputation for bad quality. In the exclusive but fickle luxury car market, this was fatal; instead of buying a Jaguar, customers flocked to Mercedes-Benz or BMW. Abroad, commentators as usual talked of 'the English disease' and Leyland cars, including Jaguar, were fast becoming synonymous with outdated designs and shoddy workmanship. Those with access to inside information on the motor industry grapevine delivered their verdict: if you get a good Jaguar, it is very good, but if you get a bad one, Heaven help you. Most people, it seemed, had only had bad ones. Admittedly, in the prevailing anti-Leyland atmosphere of the late 1970s, it was virtually impossible to find a rational or unbiased statement about the company or any of its products, but as far as Jaguar were concerned there was more than a grain of truth in the rumours. Product quality did not live up to the expectations of luxury car buyers; warranty claims were enormous, and the Americans joked that if you have a Jaguar, better have two to make sure one of them is on the road.

The main new model that Jaguar brought out in this period was launched in the Frankfurt Motor Show in September 1975 – the XJ-S coupé. Inevitably it disappointed many observers who had been hoping for an 'F-type' super sports car to replace the E-type. The XJ-S was only available in coupé form with two plus two seating, its interior was called plasticky and the styling was not liked. Although the XJ-S was the last Jaguar with styling influenced by Sir William Lyons and Malcolm Sayer (who had died in 1971) it was no beauty comparable with the E-type or the XJ saloon. It had heavy black plastic bumpers of the American impact-absorbing type, a shallow radiator grille flanked by what someone unkindly called 'bus headlamps' – in fact they were specially developed highly efficient Cibié quartz-halogen lamps – and, at the back, a banana-shaped rear window was flanked by flying buttresses which ran down to strangely-shaped rear light clusters.

*Right:*
A view of the XJ-S showing the overall styling.

However all who drove the car revelled in its behaviour, its refinement and its performance; with a measured top speed of 153mph (246km/h) the XJ-S was the fastest production model Jaguar had ever made. The fuel-injected V12 engine was to the same specification as found in the XJ12, but unlike the saloon model, the XJ-S was available with manual transmission – the ex-E-type four-speed box – as an alternative to the automatic gearbox. However only a few hundred manual cars were manufactured before this option was dropped in 1979. The basis for the XJ-S was a shortened XJ saloon floorpan, with XJ-type suspension, steering and brakes, and the XJ-S always ran on cast alloy wheels similar to those fitted to the fuel-injection XJ12 saloon from the spring of 1975.

The price of the XJ-S when launched was £8,900 (around $19,580); quite a step up from the £3,743 (around $8,235) asked for the last E-type roadster, but obviously the new car was never intended as an E-type replacement; rather it was expected to take Jaguar upwards into a new market, com-peting with the Mercedes-Benz SL range which was soon joined by two other German supercars: the BMW 635 coupé in 1976, and the Porsche 928 in 1977. On the home front, the main XJ-S competitor was the Aston Martin V8; the AC 428 had been discontinued, Jensen breathed their last in 1976, the Bristol was too aloof and the Rolls-Royce Corniche and Camargue models were much too expensive. Although no American car could compare with the XJ-S, superficially similar packages were offered in the Cadillac Eldorado and the Lincoln Continental.

Over the next few years Jaguar and Daimler just ticked over without anything much in the way of product development. In 1977, the 12-cylinder cars changed from the Borg-Warner automatic gearbox to a General Motors Hydramatic GM 400 box, and in 1978 4.2-litre cars for the USA were equipped with fuel injection instead of carburettors. This gave a valuable reduction of their fuel consumption – important under the American CAFE (Corporate Average Fuel Economy) legislation which imposed an extra sales tax on cars if the manufacturer's whole range of cars had a high average fuel consumption. This 'gas guzzler' tax added a minimum of $500 to the price of each Jaguar sold in the USA.

At the end of 1978, it was announced that on manual transmission six-cylinder cars, the old Jaguar gearbox would be replaced by the five-speed gearbox originally designed for the Rover SD1 3500. This was inevitably greeted with derision by some enthusiasts who did not relish any association between Jaguar and lesser Leyland marques; but it was a sensible thing to do as there was no point in spending money (which Jaguar did not have anyway) on producing a new gearbox when the perfectly good Rover box was available. However as the Rover box could not handle the power and torque from the V12 engine, it meant the end of the manual option on the XJ-S, and also destroyed any hope for a manual XJ12 saloon. It also meant that the time-honoured overdrive option was discontinued as superfluous.

It was also in the rather lacklustre late 1970s that Jaguar returned to racing; or to put this episode in its correct perspective, Leyland Motorsport took Jaguar back into racing. The

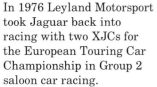

In 1976 Leyland Motorsport took Jaguar back into racing with two XJCs for the European Touring Car Championship in Group 2 saloon car racing.

chosen vehicle was the two-door XJC 5.3, and the man behind the venture was Ralph Broad of Broadspeed who had previously run a successful team of Triumph Dolomites for Leyland. Broad was now given a contract by Leyland Motorsport to prepare and run a team of two XJCs for the European Touring Car Championship in Group 2 saloon car racing. The cars were decked out in the Leyland colours of white, blue and red, and with extended wheel arches and spoilers looked the part; they were proudly shown to the press in the spring of 1976, but were far from ready to race at that time. The development story was a long battle against weight, complication and un-reliability; the first race appearance was in the Silverstone Tourist Trophy in September 1976 where Derek Bell started from pole position but the car retired with a broken driveshaft.

This was the only appearance in 1976; a pair of revised cars started in some of the 1977 Championship races but despite the fact that they were often the fastest cars on the track, unreliability dogged the Jaguars to the end. The best showing was a second place at the Nürburgring, but retirements after mechanical failures were more common. At the end of the

1977 season the whole racing programme was abandoned and the cars were retired to the Leyland Historic Vehicles museum then at Donington Park. It was rather sad that this attempt failed; had it been successful it would undoubtedly have been a shot in the arm for British Leyland and Jaguar at a time when good publicity was in very short supply. As it was, the racing cars became a symbol of how Leyland's corporate identity tried to extinguish the flame of Jaguar's independent spirit; for this reason the cars remain controversial, even as museum pieces, but in all fairness they were never more than an unimportant footnote in Jaguar's history.

In 1979, however, Jaguar took a major step forward with the introduction of the XJ Series 3 models. After almost 11 years, there was a facelift for the XJ styling, carried out with the assistance of Italian design consultant Pininfarina who had already shown his craft with an XJ12-based saloon in 1973, and the breathtaking 1978 Spyder showcar, based on the XJ-S. For the Series 3 XJ, the lower half of the car was left more or less unchanged, save for black bumpers, a new Daimler-type vertical bar radiator grille on the Jaguars, flush door handles and new rear lamp clusters; but the greenhouse was totally new. A new roof shape gave more headroom for rear seat passengers, the windows were deeper all round and curved glass was used in the side windows. The bigger glass area was a functional improvement which also brought the car's looks up-to-date, without losing any of its character; indeed, the Series 3 was far more elegant than the Series 2 which had never been as well-proportioned as the original Series 1 XJ, as the lengthened wheelbase had been rather obvious in the proportions of the side view.

With the introduction of the Series 3, the fuel-injection 4.2-litre engine was standardized for all markets and in non-USA specification gave 200bhp which was a useful boost for performance; the manual transmission model was now capable of 128mph (206km/h) and, significantly, also returned a fuel consumption of better than 18mpg overall. In the American market, the XJ12 was discontinued, leaving the 4.2-litre XJ6 as the only saloon model. As the 3.4-litre Daimler Sovereign had been discontinued in 1977, the smallest engine – still with two carburettors – was only offered in the Jaguar XJ6. The fuel-injected 4.2-litre engine was available in the XJ6, the Sovereign and the Sovereign Vanden Plas, and there was a parallel line-up of models with the V12 engine: XJ12, Double-Six and Double-Six

Vanden Plas. On all cars the interior trim and equipment were improved; one particularly welcomed new feature was an intermittent wipe facility.

When Egan took over the reins of Jaguar in 1980, this was the model range he inherited – supplemented by the XJ-S and the Daimler limousine. His first priority was to improve the build quality of these products. Adding to all Jaguar's other problems was the recent move of body manufacture to Pressed Steel Fisher's Castle Bromwich factory which was located near the M6 on the northern outskirts of Birmingham; this was 15 miles away and made more logistic sense than shipping bodies up from Pressed Steel Fisher's Cowley factory. But it took time before quality reached an acceptable level, in particular there were problems with the all-new paint plant where Jaguar bodies were sprayed with thermoplastic acrylic paint. Eventually this was sorted out, and Jaguar later assumed total control of the body plant at Castle Bromwich which is now one of the company's three factories. Egan also persuaded Jaguar suppliers and sub-contractors to improve and maintain quality levels, and motivated his own workforce by instituting 'Quality Circle' discussion groups throughout the factories. Slowly but surely things began to improve, and from 1981 Jaguar production rose, responding to renewed demand in all markets.

An important improvement was made to the V12 engine in 1981. This was the introduction of the 'Fireball' combustion chambers invented by the Swiss engineer, Michael May. As opposed to the original flat cylinder head design on the V12, the new May system had the combustion chambers machined in the head; they were designed to create a swirling motion of the mixture from the inlet valve across to a deeper chamber around the exhaust valve and sparking plug. The effect is that it becomes possible to use a very high compression ratio – no less than 12.5 to 1 – but with a very lean mixture. The result was dramatically better fuel consumption figures, and as there was also more power available (295bhp) Jaguar took the opportunity of fitting a higher final drive ratio. The re-named XJ12 HE (for High Efficiency) returned 16mpg on test, with 20mpg within the bounds of possibility for most drivers; acceleration times were fractionally slower but top speed was marginally improved. The Jaguar HE saloon could be identified by a new design of alloy wheels, with a multitude of drilled holes. The revised engine also went into

*Above:*
The Lister XJ-S with, *below and below opposite*, engine and interior details.

*Opposite page, top and centre:*
The Daimler Double-Six HE.

*Opposite page, bottom:*
The XJ-S in action.

the XJ-S which had another new, five-spoke wheel design and into the Daimler Double-Six which retained the old type of alloy wheels.

The Vanden Plas badge was applied to Jaguar models in 1981; both the XJ6 4.2 and the XJ12 HE were offered with Vanden Plas levels of trim and equipment in export markets where Daimlers were not sold. A year later, Daimlers were withdrawn from all European markets and the marque was for a time sold almost exclusively in Britain. When the 1984 models were introduced in late 1983, it was announced that the Vanden Plas versions would be dropped from production, to avoid any confusion with the Austin Rover Group which was now using the Vanden Plas name on luxury versions of the Metro, Maestro and Rover cars; the only exception was the American market where Austin Rover were not then trading, so a Jaguar Vanden Plas continued to be marketed in the USA. The Daimler saloon range was cut back to two models; the 4.2 and the Double-Six HE. The Sovereign name was transferred to Jaguar and was applied to a new luxury version of the XJ6 4.2 model as well as a revised XJ12 HE. Basically, this range took Jaguar and Daimler through 1984 and 1985.

Meanwhile the Jaguar name had made another comeback in racing. This time the initiative had come from Tom Walkinshaw Racing who had entered two modified XJ-S cars in the 1982 European Touring Car Championship, which was now run under FISA's new Group A rules which allowed only limited modifications from standard specification. The TWR Jaguars, among other victories, won the 1982 Silverstone Tourist Trophy, and for the 1983 season they received official and unstinting support from Jaguar. A highly satisfactory two seasons followed; in 1983, the Motul-sponsored cars in their white and green livery scored five firsts, two second places and two third places including a 1-2 win at the Osterreichring. It was however a disappointment that the TT win was not repeated – both Jaguars retired – especially as a fluke victory went to the Rover 3500 Vitesse; perhaps still allied to Jaguar in BL but very much considered a rival! Otherwise the BMW 635 coupés dominated the season, and BMW-driver Dieter Quester won the championship with Tom Walkinshaw in second place.

In 1984 this position was reversed. The three cars in the TWR-Jaguar-Motul team scored 1-2-3 victories in Sicily and Czechoslovakia, as well as five other wins, and Walkinshaw personally accumulated four firsts, two second places and

two third places, sufficient for him to win the championship 21 years after Peter Nöcker had won the very first European Touring Car Championship in Lindner's Jaguar Mark II.

In the USA, Bob Tullius and Group 44 had taken to the XJ-S in 1976 when they stopped racing the E-type. In the following two years, Tullius each year became the champion in Trans-Am Category 1 racing, and in 1978 Jaguar was awarded the manufacturer's championship in this category. For a period Tullius then raced Triumph TR 8s but for the 1983 racing season, he returned to the Jaguar V12 engine as the motive power for a far more ambitious project: a sports-racing prototype to be run in the IMSA Camel GT championship, the local equivalent of the FISA Group C World Endurance Championship, consisting of 17 races over a closely-packed season from February to November. Individual events varied from the Daytona 24-hour race and the Sebring 12-hour race, to short races over 3 hours or 500 kilometres.

Tullius' mid-engined Jaguar XJR-5 challenger was designed by Les Dykstra and was completely built in his own workshops in Winchester, Virginia; but the engine was authentic Jaguar V12 even if Tullius bored it out so that capacity was 6 litres and power some 600bhp! Obviously a believer in the old adage that there is no substitute for litres, Tullius eschewed the use of turbocharging. He was rewarded with four wins in the 1983 season and accumulated enough points to come second in the championship; his antics attracted favourable notice at Browns Lane and on one occasion John Egan himself flew out to see Tullius race the green-striped white car with the Jaguar name prominently and proudly displayed on nose and flanks.

The 1984 season was not quite so successful; of the Group 44 team, British driver Brian Redman was highest placed as number six in the championship, and the only win for the XJR-5 came in the Miami Grand Prix. One reason why

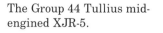

The Group 44 Tullius mid-engined XJR-5.

Group 44 did not do so well in the 1984 championship was that they missed out several important American races to come to Europe for Le Mans. Two XJR-5s duly appeared for the 24-hour race in June, with official Jaguar factory backing, and although neither finished the race, they did not disgrace themselves. The psychological impact of a Jaguar back at Le Mans for the first time since 1964 could not be overestimated, and the publicity which the company got out of this first attempt was invaluable. Jaguar's return to Le Mans, and the company's involvement with motor sport in general, was a pointer to future developments.

Another preview of Jaguar's future was given in 1983 with the unveiling of the first new XJ-S models since 1975. At long last, here was the factory's own open version of the XJ-S – after several private conversion jobs – even if Jaguar, under the influence of US safety legislation, felt compelled to incorporate a rollover bar and make the car a two-seater at that. The XJ-SC Cabriolet

was considered a great improvement over the styling of the original coupé as the awkward flying buttresses had been lost.

More important was what had gone under the bonnet – the first all new Jaguar engine since the appearance of the V12. The new engine was called the AJ6 (for Advanced Jaguar) and was destined to replace the XK engine as the main powerplant for future Jaguars, including the XJ 40 saloon. It was revealed to be a 3,590cc in-line six with almost square dimensions of 91 x 92mm bore and stroke. Like the V12 it was made entirely from aluminium alloy; it is quite likely that the AJ design had begun as one bank of the V12 engine but during years of development there had been so many changes that the final product was totally different. Like the XK, the AJ6 had two overhead camshafts, and if there were a few raised eyebrows over the fact that Jaguar chose to stick with chain drive rather than use a toothed belt to drive the camshafts, there was universal

The AJ6 (Advanced Jaguar) engine line.

*Right:*
The new AJ6 engine.

*Below:*
The 1983 XJ-S cabriolet.

approval for the cylinder head design with four valves per cylinder. With a 9.6 to 1 compression ratio and Lucas/Bosch electronic fuel injection, the engine developed 225bhp at 5,300rpm.

The AJ6 was in all respects a much more modern design than the XK. It was lighter and more powerful and was also capable of far more development and would make life easier for Jaguar's engineers trying to cope with current and future emission standards in both the USA and Europe. One slight problem with the AJ6 however was its bulk; it was not exactly a compact engine, even for a 3.6 litre straight six, and although it was installed at a slight angle from the vertical it was still necessary to add an admittedly discreet bulge to the XJ-S bonnet to clear it. Production of the AJ6 began on a very modest scale; undoubtedly Jaguar saw the advantage of being able to try out the design in the limited-production sports model, just as they had with the XK engine in 1948 and the V12 in 1971. The new six-cylinder engine was offered in both the XJ-S coupé and the cabriolet, while the V12 was available only in the XJ-S HE coupé which continued in production. However a V12 cabriolet was added to the range in 1985. The six cylinder XJ-S 3.6 was not offered with automatic transmission but only with a new manual five-speed all-synchromesh gearbox supplied by the German Getrag company.

With a top speed of 141mph (227km/h), the XJ-S 3.6 lost surprisingly little to the V12 on performance, and its fuel consumption was much better than the V12 – comparable in fact with that of the fuel-injected 4.2-litre saloon. Early road tests indicated that the AJ engine had yet to reach the same level of refinement as the XK engine, but undoubtedly Jaguar's engineers were working hard to rectify any shortcomings in the AJ6 engine design before the launch of the XJ 40 saloon model which, after several false hopes, was postponed until 1986. Obviously the new engine had to be right for this car which was so important for Jaguar's future, but if one judges by past performance Jaguar will have an estimated 30 years in which to develop the AJ6 design further!

*Left:*
The rear of the XJ-S cabriolet.

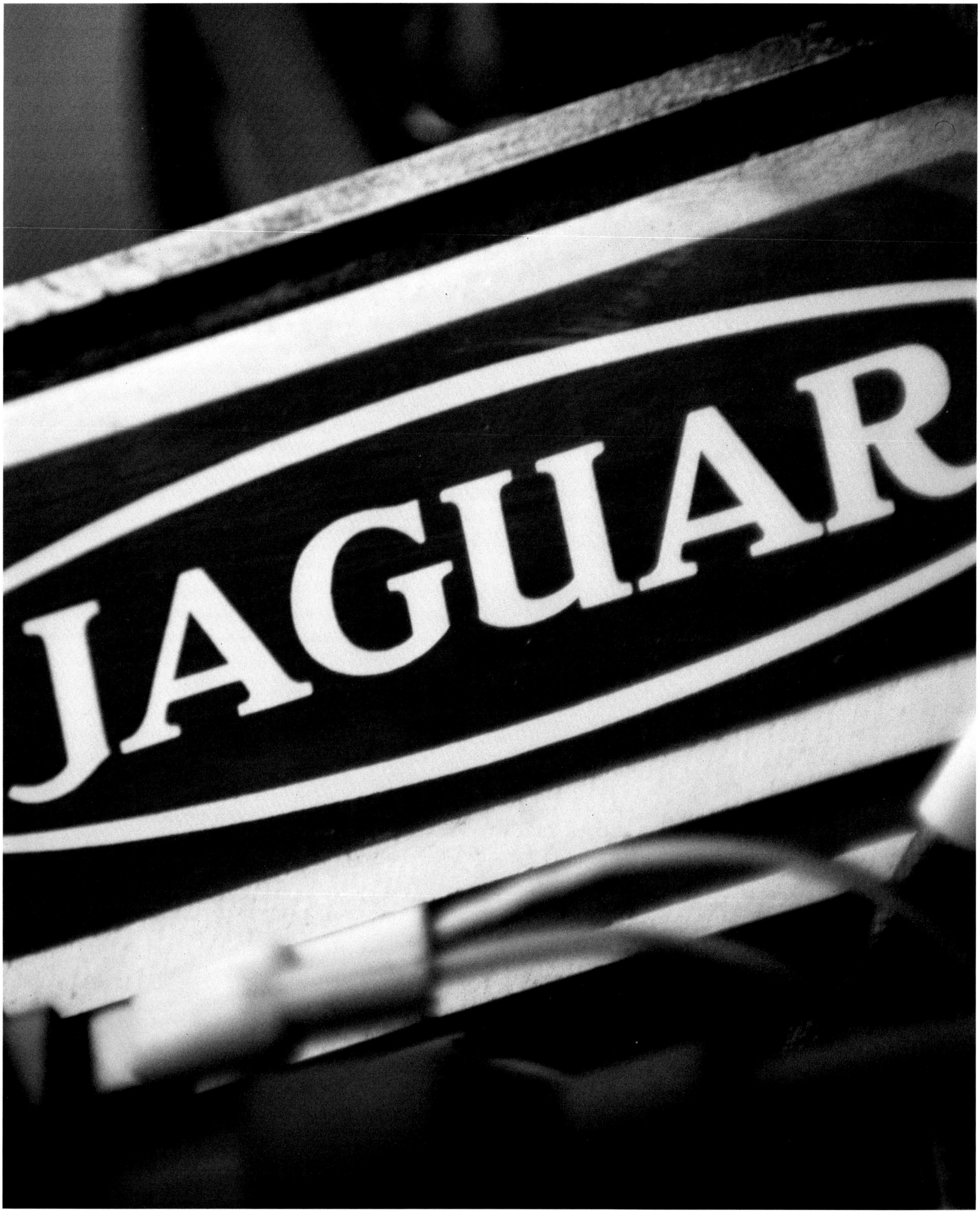
JAGUAR

# RETURN TO INDEPENDENCE
## 1984-1985

Borrowing terminology from the Chinese calendar, 1984 could be described as the Year of the Jaguar. Jaguar's success in touring-car racing, Jaguar's return to Le Mans, Jaguar's increased production, Jaguar's record sales in the USA – all at one time or another hit the headlines. However, the biggest news story of all concerned Jaguar's privatization.

It was the avowed intent of Margaret Thatcher's Tory government, and of BL chairman, Sir Michael Edwardes, to return BL companies from state ownership to the private sector. So far the unencouraging financial results of the corporation – despite marked improvements from 1980 onwards – had prevented this intention from being carried out. True, smaller parts of BL such as Alvis, Coventry-Climax, Prestcold or the Leyland tractor business had been sold off as Edwardes cleared the decks of the non-mainstream operations. Stockmarket rumours made Unipart and Land Rover early candidates for privatization, but the bulk of BL, i.e the Austin Rover Group and Leyland Vehicles, was evidently not yet saleable. The much-improved performance of the Jaguar company eventually made it clear that this would be the first of BL's larger operating companies to be sold, via a stock market flotation.

Behind the scenes, preparations began as early as 1982 when BL set up a new subsidiary company called Jaguar Cars (Holdings) Limited, with Ray Horrocks as chairman and John Egan as managing director. Originally purely a holding company, this took over the operating company Jaguar Cars Limited and a number of other subsidiaries including dormant companies such as SS Cars, Daimler and Lanchester. By a formal agreement coming into effect on 1 January 1983, Jaguar Cars Limited acquired the Jaguar and Daimler business from BL Cars Limited (which then became the Austin Rover Group Limited). BL's overseas subsidiaries in the USA and in Canada were transferred to Jaguar as well. Jaguar were now established as a completely separate entity within BL, only sharing the soon to be privatized parts operation, Unipart, and some overseas distribution companies. Gradually, however, Jaguar would establish their own subsidiaries in many important markets. While Jaguar had controlled the Castle Bromwich body plant since July 1980, the company continued to rely on Austin Rover's Swindon factory for the supply of pressed steel body panels, for the time being.

During 1983 rumours abounded about the forthcoming Jaguar flotation. One side effect of this was that the price of the few remaining privately-owned BL ordinary shares doubled within a few months, speculators obviously expecting a bonanza for BL shareholders when Jaguar was privatized.

When it became clear that they would be disappointed in their expectations, BL shares quickly drifted lower again. John Egan meanwhile had become the subject of what amounted to a personality cult. He was fast becoming the darling of the media, his face and voice familiar to millions of TV viewers. Egan was surely the first motor industry boss since Miles Thomas (the vice-chairman of Morris Motors until 1948) to be given the run of the leader page in *The*

*Opposite page:*
A Jaguar badge.

*Sunday Times.* He was increasingly seen as the personable, almost glamorous, spokesman for the motor industry as a whole. To give the media their due, they were now as eager to report good news about Jaguar as they had been to report bad news about British Leyland in the recent past. One of the more unlikely stories that emerged was the formation of a Jaguar works brass band which played a specially composed 'Jaguar March'! It did not make the Top Twenty but might have been John Egan's choice for the mythical desert island . . .

Before the plans to sell Jaguar could be finalized, there was a difference of opinion to be resolved between BL's board of directors on one side, and the government (supported by Jaguar's management) on the other. The BL directors considered it advantageous for BL to retain a large minority shareholding in a privatized Jaguar, as a safeguard against take-over bids from other motor manufacturers. The government, and John Egan's team, preferred the clean-break solution, although with some preference for Jaguar employees in the allocation of shares. In view of the size and value of the Jaguar business, such options as a management buy-out or a straight sale to another company – both stratagems had been employed in previous smaller BL privatizations – were ruled out. The only possible purchaser for the company as a whole would be an existing foreign motor manufacturer, but such a solution would obviously be politically unacceptable to all parties concerned. Nevertheless, rumours mentioned General Motors, Mercedes-Benz, BMW and Toyota as being interested in buying Jaguar. And so they probably would have been, had they been given the chance!

In the spring of 1984, it was finally decided to float the entire company publicly with preference for Jaguar and BL employees, and for existing BL shareholders to take up a maximum of 15 per cent of the shares. Jaguar management and employees were also to be given a small shareholding each under the company's employee share scheme, as it turned out an average 245 shares to the value of some £405 (around $480) at the price of issue. At the beginning of May, Ray Horrocks stepped down as chairman of Jaguar Holdings. While he remained as a non-executive director, the chairman's job was taken over by Rank-Xerox chairman Hamish Orr-Ewing. Although Orr-Ewing had a motor industry background, having worked for both Leyland and Ford, and although he turned out to be a car enthusiast with a vintage Rolls-Royce and a pristine E-type in his stable, it was regarded as a surprising appointment. Having a City-based non-executive chairman as a figurehead was more of a BL idea than a Jaguar tradition. Sir William Lyons had always 'lived above the shop', and had been very much a hands-on chief executive. As we shall see, Orr-Ewing was not to remain the company's chairman for any length of time.

The final prospectus was published by merchant bankers, Hill Samuel & Co, at the end of July 1984. In broad terms, the authorized share capital of Jaguar Cars Holdings which now changed its name to Jaguar plc (public limited company) would be £60 million (around $72 million at the time), of which £45 million (around $54 million) would be issued in 180 million shares of 25 pence each. The sale price was pitched at 165 pence per share, which put a value of £297 million (around $356 million) on Jaguar. There were some protests. BLISS – the British Leyland Independent Shareholders' Society, led by Noel Falconer – were annoyed that they were not given concessionary rates when applying for shares and also argued that it was damaging for BL to sell off its most profitable subsidiary. MPs from all parties in the House of Commons Trade and Industry Select Committee felt that piecemeal privatization of BL subsidiaries would be detrimental to the privatization of the group as a whole; perhaps it would be better to wait and sell all of BL together. Similar sentiments were expressed by Sir Richard Dobson, a former non-executive chairman of BL who had resigned in 1977. In a letter to *The Times* he expressed concern over the possible fate of an unprofitable BL rump left after the sale of the profitable subsidiaries. There was also the feeling expressed by some columnists in the business pages of the newspapers that there could only be political reasons for selling Jaguar, and that if the company had to be sold, the share price was too low. But in the prevailing euphoria, no one wanted to listen to such negative talk. When the share application list closed on 3 August, it was estimated that the share issue had been oversubscribed more than eight times.

It was quite deliberately decided that Jaguar plc should have a large number of small shareholders. The publicity campaign around the offer, and the prospectus itself, were clearly aimed at attracting small private investors. When shares were allocated, applications for a small number of shares were usually approved. The minimum number of shares it was possible to apply for was a lowly 100. On the other hand, applications for

No.

## JAGUAR plc

(Incorporated under the Companies Acts 1948 to 1981)

No. of Shares

**This is to Certify** *that the above-named is/are the Registered Holder(s) of*

*fully paid Ordinary Shares of 25p each in* **Jaguar plc** *subject to the Memorandum and Articles of Association of the Company*

**Given** *under the Seal of the Company.*

This certificate must be deposited with the Registrars of the Company before any transfer of all or any of the Shares comprised herein can be registered.

*Left:*
A blank example of the share certificate.

Copies of this Offer for Sale, which comprises listing particulars with regard to Jaguar in accordance with The Stock Exchange (Listing) Regulations 1984, have been delivered for registration to the Registrar of Companies as required by those Regulations. Application has been made to the Council of The Stock Exchange for the whole of the issued ordinary share capital of Jaguar to be admitted to the Official List.

The Directors, BLMC and BL are responsible for all the information contained in this document and have taken all reasonable care to ensure that to the best of their knowledge such information is in accordance with the facts and contains no omissions likely to affect the import of this document. Coopers & Lybrand are responsible (together with the Directors, BLMC and BL) for the information contained in the Accountants' Report and have taken all reasonable care to ensure that to the best of their knowledge such information is in accordance with the facts and contains no omissions likely to affect the import of this document. In addition, Coopers & Lybrand and Hill Samuel are responsible for the information contained in their respective letters relating to the profit estimate and have each taken all reasonable care to ensure that to the best of their knowledge such information is in accordance with the facts and contains no omissions likely to affect the import of this document.

## JAGUAR plc

(Registered in England No. 1672066 under the Companies Acts 1948 to 1981)

### Offer for Sale

by

**Hill Samuel & Co. Limited**

on behalf of

**BLMC Limited**

(a wholly-owned subsidiary of BL Public Limited Company)

of

177,880,000 Ordinary shares of 25p each

at 165p per share

payable in full on application

and underwritten by

Hill Samuel & Co. Limited

J. Henry Schroder Wagg & Co. Limited          Lazard Brothers & Co., Limited

Kleinwort, Benson Limited          S. G. Warburg & Co. Ltd.

The Application List for the Ordinary shares now offered for sale will open at 10.00 a.m. on Friday, 3rd August, 1984 and will close as soon thereafter on the same day as Hill Samuel may determine. The procedure for application and an Application Form are set out at the end of this Offer for Sale.

larger numbers were reduced, and as far as possible multiple applications from would-be profit takers, the so-called 'stags', were weeded out. In consequence, Jaguar ended up with rather more than 120,000 shareholders in the first instance. This number was quickly halved when trading in the shares began and numerous investors, large and small, sold out for a quick killing. And a killing it was: within six months of the issue, Jaguar shares were being traded on the stock exchange at more than double the issue price. Arguably the Jeremiahs who had complained that the issue price was too low had been proved right! The highest recorded price for Jaguar shares was 632 pence, reached in February 1987.

The conditions which pushed up the value of Jaguar shares so rapidly were far from ordinary. Throughout the closing months of 1984 and the beginning of 1985, the pound continued to fall against the US dollar. Where in 1980-81, the exchange rate had been $2.40 to the pound, the value of the pound had now been halved, and at one stage there was almost parity between the

*Left:*
The prospectus for the new privatized company, Jaguar plc, was issued at the end of July 1984.

two currencies. The four years of the falling pound were of immense benefit to the company's export business, particularly in the all-important American market. Throughout this period, the USA regularly took 50 per cent or more of all Jaguar cars produced, and every car sold in the USA brought more and more profits to the company. The pre-tax profit for the financial year (which was the calendar year) increased from £50 million in 1983, to £91.5 million in 1984 and peaked at £121.3 million in 1985.

Then there were the recurring rumours that one or other of several parties were building up large shareholdings in Jaguar, preparatory to a takeover bid. General Motors, Ford and Volkswagen-Audi have all been mentioned as Jaguar suitors. If any of these companies have been building up a stake in Jaguar, they have covered themselves well, to avoid having to declare an interest in the company. Under British law, any shareholding of more than 5 per cent of a company's capital held in the same name must be publicly declared. From the statistics of shareholders published in Jaguar's annual reports it is evident that the number of shares held by banks and nominees has increased steadily over the years, and by March 1989 had reached 48 per cent. On the other hand, although a large percentage of shares are still known to be owned by US investors, the number of shares held in American depositary receipts peaked at just over 49 per cent in March 1987 (but may have been even higher at other times, according to newspaper reports). There is one – or rather two – safeguards against a possible takeover bid by a foreign car manufacturer. Firstly, there is the so-called 'golden' or special share held by the Secretary of State for Trade and Industry. This enables the minister to veto any takeover bid until the date of expiry of the share, which is 31 December 1990. The second safeguard is the publicly declared intent of Sir John Egan and his directors, that they would resign from the company if Jaguar were subject to an unfriendly takeover bid.

What will happen in 1991 remains to be seen. What is certain now is that Jaguar are extremely vulnerable to currency movements. The increasing value of the pound, particularly against the US dollar but also against the currencies of other major Jaguar markets, has adversely affected the company's profits which, despite increasing turnover, have fallen well below the 1985 peak. Furthermore, the company have seen major capital expenditure in connection

with the XJ40 project, the launch of the new model in 1986 and the new engineering centre at Whitley. In the wake of the Wall Street crash in October 1987, there was a marked reduction in the demand for luxury cars in the American market, and this also affected Jaguar – though not so badly as, for instance, Porsche. Jaguar were fortunately able to redirect much of their production to the home market or to other export markets, and so total production and sales figures have kept on increasing, although US sales have declined. They are now showing signs of picking up again, however.

History tells us that investment in any motor manufacturing company is of a speculative, even risky, nature. There have been many more failures than success stories in car manufacture. No one needs reminding of the failure of British Leyland. Also within recent memory are the enormous losses sustained by Renault (even greater than those of BL!), as well as the almost-failures of Volkswagen in the 1970s, and of Chrysler in the 1980s. The stock market has certainly censured Jaguar because of the declining profits in recent years. But the company are doing many things right, and, given half the chance, ought to survive as a long-term success story. That is not to say that Jaguar are not vulnerable. Apart from the influence of the exchange rate, there is the as yet limited product range. Jaguars are luxury saloons or GT cars and

*Left:*
Sir John Egan, the
Chairman and Chief
Executive of Jaguar plc.

this market is particularly fickle. The company is often compared with BMW or Mercedes-Benz but both of these two German competitors have far more extensive product ranges and can always make a few more small saloons or diesel taxis should they lose sales of luxury cars. Furthermore, Mercedes-Benz have an extensive commercial vehicle business and have diversified into numerous other areas, from aerospace to household appliances. It could also be argued that if the Jaguar company were a subsidiary of a larger concern, this would to some extent constitute a safety net.

Soon after privatization, the argument about which direction the company should take surfaced within the Jaguar board. The chairman, Hamish Orr-Ewing, and the other non-executive directors (of whom one was Ray Horrocks), felt that Jaguar should diversify by acquiring other businesses or should look for a partner in the motor industry. The executive directors, led by John Egan, were against this. Egan felt that diversification could lead to problems and he was strongly in favour of the company remaining independent. Matters came to a head in March 1985, when, following a board meeting, Orr-Ewing stepped down. Egan was appointed as the new chairman. Later in the year, both Orr-Ewing and Horrocks formally resigned from the Jaguar board. In their place was appointed one other non-executive director, Sir Austin Pearce, a former chairman of British

Aerospace. The only other non-executive director is Edward Bond, formerly finance director of the Beecham Group, while the executive directors, in addition to Sir John Egan, are Michael Beasley (assistant managing director), John Edwards (finance director), Kenneth Edwards (personnel director and company secretary) and Graham Whitehead (president of Jaguar Cars Inc and chairman of Jaguar Canada Inc, the company's subsidiaries in the USA and Canada).

Initially, Jaguar plc had an honorary president – Sir William Lyons, the founder of Jaguar Cars. While he lived to see the privatization successfully completed, and was kept informed and involved by John Egan personally about the plans for new models and the future of the company, he would not see the new generation of Jaguar cars come to fruition. On 8 February 1985, Sir William, at 84 years of age, died peacefully in his home at Wappenbury Hall near Leamington Spa. He had been in failing health for some five years but, although obviously frail, he still managed a tour of the 1984 Motor Show, one of his last appearances in public. In the closing months of his life, it must have given him the greatest satisfaction to see the company which he founded being restored to successful independence. Sir William fully approved of Egan's management and the way in which the company had been turned around. He was still a well-known figure at Browns Lane where he continued to appear regularly, especially in the engineering and styling departments where the XJ40 (and other new models) were taking shape. Younger members of staff might have been given to refer to him, less than respectfully but always fondly, as 'Swilly' – but only behind his back. Sir William always maintained a formal relationship with even the most senior members of his staff. *He* was undoubtedly *Sir* William. They in return were addressed by 'Mr' and their surname, unless they were in Sir William's doghouse when he would drop the 'Mr' and address them by surname only! Sir William is remembered as a disciplinarian, at times as a bit of a martinet, but always unfailingly polite and scrupulously fair in dealing with his employees. His best memorial will always be the cars and the company that he created. Sir William Lyons will not be forgotten as long as the Jaguar tradition lives on – Sir John Egan, for one, will make certain of that. A further sad occurrence was the death on 31 March 1986 of Lady Greta Lyons, widow of Sir William, at the age of 84. They were survived by two daughters, Mrs Patricia Quinn (formerly Mrs Appleyard) and Mrs Mary Rimell.

# BACK ON TRACK!
# 1985-1986

Nothing could be guaranteed to stir the blood of enthusiasts everywhere more than the return of Jaguar in 1985 to sports car racing. The first appearance of a Jaguar, the American XJR-5 car, at Le Mans in 1984, had increased anticipations, and so had Tom Walkinshaw's win of the European Touring Car Championship in the Motul XJ-S. In the winter of 1984-85, rumours grew about a Walkinshaw-Jaguar project to challenge Porsche's dominance in Group C sports car endurance racing.

Tom Walkinshaw had borrowed a Group 44 XJR-5 car which had been displayed in the British Motor Show in October 1984, and this car was tested extensively by the Kidlington-based team. The car was fitted with a 48-valve version of the 6-litre V12 engine, and was run at Donington Park in March 1985. Martin Brundle drove the car which had been repainted in a British Racing Green livery. While the Donington Park test runs served their purpose as far as engine development was concerned, the initial idea of the Walkinshaw team running a modified XJR-5 was abandoned as the car was found to be too heavy to be competitive in Group C racing. Instead it was decided to proceed with a new car which was to be named the XJR-6. This was announced at the beginning of May 1985, when it was also announced that there was now no intention of running the TWR car at Le Mans. Instead it was intended that the racing debut of the XJR-6 should take place at Hockenheim in July, while Group 44 would once again field two cars at Le Mans. Meanwhile, Tom Walkinshaw announced that the TWR team would not contest the 1985

*Opposite page:*
The Silverstone 1000km race, May 1986: the Schlesser/Brancatelli Jaguar XJR-6, which finished seventh. The race was won by the Cheever/Warwick XJR-6.

touring car championship; they would obviously have their hands full with the new cars! For the benefit of *Autocar* magazine, Walkinshaw took an XJ-S to the Vauxhall proving ground at Millbrook, and put in a record lap at 176.16mph. Then the three XJ-S racing cars were shipped to Australia. In October 1985, John Goss and Armin Hahne drove to victory in the 1000km race at Mount Panorama, Bathurst, NSW, with Walkinshaw and Win Percy in third place. This was effectively the swan-song for the Group A XJ-S, although the cars were seen again at Fuji in Japan in 1986, and in two New Zealand races in early 1987. They were not successful on either of these occasions, and the homologation for the car had expired at the end of 1986.

In the USA, Bob Tullius and Group 44 continued to contest the IMSA Camel GT Championship with the XJR-5 cars. However, the 1985 season was not to be greatly more successful than 1984 had been. The best result was the 1-2 Jaguar win at Atlanta in April, Haywood and Redman being followed home by Tullius and Robinson. But this was Jaguar's only win of the season. All four drivers were among the top ten in the championship at the end of 1985, Haywood's third place overall being the best individual result. The decision had been made for Group 44 to contest the full racing season in the USA, and to appear at Le Mans with two cars. Although they built two cars specially for Le Mans, the extra effort involved undoubtedly put some strain on the team as a whole and possibly deprived them of further wins in the IMSA championship.

The two Group 44 cars were duly brought over to Europe for the Le Mans 24-hour race on 15-16 June 1985. The cars were more powerful than the 1984 entries and showed improved lap times. Still rather heavy, they were capable of some 212mph, somewhat slower than the 228mph of the Porsche 956B. The Jaguar drivers were Tullius, Robinson and Ballot-Lena in car number 44, with Redman, Haywood and Adam in car number 40. Both the Jaguars ran consistently but were never among the race leaders. Then, in the early hours of the morning, the Redman/Haywood/Adam car was put out of the race when a CV joint failed. The other car was plagued with a misfire and twice had to have its electronic engine management system changed. Towards the end of the race, more serious trouble occurred – the engine broke, and a piston was lodged in the cylinder head. The car continued on 11 cylinders and made it to the finish in 13th place, having completed 323 laps, 50 laps behind the winners. Historically, this was a most important occasion – the first time since 1963 that a Jaguar had finished at Le Mans.

In Tom Walkinshaw's workshops at Kidlington, the first XJR-6 car was nearing completion in the weeks after Le Mans. The new car had been designed by Tony Southgate, whose previous experience included work for Lola, BRM and Lotus. His last work before joining Walkinshaw in 1984 had been concerned with the Ford RS200 rally car. The XJR-6 which came off his drawing board was a thoroughly competitive Group C challenger, incorporating the most modern technology in its carbon-fibre composite monocoque structure. The engine was the 24-valve version of Jaguar's 6-litre V12. Normally aspirated, this was estimated to produce around 630bhp. Because of the fuel consumption restrictions in Group C, the 48-valve version of the engine, as tested by Walkinshaw in the borrowed XJR-5, was held back for the time being. A five-speed gearbox developed by March engineering was fitted. The car was tested and announced at the beginning of July 1985, but it was found impossible to have two cars ready for Hockenheim and so the decision reluctantly was taken to scrap the entry for this race.

Instead the first race for the new challenger came in August. The venue for the debut of the XJR-6 was the Mosport 1000 kilometre race held in Ontario, Canada. The two cars were entrusted to Martin Brundle and Mike Thackwell (no 51), and Jean-Louis Schlesser and Hans Heyer (no 52). The cars ran in the green TWR-Jaguar livery; while Castrol had provided some backing, a major

sponsor had not yet been found. The two cars started in third and fifth position on the grid, and Martin Brundle got off to a spectacularly good start which put him in the lead on the first lap. He stayed in the lead for ten laps, until overtaken by two works Porsches. Soon after, a wheel bearing failed and the car retired. Schlesser sportingly handed over his XJR-6 to Brundle and Thackwell, and eventually they finished third behind two Porsches. It was a most encouraging result for the brand new and as yet largely untried car.

Three weeks later, the team was at Spa in Belgium facing not only the Porsche team but also the Lancias. The driver pairings were the same as they had been in Canada. Schlesser and Heyer retired after 14 laps of a troubled race. The car had oversteered alarmingly and no solution to the problem could be found during a series of pit stops. The race was marred by a collision between the two Porsches of Jacky Ickx and Stefan Bellof, which tragically cost Bellof his life. As a mark of respect, the race was halted early after 122 laps or 847km instead of 1000km. Brundle and Thackwell stayed the course and finished in fifth place. For the next race in the World Championship, at Brands Hatch, neither Brundle nor Thackwell was available to drive, Brundle having to return to Ken Tyrrell's Formula 1 team. Hans Heyer was partnered by Jan Lammers, and Alan Jones joined Schlesser in the other car but this was not to be an auspicious occasion as both cars retired with broken engines.

Over the same weekend that saw the XJ-S win at Bathurst, the next round of the sports car championship took place at Fuji in Japan. The two Jaguars, driven by Thackwell/John Nielsen and Hans Heyer/Steve Soper, both had engine failures in practice but were rebuilt in time to qualify. The start of the race was delayed several times owing to the appalling weather conditions. After only a few laps, the TWR-Jaguar team decided to withdraw, in common with the works Porsches and most other European entrants. If rain had been the problem in Japan, the heat was almost too much for everyone in the final race of the season, the Selangor 800km in Malaysia on 1 December. This was the first race for another new driver in the Jaguar, Gianfranco Brancatelli, who shared Jan Lammers' car. When this was put out of the race by a tyre explosion which caused Lammers to lose control, the Thackwell/Nielsen car was the only Jaguar in the race. Exhausted by the heat and high humidity, Thackwell had to turn the car over to his co-driver, and Lammers took over the car for the final spell. The result was a second place, close behind the Porsche of Mass/Ickx. It was the best result so far for the TWR-Jaguar, and a suitable note on which to end their first season, which saw Jaguar placed third in the manufacturers' championship after Porsche and Lancia.

After the end of the 1985 racing season, details were announced of a major sponsorship deal for the TWR-Jaguars by the tobacco manufacturers Gallaher International. The team would now be known as the Silk Cut Jaguar Racing Team, and the cars duly appeared in what has disparagingly become known as the cigarette packet livery! Schlesser and Brancatelli were retained for the 1986 season and the team was joined by two new drivers – Eddie Cheever and Derek Warwick. Jaguar also drew a demarcation line between the Silk Cut team, which would contest the World Sportscar Championship, and Group 44 which would continue to race in the IMSA series in the USA, but which would not get factory support for another Le Mans entry.

During the winter months, designer Tony

Southgate was able to reduce the weight of the Jaguars, and testing continued with the 48-valve engines as well as with a new twin-disc front brake set up. For the first race of the season, at Monza in April, the lightened 'Mark II' XJR-6 cars still ran with the 24-valve engines. Two of the modified cars were prepared and a 1985 specification car was held in reserve. The race at Monza was the first of a new-style short sportscar race, of only 365km. The Cheever/Warwick car retired with a broken driveshaft coupling, while Schlesser and Brancatelli went on almost to the finish. They were running low on fuel, and on the last lap but one the fuel pickup went on strike. Afterwards it was found there were still eight litres left in the tank.

On 5 May 1986, in the Silverstone 1000km race, the Jaguars finally demonstrated what they were capable of. The two XJR-6 cars now ran with engines of 6.5 litres. The driver pairings were the same as they had been at Monza and they faced a formidable lineup, the main opposition coming from ten Porsches of the 956/962 family, but the Martini-Lancia and Sauber-Mercedes had to be

*Below:*
The winning XJR-6 in the 1986 Silverstone 1000km race.

*Above:*
A pit stop for the Schlesser/
Brancatelli XJR-6 during
the 1986 Silverstone
1000km race.

*Opposite page:*
The Brancatelli/Hahne/
Percy XJR-6 number 53 at
Le Mans in 1986.

taken seriously as well. The win of the Cheever/ Warwick Jaguar in this important British race was tremendously popular with the spectators, who saw the two Jaguars cruise over the finishing line in close company (the Schlesser/Brancatelli car finished in seventh place). The main challenge had come from the Lancia, but when this car retired with failing fuel pressure, Jaguar had the race in the bag. None of the Porsches could catch up – Bell and Stuck in second place were two laps behind the winning Jaguar. For the first time since the 1957 Le Mans, a Jaguar had won a World Championship sports car race.

Hopes were understandably high as Tom Walkinshaw prepared his team for their first assault on the 24-hour classic, held rather earlier this year than traditionally, on 31 May to 1 June. Three cars were prepared for the race, and three drivers were allocated to each car. Warwick, Cheever and Schlesser had car no. 51. For car no. 52, two of the Le Mans experienced Group 44 drivers, Redman and Haywood, were joined by Hans Heyer. The third car, no. 53, was driven by Brancatelli, Armin Hahne and well-known saloon car racer, Win Percy. On the test day in early

May, two of the Jaguars had easily proved them- selves to be the fastest cars on the track. The team's three cars eventually qualified to start in fifth, seventh and fourteenth positions on the grid, Cheever having put in the best qualifying lap for the team. As ever at Le Mans, Porsches were domi- nant in numbers. It looked as if this was going to be a straight Porsche versus Jaguar battle, with the Sauber-Mercedes team somewhere in the background!

So indeed it turned out to be. The three Jaguars were fairly consistently among the five leading cars in the race, but after less than four hours Hans Heyer stopped on the track with apparent fuel pump failure. Next to drop out was Win Percy, whose first Group C race this was, as his car broke a driveshaft. Then at 0835 hours on Sunday morning, the third Jaguar, at that time lying in second position with Schlesser at the wheel, suffered a tyre explosion which destroyed most of the rear bodywork. Schlesser was able to drive the remains of the car back to the pit where the mechanics could only shake their heads and pack up. They went home, leaving a message on the wall: 'We'll be back'. The final result of the

race was that Porsches finished in the first seven places, as well as ninth and tenth.

There was better news for Jaguar later in June when John Egan was knighted in the Queen's birthday honours list for his services to British industry. It was a deserved recognition for his outstanding achievements at Jaguar but, in Sir John's own words, it was also a recognition of the efforts of everyone who had contributed to the renaissance of Jaguar Cars. The honour was shared by thousands of members of the Jaguar family.

Tom Walkinshaw's Silk Cut racing team still had most of the racing season in front of them. While there was not to be a repeat of the Silverstone victory, the cars ran consistently well for the remainder of the season. In the short Norisring race in Germany at the end of June, Cheever and Warwick were second and third respectively, with Schlesser in a distant 17th place after his throttle had jammed and delayed him for 12 laps. Two cars started at Brands Hatch in July, Warwick being paired with Schlesser and Cheever with Brancatelli. They finished fourth and sixth respectively. Next the team went to Jerez in Spain, but this was an embarrassing occasion as all three Jaguars were involved in an accident on the first lap.

While the three cars were able to continue the race, the Schlesser/Brancatelli and Cheever/Brundle cars both retired with driveshaft failures. The accident had landed Derek Warwick in a sandpit where he lost precious time digging the car out. He put in a spirited performance after having extricated himself, and together with co-driver Jan Lammers, finished in third place.

It would have been particularly sweet for Jaguar to have trounced the Porsches on their home ground, the Nürburgring, which was the setting for the next race in the series. The weather was bad and visibility poor. After a number of incidents, the race was stopped and then restarted. As Derek Warwick had damaged one of the Jaguars in practice, only two of the XJR-6s came to the start, with three drivers to each car, the final crews being made up of Warwick/Lammers/Brancatelli, and Cheever/Schlesser/Heyer. In the event, both Heyer and Brancatelli dropped out. In the race, Cheever was an early retirement with gearbox failure, and in the second part of the race, the Warwick/Lammers car was put out with engine failure. The surprise winner was the Mercedes-engined Sauber.

At Spa in September, the Jaguar of Warwick/

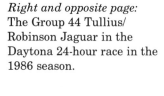

*Right and opposite page:*
The Group 44 Tullius/ Robinson Jaguar in the Daytona 24-hour race in the 1986 season.

*Previous page:*
Car number 51, driven by Warwick/Cheever/Schlesser, in the 1986 Le Mans race.

*Previous page inset:*
The Brancatelli/Hahne/Percy car number 53.

Lammers came close – so close! – to winning. Less than a second separated it from the winning Porsche at the finish which was considered to be one of the most exciting seen in Group C racing. The only other Jaguar in the race finished fifth, in the hands of Cheever and Schlesser. The final sports car race of the season was at Fuji in Japan in early October. Jan Lammers had trouble when a wheel bearing failed on his Jaguar; this car was also driven by Schlesser and Brancatelli and, after problems with the gearchange, eventually finished in 17th place. Eddie Cheever started in the other car and then handed over to Derek Warwick. At the finish of the race, it was first thought they had finished in second place which would have given Warwick the driver's champion-ship title. Alas, it was due to a timekeeping error. Cheever and Warwick had come third, so Derek Warwick had to be content with a third place in the championship, while the Silk Cut Jaguar team was a joint third (shared with Rothmans Porsche) in the team championship for 1986.

In the USA, the Group 44 team had contested the entire series of IMSA championship races with two new cars, the 6.5-litre-engined XJR-7 models. As in the previous year, the drivers were Brian Redman paired with Hurley Haywood, while team boss Bob Tullius and Chip Robinson shared the other car. It was not a good season for the team. They had 31 starts in 16 races; a crash at Riverside in April meant that only one car was available to start at Laguna Seca in May. On the other hand this single entry resulted in a second place, the team's best result so far. There were two more second places to come, but it was not until the final race of the season that Group 44 found its form again, and scored its first win since Atlanta in 1985. On 26 October, veteran Tullius and newcomer Robinson shared the spoils of victory in the Daytona 3 hour race.

If 1985 had been promising, and 1986 had given clear proof that Jaguar were on the right track and were determined to become a leading force in sports car racing once again, it was natural that there were high hopes for the 1987 racing season on both sides of the Atlantic. For the moment, how-ever, let us break off the study of the recent racing career of the marque and return to the world of Jaguar road cars. The 1986 British Motor Show was going to be a very special occasion for Jaguar. For the first time in 18 years, the company was pre-paring to launch a major all-new saloon car model.

# XJ-40 – THE NEW TRADITION
# 1986-1987

It was only after the launch of the new XJ6 (commonly referred to by its project number XJ40) in 1986 that the long, even tortuous, saga behind its development became known to the general public. True, the existence of the new car was common knowledge. The rumour mongers and spy photographers had been busy, and the Jaguar company had long since acknowledged the fact that a new model would be launched — when it was ready. All in all the new Jaguar was the most eagerly awaited new car from a British manufacturer for many years.

But few people outside the company realized that project XJ40 had been started right back in the early 1970s, in the days of 'Lofty' England and Geoffrey Robinson. No-one at that time expected the then almost new XJ6 to survive in production for as long as it did. In the previous decade Jaguar had undertaken new model development at a prodigious pace, and it was very natural that the company should begin to look at an XJ6 replacement at a fairly early stage. It will be remembered that most previous Jaguars had been styled virtually by Sir William Lyons personally, but Sir William had retired in March 1972 and was, in his own words, trying not to interfere too much. It now fell to chief engineer Bob Knight and the recently-formed styling department under Doug Thorpe to come up with proposals for the new car. During the autumn and winter of 1972-73, early styling renderings and quarter-scale models were translated into the first full scale clay model which was eventually shown to Lord Stokes and other top executives of British Leyland. There was not, at this stage anyway, much

*Opposite page:*
The 1986 XJ6.

dissension about the way in which the new car should develop as far as engineering was concerned. Indeed, the original programme literally called for a new body to fit the existing XJ6 underframe and mechanical components. However, what was to prove the greatest problem in the development of the car was to decide in which direction the styling should develop. Ever since 1935 there had been a logical progression in Jaguar styling. Each new model had appeared as a development of its predecessor. Over the years little signature themes had been added and refined, until finally Sir William's mastery of the art had produced the original XJ6 of 1968. A great act is always hard to follow, and it must have been an awesome task for Doug Thorpe and his staff to replace what was generally conceded to be the most elegantly-styled Jaguar ever. Apart from that there were so many conflicting ideas among Jaguar's and Leyland's management which undoubtedly created a lot of confusion in the styling studio.

One school of thought would have the new model styled somewhat conservatively, in the manner of the existing car, with only a modest update. This was the way in which Mercedes-Benz and BMW went about their styling, and was also generally in keeping with traditional Jaguar thinking. This we might call the Anglo-German or European approach! On the other hand there were those who felt that the next Jaguar should be a totally modern and different — if not way-out — car. This could perhaps be described as the American approach... But there was a joker in the pack. Jaguar's new managing director, Geoffrey Robinson who had previously run BL's subsidiary company in Italy, Innocenti, favoured an Italian approach. Pininfarina had just built a very impressive show car based on the XJ12, which in due course was brought to Browns Lane for viewing. Robinson's enthusiasm for Italian design did not stop here, and Bertone and Giugiaro's Ital Design were also commissioned to submit proposals for the new Jaguar.

None of the Italian offerings, however, managed to capture the Jaguar spirit, and with Geoffrey Robinson's departure in the wake of the 1975 upheaval, they were not heard of again. Indeed, for a time it seemed that project XJ40 was floundering. To prolong the life of the existing model, it was decided to produce a Series 3 version of the XJ6 and XJ12. For this project, Italian assistance was sought and accepted. The Series 3, launched in 1979, was tastefully updated by Pininfarina. For a time Browns Lane was busy on the development of the Series 3, and XJ40 was put on one side. Some work continued throughout, both by Jaguar's own stylists and by the Italian consultants who submitted second thoughts in 1976 – also to be consigned to oblivion after viewing at Browns Lane. It was not until 1977 that XJ40 re-emerged. Where Lord Stokes had once wanted to subsume any Jaguar characteristic – except the badge – to some form of Leyland corporate styling, it was now officially acknowledged at decision-making levels in the corporation that a Jaguar should look like a Jaguar. In other words, Jaguar could return to their traditional philosophy, adhered to so successfully by Sir William Lyons.

The final style of XJ40 was developed from 1978 to 1980. It is interesting to note that this was also the period when Jaguar's independence was allowed to re-assert itself, although still of course within the BL group – the period between the appointments of Michael Edwardes and John Egan. XJ40 became a symbol of Jaguar's future. It is also interesting that Sir William Lyons resumed his habit of visiting the styling department regularly, knowing that his advice would be welcomed and respected. Therefore, the XJ40 as it finally appeared, was also a symbol of Jaguar's traditions. Many of the early proposals had been too bland or were too much influenced by contemporary 1970s fashion. The final XJ40, such as it was approved in 1980, incorporated a very traditional Jaguar front end with a radiator grille that was immediately recognizable as a descendant of Lyons' original 1935 style. Another Jaguar characteristic inherited from the XJ6 was the slight upsweep of the rear wing line. However,

there were innovations as well. After a great deal of agonizing it was finally decided that XJ40 would be a six-light saloon, with a small separate quarter-light in the rear side pillar. Previous to this all Jaguars had been four-light saloons, a style which, in 1935, had been synonymous with sports saloons. Making the XJ40 a six-light saloon also meant a farewell to the well-liked Jaguar characteristic of the extended quarterlight in the rear door. Other innovations were the introduction of large, rectangular headlamps on some models (others continued with the twin round headlamp set-up, found on all American export models due to local legal requirements) and almost equally large rectangular rear lamp clusters.

Meanwhile, the engineering of the new car had proceeded apace. A fundamental part of the concept for the new model was the development of Jaguar's own all-new aluminium alloy straight-six cylinder engine, the AJ6. There was some wrangling in the corridors of decision within British Leyland before the new engine was finally sanctioned. In some quarters within the corporation it was felt that the expense of a new Jaguar engine could not be accepted, and that future Jaguars could use a larger version of the Rover V8 engine. Wily but diplomatic chief engineer Bob Knight came up with a typical solution. He deliberately engineered the front end structure of XJ40 so that the engine bay would not accept the rather wide V8 engine. This also meant that XJ40 would not accept Jaguar's own V12 engine, but the decision was made at the time when it was believed that there was little future for the V12 and it was already scheduled to be phased out. Later on, of course, this would create something of a problem for Jaguar's engineers! But, for the time being, the threat of a Rover-engined Jaguar was averted, and the AJ6 engine programme was sanctioned. The introduction of the new engine in the XJ-S in 1983 has been described elsewhere but, for the new saloon model, an additional version of the new engine was planned – a single overhead camshaft, 2.9-litre version with two, instead of four, valves per cylinder, and with a high compression May-type cylinder head similar to that found on the V12.

With the new engines came new gearboxes. The manual box chosen was the Getrag five-speed unit which had also been introduced in the XJ-S 3.6 in 1983. After considering a number of alternatives, a German supplier was also chosen for the automatic gearbox. This was the ZF four-speed box. Jaguar developed their own unique shift pattern for the automatic box, the 'J'-gate so-called because of its shape. To the right, on the long downstroke of the J, were the normal automatic gearbox positions of P-R-N-D. Round the corner on the left were the lock-up positions for the lower ratios, 2 and 3, with again the D for drive position at the bottom. The result was a more positive feel to the 'manual' part of the gearchange, and it also minimized the risk of the driver selecting neutral or reverse by mistake.

The chassis engineering of XJ40 was less radically altered from the XJ6. The front suspension was of similar design to that of the Series 3. The rear suspension was redesigned under the guidance of Jim Randle who had been the company's suspension specialist for many years before taking over from Bob Knight as chief engineer in 1980. The suppression of noise and vibration, together with maintaining a high standard of road behaviour, had been Bob Knight's forte, and Jim Randle was committed to keeping Jaguar's lead over the competition in this respect. While superficially similar to the previous Jaguar rear suspensions, the new patented design was 'compliant', incorporating a pendulum arrangement which allowed fore and aft movement of the inner front mounting point of the lower wishbone. Anti-brake dive and anti-acceleration squat geometry was incorporated. A simplification was achieved by using only one spring and one damper each side. A self-levelling system was fitted as either standard or optional equipment on all models in the new range. The rear brakes were mounted outboard for the first time on a Jaguar with independent rear suspension. It was found that the addition to unsprung weight did not have such a significant impact as had been feared, and it certainly made brake maintenance a rather simpler affair! Anti-lock braking (ABS) specially developed by Bosch was specified as standard or as an option depending on model.

Apart from settling the difficult question of the styling, a great deal of thought went into engineering the new bodyshell. There were a number of objectives which the new design had to meet. The new car had to be more aerodynamic and more spacious than the Series 3. For simpler production, the new body should be made up of fewer but larger individual panels, and it had to weigh less. The marque's already standard-setting levels of refinement and quietness should be further improved. Finally, corrosion protection and paint quality had to be better than ever. It is to the credit of the design team that these objectives were reached. While the drag coefficient of 0.37 may not look impressive compared with those figures quoted by other manufacturers, taken in combination with the frontal sectional area it made the XJ40 one of the most aerodynamic cars in its class and at the same time preserved high-speed stability. Interior space was usefully improved and, with the petrol tank relocated to a safer place above the rear axle, the boot was increased in size and had a more practical shape.

For the first time on a Jaguar body, the entire body side frame was pressed in one piece – the so-called monoside. There was a 25 per cent reduction in the total number of pressings involved in making up each bodyshell. Many of the pressings had also been made much simpler. For instance, the characteristic headlamp eyebrows of the Series 3 – another long-standing Jaguar styling characteristic – had been lost, but this not only simplified the pressing of the headlamp surround: other benefits were improved aerodynamics and the avoidance of a possible rust-trap. The ultimate weight saving of 18lb (8kg) of the XJ40 bodyshell over that of the Series 3 may sound insignificant, but coupled with lighter engines, lighter front suspension sub-frames and weight savings made in other areas, it meant that the new car was between 150 and 200lb (78 and 90kg) lighter than its predecessors, depending on specification.

To achieve improved refinement, the flexible mountings for suspension subframes and power units were improved. The experience gained with the AJ6 engine in three years of service in the XJ-S, together with the 5½ million road test miles clocked up by 400 prototype and pre-production XJ40 cars, resulted in the engine being much smoother and more refined in the new saloon model. In addition, the inside of the passenger cabin was completely insulated with barrier foam to damp out vibration and absorb noise. Finally, a substantial investment was made in the Castle Bromwich body plant, totally controlled by Jaguar even before the company was privatized in 1984, which ensured that every bodyshell would undergo extremely comprehensive rust-preventing treatment. A new paint plant was installed, and Jaguar chose to use clear over base paint for a deeper finish, even on cars finished in non-metallic colours.

There were certain aspects of the new design which were subject to changes at a fairly late stage. When the final XJ40 style was shown to selected potential Jaguar customers in so-called clinics in the UK in 1980 and 1981, the exterior design was given uniformly high marks but the interior was at first not so well liked. As originally planned the interior was very modern in concept and execution, to the point where Jaguar's traditional wood and leather ambience had been somewhat left behind. This was not what customers expected of a Jaguar. Interior design is as important as exterior design, if not more so, to the way in which the image of a quality car is perceived. For instance, the high-tech functional interior found on many German cars perfectly mirrors the expectations of BMW or Mercedes-Benz customers, but would be too spartan and clinical for a Jaguar. On the other hand, the vulgar ostentation of some American cars equally was to be avoided. So there was some last-minute rethinking in the interior design department, and XJ40 duly acquired a traditional Jaguar wood and leather interior. One modern feature was retained – an all-electronic instrument display featuring a combination of analogue and digital displays, and with a built-in computer. When XJ40 was launched this was a major subject for criticism in the press, and remains the car's least liked feature. Undoubtedly it is scheduled for revision when the time comes for a facelift!

In all important aspects, however, the XJ40 design was 'frozen' in 1980–81, and construction of the first prototype began. In July 1981, Jim Randle could take this car for its first spin in the factory grounds. Now the hard slog began to make the car ready for production. Over the next five years the longest and most arduous testing programme in the history of Jaguar took place. XJ40 prototypes, partially camouflaged in characteristic disguise panels, became a fairly regular sight on many Midlands roads. Extensive use was made of the BL Technology test track at Gaydon south of Warwick. But Jaguar's test team also went further afield, and XJ40 prototypes were shipped to Australia as well as North America to be exposed to every possible hardship, from the Arctic temperatures of the Canadian winter, to the scorching heat of the desert in Arizona or Australia's Northern Territory. There was continuous high-speed running at the Nardo test track in Italy and prototypes were even run in the Middle East to ensure that they could stand up to local conditions in this potentially lucrative market.

Meanwhile, the production facilities in the Jaguar factories were re-equipped and improved. Of the total bill of £200 million spent on project XJ40 'only' £50 million was spent on design and development with £150 million going towards capital expenditure in the three factories. The tooling cost £70 million, and another £25 million was spent on body assembly and painting facilities at Castle Bromwich. £45 million went into Radford, mostly spent on a new transfer line for AJ6 engine production. The cost of equipping a pilot production assembly line at Browns Lane, and of improving existing assembly facilities in readiness for full-scale production of the new car, was put at £10 million. At the same time, John Egan's programme to improve productivity as well as quality was put into action. 'Quality circle' discussion groups were instituted in the factories. Jaguar persuaded their component suppliers to improve quality. Apart from anything else, there is no doubt that both Egan's personality and the positive spirit generated up to and after the 1984 privatization were enormous morale-boosters to Jaguar employees and everyone connected with the company, in the period leading up to the XJ40 launch.

It is possible that the new car could have been launched earlier than it was. At one time it was thought it might have been introduced before the company was privatized. But John Egan, and no less Jim Randle, were insistent that the car had to be if not perfect, then at least *almost* perfect, before they would agree to series production and the public launch. This was delayed several times until the decision was finally made in 1984 to go for a launch just before the British Motor Show in October 1986 – two years in the future. John Egan made it clear that the XJ40 would not be produced for sale until they were confident that it was the best car in the world. However, for practical and commercial reasons a decision had to be made to commit to a target date, and once the decision had been made it could not be altered.

Luckily there were few problems in the final countdown to introduction. The final specification details were settled in 1985. The manufacture of pre-production or pilot build cars proceeded until some 400 such cars had been made by June 1986. Series production began in July. A pre-preview of the new car was given to the Institute of Mechanical Engineers in London in August when Jim Randle delivered a paper on the development of the XJ40. This was the occasion when, for the first time, a complete car was introduced into the Institute's lecture hall. A special trolley had to be designed to carry a wheel-less XJ40 on its side through rather narrow double doors! In September, the press launch took place in Scotland, Jaguar eschewing exotic foreign locations in favour of a demanding Highlands test route. The official launch date was 8 October but

*Opposite page:*
The top of the XJ40 range was the Daimler 3.6, which was unveiled at the Paris Motor Show in October 1986.

on 7 October, evening parties were given to invited customers by Jaguar dealers throughout the UK who each had one or more examples of the new model in their showrooms. Jaguar's own employees, their families and other specially invited guests had already been shown the new car in a special series of presentations, the so-called J-days, held in the National Exhibition Centre between Birmingham and Coventry. And finally, the public at large were shown the new car. An example had been added to the Jaguar stand in the Paris Motor Show, overnight, between 7 and 8 October, and then finally revealed with the wraps being pulled away mid-morning on launch day. A week later the British Motor Show opened, and once again a Jaguar was the star attraction of the show.

It was revealed on launch day that there was a total of five derivatives of XJ40, and that the Jaguar versions would be known as XJ6 and Sovereign respectively. With the six-cylinder versions of the Series 3 being phased out (the final cars were made in April 1987) Jaguar saw little risk for confusion by carrying over the model titles to their successors. Each of the Jaguars was offered with the 2.9-litre or the 3.6-litre engines, and the differences between XJ6 and Sovereign were limited to trim and equipment – the Sovereign models having as standard air conditioning, anti-lock braking, cruise control, self-levelling rear suspension and other features which were extra-cost options on the XJ6. The XJ6 2.9 litre was brought in at a retail price of just under £16,500 in standard form with manual gearbox, reinforcing Jaguar's reputation for value for money and causing some consternation in the Austin Rover Group as it undercut the most expensive Sterling version of their recently introduced Rover 800 series. Admittedly the cheapest Jaguar had cloth rather than leather trim, so in retaliation Austin Rover sales personnel nick-named it the Jaguar 'City' after their own bargain-basement Mini and Metro models! At the top of the XJ40 range was a single Daimler 3.6-litre model, with more luxurious interior trim including individual rear seats. This was also fitted as standard with an electric sunroof, heated front seats and a limited-slip differential, and retailed at £28,500 when introduced. The Daimler could, as ever, be distinguished by the fluted radiator grille surround. Both this and the Jaguar Sovereign models had the single rectangular headlamps, while the XJ6 featured double round headlamps.

Press reception was universally favourable, the most serious criticisms concerning the instruments and minor controls. The styling – the one area of the car which had caused Jaguar more heartache than any other – was well-liked but many commentators pointed out that the new car looked so very similar to the model it replaced! While it was accepted that the new XJ6 represented evolution rather than revolution in Jaguar's scheme of things, the respected periodical *Motor Sport* suggested that an opportunity had perhaps been missed in that the new car did not seem to represent a very big advance over the old model. They were obviously aware that they were looking at a six-year old design. Some writers also questioned the rectangular headlamps and rear lamps, neither of which it was felt was quite Jaguar. But generally, the new XJ6 was given an enthusiastic welcome for its dynamic as well as static qualities. Public reaction was perhaps predictable in view of the reception given to previous Jaguar models, notably the original XJ6. In the first few months after launch when the new models were still in somewhat short supply, a black market for 'second-hand' new Jaguars sprang up, with delivery-mileage cars changing hands at well over list price. The company was doing everything to prevent this sort of thing happening in so far as it involved their distributors and dealers, but in any case the black marketeering died out as the supply situation was improved with another assembly line coming on stream in 1987.

The new cars were also launched in many export markets before the end of 1986, but the North American introduction was purposely delayed until the spring of 1987. Not only was the USA Jaguar's single most important market (by now taking 50 per cent of production so it was necessary to build up much larger stocks

*Below:*
The Jaguar Sovereign.

preparatory to the American introduction) but, as usual, local requirements dictated the development of rather different models from those sold in Europe, and the added complication of building North American specification cars was best avoided in the first hectic months of production. After press and public launches, the new cars went on sale in the USA on 5 May 1987, by which time they were described as 1988 models (following the American model year practice). Two models were introduced, both with the 3.6-litre engine adjusted to run on lead-free petrol and equipped with a catalytic converter for the exhaust system. The North American specification cars all had the twin round headlamp set-up. The base model was the XJ6 but this was in fact equipped to a level comparable with that of the home-market Sovereign model. Jaguar kept to the Vanden Plas label for American use, and this luxury version was virtually trimmed and equipped to the specification of the UK market Daimler model. All American cars were fitted with automatic transmission as standard, a manual option not being quoted.

In the three years or so that have elapsed since its launch, the new generation XJ6 has proved to be a worthy heir to the Jaguar tradition. From fewer than 4,000 cars in 1986 production has built up to more than 32,000 in 1987 and almost 39,000 in 1988 and the new Jaguar is now a relatively common sight on British roads. Although Jaguar will now admit that there were teething troubles with the new model, and although there has been at least one well-publicized recall, in general the cars have lived up to expectations in service. It has been a successful three years for the car, and for the company. Prices have, of course, crept up but at the time of writing the cheapest XJ6 2.9 was still under £20,000 with the Daimler at £34,500.

Apart from detail retouches, no changes have been considered necessary to the five models in the range.

Alongside the new models, the last survivors of the Series 3 are still in production: the Jaguar Sovereign V12 and the Daimler Double Six, which offer the additional refinement and performance of the V12 engine at very little extra cost over the most expensive six-cylinder cars to customers who are prepared to accept the old body styling and who know they are buying a new car which has only a limited life expectancy as a production model. Perhaps the knowledge that they are buying an instant classic is an added attraction for V12 customers! The XJ-S is still very much there, enjoying steadily increased sales; in 1987 for the first time more than 10,000 XJ-S models were delivered in a 12-month period. This model has been the focus of further development since the introduction of the V12-engined Cabriolet in 1985. In 1987, the six cylinder XJ-S models were offered with optional automatic transmission. Then the six cylinder Cabriolet was discontinued, soon followed by the V12 Cabriolet model, replaced at the 1988 Geneva Motor Show by the Convertible which is offered only with the V12 engine. On the Convertible Jaguar have finally done what many observers felt they should have done in the first place; they have taken off the roll-over bar and removed the fixed side window frames, producing the first completely open Jaguar since the demise of the E-type in 1974. The XJ-S Convertible is a car of considerable elegance which has given the model a new lease of life. It is also the most expensive model in the Jaguar range, at close to £40,000. In addition to the Convertible, the XJ-S Coupé with either the AJ6 or the V12 engine, continued in production in 1989.

*Above:*
The Jaguar Sovereign.

*Above left:*
The Jaguar XJ6 2.9 manual.

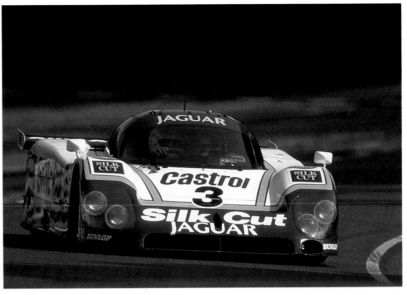

# ON TOP OF THE WORLD
## 1987-1988

In early 1987, the TWR-Jaguar XJR-6 had won a rather special recognition. Most unusually for a racing car, it was chosen as the recipient of one of the Design Council Awards, as being exceptional in design and innovation. Unbeknown to the Design Council, Tom Walkinshaw and Tony Southgate were already busy on the replacement for the XJR-6. The result of their labours over the winter months was an even more spectacular car, launched in March 1987 just before the beginning of the new racing season.

Of the previous year's drivers, Jan Lammers and Eddie Cheever chose to stay with the Silk Cut Jaguar team, while Derek Warwick and Schlesser went off in search of pastures new. New recruits were John Watson and Raul Boesel, while the Danish driver, John Nielsen (who had previously had two drives for the team, in Japan and Malaysia in 1985) was engaged to complete the line up on those occasions when Cheever, due to other contractual obligations, would be unable to race with the Jaguar team. A new livery for the Silk Cut Jaguars was revealed at the Amsterdam Motor Show in February, but details of the actual 1987 racing cars were kept under wraps for another month. The new season's car emerged as a logical development of the original XJR-6 but was so completely revised throughout as to justify giving it a new name – the XJR-8. (The XJR-7 title had already been bagged for the new racing Jaguar from Group 44 in the USA!)

The 7.0 litre V12 engine was now said to give up to 700bhp. In tests at Silverstone, the new car lapped the circuit an amazing five seconds faster than the XJR-6 at an average speed of more than

*Opposite page:*
The five XJR-9 Jaguars entered in the 1988 Le Mans 24-hour race, which was won by car number 2 (*centre*) driven by Lammers/ Dumfries/Wallace, with car Number 22 (*bottom right*) in fourth place.

150mph, and only one tenth of a second slower than the Formula 1 lap record of this circuit. The revisions to the design did not stop with the engine. There were improvements to the suspension, the transmission and the bodywork, which was much lighter than that of the XJR-6. Lighter wheels were fitted with Dunlop's latest Kevlar-based tyres. Two distinct versions of the XJR-8 were developed. There was a high downforce sprint version for the shorter races now becoming popular in the championship series. This could be distinguished by the spatted rear wheels. With an eye to the Mulsanne straight at Le Mans, a special Le Mans version was being developed alongside the Sprint car. This was of very low build, with an inclined engine, and a special low-drag aerodynamic body.

The first race of the season was at Jarama in Spain on 22 March. This was an occasion when history, for once, repeated itself. Those with long memories looked back to the 1951 Le Mans, when the C-type Jaguar had won its very first race; 36 years later, Jaguar would repeat this remarkable feat. Eddie Cheever and Jan Lammers put the two Jaguars in first and second positions on the starting grid. The Cheever/Boesel car went into an early lead but was twice delayed, first by an oil leak and then by what appeared to be a problem with the fuel pickup. This allowed their team mates Watson and Lammers to take the lead and only the Rothmans-Porsche of Stuck and Bell could offer a challenge. In a reversal of events at Spa in 1986, it was the turn of the Jaguar to lead home the Porsche by a margin of seconds. Complementing the fine win of Watson and

Lammers was a thoroughly deserved third place for Cheever and Boesel. No wonder they threw a party in the Jaguar team to celebrate!

Once the Jaguars had got under way there was no stopping them. Looking at the table of results for 1987, it seems that Watson/Lammers and Cheever/Boesel deliberately took turns to win, keeping up the excitement in the struggle for the championship. If there really was a pre-planned scheme behind the changing fortunes of the two Jaguar cars in subsequent races during 1987, it would certainly explain why it was the turn of Cheever and Boesel to take the laurels at Jerez, also in Spain, in the week after the Jarama race. There was more to it than that. Lammers had started from second position on the grid and had held on to this position until delayed by a wheel bearing failure. This put the two works Porsches well ahead of Cheever in the other Jaguar. When Watson took over Lammers' car, it was only to be stranded soon after with driveshaft failure, apparently caused by the notoriously bumpy surface of the Jerez circuit. Both of the works Porsches had gearbox problems which were to put one of them out of the race, and ultimately the Cheever/Boesel Jaguar went into the lead. It stayed there until the finish.

At Monza in Italy on 12 April, John Nielsen got his first drive in an XJR-8, joining Raul Boesel, while Watson and Lammers again shared the second Jaguar. This might have been a 1–2 for the Jaguars, but towards the end of the race the heavens opened. Raul Boesel left it just too late to go into his pit for a change of tyres, and instead skidded off the now very slippery circuit to get stuck in a gravel trap. The Lammers/Watson car was comfortably in the lead, two laps ahead of the best Porsche, and ensured the third win in as many races for Jaguar. With the cancellation of the Vallelunga race, the world championship series now headed for Britain and Silverstone. Local enthusiasts were looking to Jaguar to repeat their 1986 victory and they were not disappointed. The team had three cars at the start. John Nielsen teamed up with Martin Brundle to give the Le Mans version of the XJR-8 its race debut. Deliberately punishing the car to give it a good workout prior to Le Mans, they ended up with a broken valve spring which put them out of the running. The other two Jaguars, driven as usual by Watson/Lammers and Cheever/Boesel, did not disappoint the enthusiasts. They fought a close battle between themselves and eventually finished first and second. It was Cheever and Boesel's turn to win, and win they did, but the Watson/Lammers car was only six seconds behind and they stayed ahead in the drivers' championship.

Come the weekend of 13–14 June, and a change of setting to Le Mans. Three Jaguars were entered, all of the special Le Mans version of the XJR-8, and they lined up in third, fourth and fifth positions on the grid. Extra drivers had been brought in for the 24-hour race, so the crews were Cheever/Boesel, Martin Brundle/John Nielsen (with Hahne as reserve driver), and Lammers/Watson (with Win Percy as reserve). The cars were timed at 219–220mph which put them among the favourites. This was not to be Jaguar's race, although if the sheer willpower and enthusiasm among the estimated 30,000 British spectators could have won the race for Jaguar, the cars would have finished 1-2-3! First to come to grief was the Lammers/Watson car. Win Percy was just settling down to enjoying his first spell at the wheel when a tyre exploded at Mulsanne, causing a monumental crash. That Percy escaped with his life, and was unhurt at that, can only be ascribed to the strength of the Southgate-designed Jaguar chassis. The car literally turned cartwheels and ended up minus most of its bodywork, as well as the rear wheels and gearbox. The Brundle/Nielsen car was quickest in the race and led the field on several occasions, but was put out of the running by a cracked cylinder head on Sunday morning. This left the Cheever/Boesel car, with Lammers now sharing the driving. A series of problems in the final stages of the race held the car back, and they eventually finished in fifth place overall.

*Below:*
Le Mans 1987: the XJR-8 of Brundle/Nielsen has to give up.

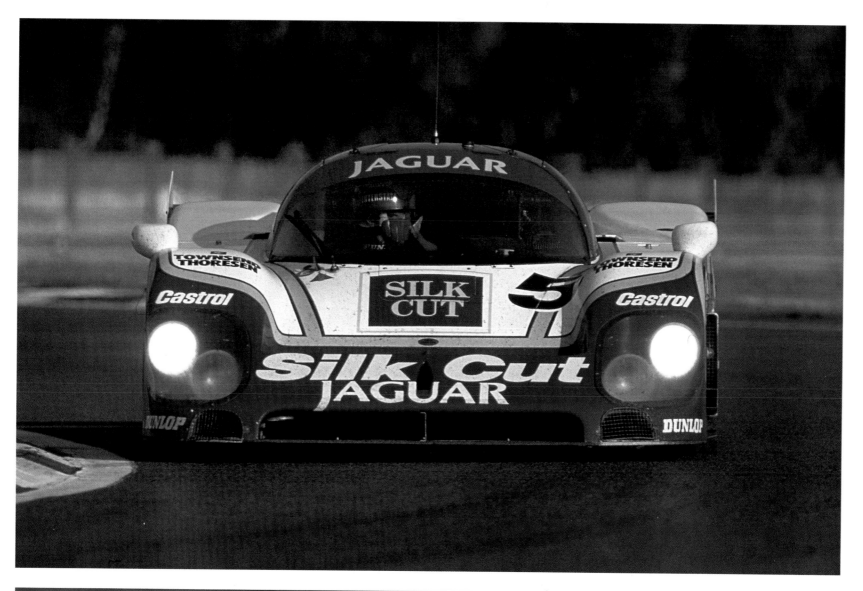

*Above:*
The Lammers/Watson car before it blew a tyre in the 1987 Le Mans.

*Left:*
The Cheever/Boesel car, which finished the race.

The bad luck from Le Mans dogged the Jaguar team also at Norisring at the end of June. Cheever and Boesel upheld the team honours, by starting and finishing in fourth position, but Lammers and Watson retired with transmission failure after 42 laps of the 154-lap race. Cheever and Boesel were now in second place for the drivers' championship, having been displaced by Stuck and Bell who were the Le Mans winners, while Watson and Lammers were third. As far as the team championship was concerned, Silk Cut Jaguar had a comfortable lead. They were to prove unassailable for the rest of the season.

At Brands Hatch in July, the team found its form again. In Cheever's absence, Boesel was teamed up with John Nielsen, while Lammers and Watson shared the other car as usual. They started in first and second positions and Boesel/Nielsen were the ultimate winners, followed by a privately-entered Porsche, with Lammers/Watson third. The rest of the season was a Jaguar benefit. Cheever was back for the Nürburgring race at the end of August, where he and Boesel won comfortably. The Lammers/Watson sister car had kept pace with the leaders in the early stages of the race but retired with a valve failure. At Spa in September, the Silk Cut team fielded three Jaguars. Raul Boesel was given a new car to drive, shared with Martin Brundle and Johnny Dumfries. Lammers and Watson kept to their well-established partnership, and Eddie Cheever was paired with John Nielsen in the third car. This time a Sauber-Mercedes took the pole position, and the Jaguars started in the third, fourth and sixth positions — with the Boesel/Brundle/Dumfries car as tail-end Charlie. Their impeccable driving eventually brought them victory, followed home by the Lammers/Watson car, then a Porsche to spoil the Jaguar cavalcade, and then Brundle/Nielsen in fourth place. After this race, Boesel had clinched the drivers' championship, and the Silk Cut Jaguar team had more than double the points of the Porsche team which was second in the team championship. There was perhaps just a slight feeling of anti-climax as Lammers/Watson and Boesel/Dumfries took first and second places in the last race of the season, at Fuji in Japan on 27 September.

Not forgetting the many successes scored by Jaguar racing cars in the 1950s, 1987 was the most remarkable racing season for the marque so far. For the first time, Jaguar had won the world championship for sports cars — a feat which had always eluded them in their Le Mans-winning heyday — and four of the team's drivers occupied the first four places in the drivers' championship. The Brazilian driver Raul Boesel was first, Watson and Lammers were joint second, and Cheever fourth. There were wins in eight out of ten races, as well as three second places, and two third places. In three races, there had been Jaguar 1–2 wins. Truly 1987 was a year to remember for everyone in Tom Walkinshaw's team, and everyone at Jaguar!

In the USA, Bob Tullius and Group 44 had entered what would be their final season of racing with Jaguar-engined sports cars. Their efforts were concentrated on a single developed 650bhp XJR-7 car. Both Brian Redman and Chip Robinson had left the team, so Bob Tullius and Hurley Haywood were joined by newcomer John Morton. A smaller number of races was scheduled for the IMSA Camel GT series than in previous years. The car retired in the first two races of the season, but at Riverside in April Morton and Haywood won the race, beating the former Jaguar team driver Chip Robinson (now at the wheel of a Porsche) into second place! Morton and Haywood repeated their win at West Palm Beach in June, again beating Robinson's Porsche by a margin of two seconds. This time Chip Robinson was partnered by Derek Bell who had come fresh from winning Le Mans (again). The swan song for the Group 44 Jaguar came with victory at West Palm Beach in June, but by then it had already become known that Tullius would switch his attention towards running an Indy car team in 1988, while the British TWR-Jaguar team, with sponsorship from Castrol, would take up the challenge of running a team in the IMSA series in the USA, as well as continuing to contest the World Championship in the following season. Although the team continued to run for the remainder of the 1987 IMSA series, there was no better result than a third place at Watkins Glen, and eventually the championship fell to former Jaguar driver Chip Robinson in a Porsche 962.

The outlook for the 1988 racing season was excellent, and prospects were enlivened by the announcement that Mercedes-Benz would return officially to racing with the Sauber team. This was a promise that the interrupted Jaguar v Mercedes duel of 1955 would be resumed! The TWR-Jaguar team was preparing six new cars of the modified XJR-9 design, three for the sports-prototype World Championship series, three for the IMSA series. Although basically similar in design, the IMSA cars had a different rear suspension and 6-litre engines, where the World

Championship Group C cars had 7-litre engines. The principal drivers for the sports-prototype championship were Martin Brundle, Eddie Cheever, Jan Lammers and Johnny Dumfries. The IMSA team, sponsored by Castrol and based near Chicago, could count World Sports Car Champion Raul Boesel among its drivers, together with John Watson, John Nielsen, Danny Sullivan and Davy Jones. However it was expected that there would be some interchange of drivers between the two teams.

The American racing season opened with the 24-hour race at Daytona in Florida on 30−31 January. Here, the Castrol Jaguars were up against a mighty line up of Porsches, and there was also a single Group 44 Jaguar XJR-7 which was now considered something of an outsider. Unable to match the fastest Porsches for speed in practice, the Jaguar of Lammers/Sullivan/Jones was nevertheless second on the grid, with the two other cars, driven by Brundle/Nielsen/Boesel and Cheever/Dumfries/Watson not far behind. As the race unfolded, the Group 44 XJR-7 was an early casualty with a blown head gasket, while the three Castrol Jaguars stayed consistently among the top five cars until early on Sunday morning, the Lammers/Sullivan/Jones car retired with engine trouble. With both of the leading Porsche challengers running into trouble, the final result was a Jaguar victory, for the Brundle/Nielsen/Boesel car (with Lammers sharing the driving in the final stages). A Porsche was second, and the other remaining Jaguar third. In the next IMSA race at Miami on 28 February, Jaguar's fortunes were reversed. Brundle and Nielsen were placed second behind a Porsche, by a margin of four thousandths of a second which must be a record for a close second place! Team-mates Lammers and Jones finished sixth.

In Europe, the racing season began at Jerez in Spain on 6 March. Three of the TWR/Silk Cut Jaguars came to the start of the 800km race − drivers being Brundle/Cheever, Lammers/Dumfries and Nielsen/Watson with Andy Wallace as a third driver. This race marked the debut for the official Mercedes-Benz team, and the single Sauber-Mercedes car was first on the grid, with the Jaguars in second, third and fourth position. In the race, two of the Jaguars were put out of action almost simultaneously by gearbox trouble, and the Nielsen/Watson/Wallace car lost a lap after the quick-thinking Wallace had run the car over the grass verge, successfully avoiding another car which had skidded across the track. The team almost caught the Mercedes but in the end had to be content with a well-deserved second place. A week later, the Jaguars had their revenge at Jarama, with Cheever and Brundle leading the Mercedes home, followed by Nielsen and Watson in third place. Lammers and Dumfries were unlucky; Dumfries lost the car which went into a gravel trap and stuck there. So after the two Spanish opening races, it was Jaguar 1, Mercedes 1.

The next American race was the 12-hour at Sebring on 19 March, Here, the Brundle/Nielsen/Boesel Jaguar retired in the second hour with engine trouble, while the other car − crewed by Lammers, Jones, Sullivan and Nielsen − was delayed by a number of problems, culminating in a complete transmission replacement undertaken in just under an hour. They continued to the end of the race but, understandably, could do no better than a seventh place. At Road Atlanta on 10 April, Nielsen and Watson were just pipped to the post by the Electramotive-Nissan − the first victory for this American-Japanese team. Davy Jones and Andy Wallace in the other Jaguar were placed fourth. On the same day at Monza in Italy, the Silk Cut Jaguars had better luck but the race was not without diversions. Jan Lammers had to be push-started by the marshals and he later had a minor collision with the Sauber-Mercedes. When Johnny Dumfries took over this car, he again had the bad fortune to spin off the track into a gravel pit. Meanwhile, the other Jaguar of Cheever and Brundle built up a comfortable lead over the Mercedes, and eventually won the race with a lap in hand.

At the beginning of the 1988 season, it had been predicted that the IMSA GT championship would be a straight battle between the TWR-Castrol Jaguars and the various Porsche teams. But after Road Atlanta, there was no stopping the 'new boys' in the Electramotive-Nissan team − they enjoyed eight wins in eight consecutive races, usually leaving the Jaguars and the Porsches to fight it out for second place. At West Palm Beach on 24 April, Nielsen and Brundle retired halfway with transmission trouble, while Lammers and Jones were second after the winning Nissan. Brundle and Nielsen were second at Lime Rock on 30 May, with Lammers and Jones third, and exactly the same results were achieved at Mid-Ohio on 5 June. At Watkins Glen on 3 July, one of the Jaguars retired early with engine trouble, and the other car was involved in a collision, owing to rear suspension damage sustained when it had blown a tyre earlier in the race. On 17 July at Road America, the two Jaguars finished fourth

*Above:*
The 1988 Silverstone 1000km race: Martin Brundle in the winning Jaguar; and (*right*) with Eddie Cheever on the winners' stand.

and fifth, having to give way to two Porsches as well as the winning Nissan, while at Portland on 31 July, for the first time there were two Nissans entered. They finished first and second with the Jaguars in third and fourth place.

So it went on. At Sears Point on 14 August, the Jaguars were second and third after the Nissan, and even if the Nissan for once was beaten at San Antonio on 4 September (the car retired), this merely gave a victory to Porsche, with a second place to Jaguar. At Columbus on 2 October, the Nissan was back on form, and the single Jaguar entered could do no better than finish tenth and last. At least the TWR-Castrol Jaguar team finished the season in style for in the last race in the series, at Del Mar on 23 October, Lammers and Brundle scored Jaguar's first win since the Daytona race ten months before. Theirs was the only Jaguar in the race after John Nielsen had crashed in practice. The result of the championship was Australian Nissan driver Geoff Brabham, first, and John Nielsen second for Jaguar, while in the manufacturers' championship, Jaguar had to be content with a third place after Porsche and Nissan.

In the World Sports Car Championship, the TWR-Silk Cut Jaguar team had been doing much better. Going back to 8 May, Jaguar scored their third consecutive victory, in the 1000km race at Silverstone. It was also the third time in as many years that a Jaguar had won this particular race, much to the delight of the thousands of local fans. The race saw an exciting duel between the Cheever/Brundle Jaguar and the two Sauber-Mercedes cars, which was ultimately decided in favour of the British car when Brundle gained a crucial half-minute lead over the quickest Mercedes. Unfortunately, the other Jaguar, driven by Lammers and Dumfries, ran out of fuel with five laps to go; apparently the computer monitoring fuel consumption had been

malfunctioning, leading Johnny Dumfries into thinking that he had 11 litres left when there was none. Otherwise they might have finished the race in third or even second place. But it was a fine and satisfying victory for the Cheever/Brundle Jaguar, and the team now set about preparing for Le Mans with understandably high hopes.

The line-up of cars that eventually came to the start at Le Mans on 11 June was not quite what had been expected. After experiencing tyre problems in practice, the Sauber-Mercedes team decided to scratch their two entries at the last moment. The prospect of a three-cornered battle between Jaguar, Mercedes-Benz and Porsche therefore evaporated. Also of note was the fact that, in addition to the usual horde of privately-run Porsches, a Porsche works team of three cars made its first appearance on a race circuit for quite some time. Jaguar fielded an impressive line up of five cars, with Brundle/Nielsen being the quickest in practice, setting up the fourth fastest qualifying time. The three works Porsches were noticeably quicker. The second Jaguar, driven by Lammers and Dumfries together with Andy Wallace, was sixth on the grid. Danny Sullivan, Davy Jones and Price Cobb started in ninth position, and the fourth Jaguar – driven by Derek Daly, Larry Perkins and Kevin Cogan – was eleventh. Just behind, in 12th position, Le Mans oldtimer and previous winner Henri Pescarolo gave a hand to John Watson and Raul Boesel in the fifth and last Jaguar. Otherwise there were Porsches all round them, although a Japanese challenge materialized at Le Mans as it had in the American IMSA championship – but it was Toyota rather than Nissan which was to the fore at Le Mans, a Toyota starting in eighth place as the quickest car which was neither a Jaguar nor a Porsche.

As the race got underway, it became clear that this was primarily a battle between the works

*Far left:*
Le Mans 1988: Larry
Perkins, whose car was to
finish fourth.

*Left:*
Three of the five Jaguar
works cars at Le Mans 1988.

*Below:*
Some of the jubilant
supporters and (*bottom*) the
winning Jaguar drivers.

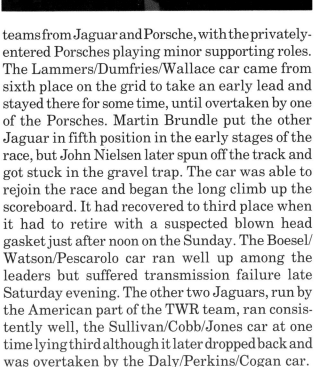

teams from Jaguar and Porsche, with the privately-entered Porsches playing minor supporting roles. The Lammers/Dumfries/Wallace car came from sixth place on the grid to take an early lead and stayed there for some time, until overtaken by one of the Porsches. Martin Brundle put the other Jaguar in fifth position in the early stages of the race, but John Nielsen later spun off the track and got stuck in the gravel trap. The car was able to rejoin the race and began the long climb up the scoreboard. It had recovered to third place when it had to retire with a suspected blown head gasket just after noon on the Sunday. The Boesel/Watson/Pescarolo car ran well up among the leaders but suffered transmission failure late Saturday evening. The other two Jaguars, run by the American part of the TWR team, ran consistently well, the Sullivan/Cobb/Jones car at one time lying third although it later dropped back and was overtaken by the Daly/Perkins/Cogan car.

But it was the Lammers/Dumfries/Wallace car which held most of the attention. Soon after midnight, it was back in the lead, and stayed there for the rest of the race, with the quickest of the works Porsches only briefly getting in front when the Jaguar had a long pit stop to have its windscreen changed. When, soon after, it was the Porsche's turn to get stuck in the pit with fuel pump trouble, the Jaguar re-established its lead. Towards the end of the race tension mounted as the Porsche began to haul in the Jaguar, especially when the British car made a late pit stop for fuel, but at 3pm on Sunday afternoon, the Jaguar was still in front, though the Porsche was on the same lap, less than a minute behind. The Daly/Perkins/Cogan Jaguar finished strongly in fourth place, while the last of the three surviving Jaguars, the Sullivan/Jones/Cobb car, was 16th. So, after 31 years, a Jaguar had won at Le Mans again. The 1988 Le Mans victory put the seal of success on Jaguar's return to racing. Winning the

*Above:*
Brands Hatch 1988: Martin
Brundle in the winning car.

after the Le Mans *débâcle*. A close battle between the leading two teams ensued, decided here in favour of the Germans. The Jaguars were placed second (Brundle and Nielsen), and third (Lammers and Dumfries). The tables were turned at Brands Hatch on 24 July. Three Jaguars came to the start, but the team suffered two retirements. Watson and Jones went out early with engine trouble, and the Lammers/Dumfries car had to retire when some of the wiring caught fire late in the race. But John Nielsen, Martin Brundle and Andy Wallace brought the leading Jaguar home in a fine first place, followed this time by a Porsche and the Mercedes in third place. This race was the first occasion when the TWR-developed 48-valve version of the V12 engine had been used in anger, fitted to the Watson/Jones car. This developed some 750bhp, but the weight of the car had also increased by some 70kg.

If the Jaguars had now won both the championship races held in Britain, perhaps there was some justice in the victory of the Mercedes on its home ground, the 1000km race at the Nürburgring held on 3 and 4 September. The race organizers had come up with the novel and controversial idea of holding two 500 kilometre races on subsequent days, with the winner being decided on aggregate. The Mercedes had won the Saturday race, with Lammers/Dumfries and Brundle/Cheever in the

1987 World Championship was all very well, but the psychological impact of the historic Le Mans win could not be overlooked when one remembered Jaguar's glorious history in this one event.

After Le Mans, it was back to business as usual for the TWR-Silk Cut Jaguar team. The customary two cars were fielded at Brno in Czechoslovakia on 10 July. Once again, they were up against the Sauber-Mercedes team which returned to the fray

*Right:*
The winning drivers.

Jaguars second and third respectively. In the Sunday race, Johnny Dumfries ran out of road and badly damaged the car against the barrier. While the car was able to rejoin the race after a long pit stop, it eventually finished eighth on aggregate, while team mates Brundle and Cheever were second, both in the Sunday race and on aggregate, with the Mercedes winning the Sunday race as well.

The last European race in the Championship series, held at Spa on 18 September, again brought victory to a Sauber-Mercedes, but Lammers and Brundle were a close second in the Jaguar, the other Jaguar having retired early in the race. The Spa result put the TWR-Silk Cut Jaguar team so far ahead in the teams' championship that their lead was unassailable, and Jaguar driver Martin Brundle now also eased ahead of the leading Mercedes driver Jean-Louis Schlesser in the drivers' championship. With two rounds to go, Jaguar were World Champions for the second year running. What had yet to be decided was the outcome of the drivers' championship where Brundle had only a very narrow lead. This was settled in Brundle's favour at Fuji in Japan on 9 October, where Cheever and Brundle scored a decisive victory over the assembled Porsche teams; on this occasion, Mercedes could do no better than a fifth place. The Lammers/Dumfries car was unlucky. A front tyre deflated and sent Lammers into the barrier, the damage being too serious for the car to rejoin the race.

With the championship in the bag for Jaguar and Martin Brundle after Fuji, the final race, at Sandown Park in Australia on 20 November, was an anti-climax. This poorly-supported race, in addition to the Jaguar and Mercedes teams, attracted only three entries in Group C1 – two Porsches and an Australian-built Veskanda-Chevrolet. The result was a 1–2 for Mercedes, with Cheever/Brundle in third place, and Lammers/Dumfries in fourth.

If, at the beginning of the 1988 racing season, one had asked Tom Walkinshaw what his goals were for the two Jaguar teams, he might have admitted he hoped to win both the World Championship and the IMSA Championship as well as the Le Mans 24-hour race. In the event, the TWR–Castrol Jaguar team had a disappointing season in the USA, but the other two goals were reached by the TWR–Silk Cut Team, and two out of three can't be bad! Jaguar had won six out of eleven races in the World Championship, while in addition to Martin Brundle winning the drivers' championship, his team mate and regular co-driver, Eddie Cheever, was fourth. In the IMSA series, Jaguars had won only two of the 15 races, but at least Jaguar driver John Nielsen was second in the drivers' championship, and Jaguar was third in the manufacturers' championship. But with two World Championships under their belt, in 1987 and 1988, there was no doubt that Jaguar were back where they belonged – on top of the world.

*Left:*
Jan Lammers and Tom Walkinshaw after the 1988 Le Mans victory.

# TOWARDS THE FUTURE
## 1988-1990

A tantalizing glimpse of Jaguar's future was given in the 1988 British International Motor Show at the National Exhibition Centre, Birmingham. Dramatically unveiled by Sir John Egan himself, the stunning XJ220 prototype supercar stole the show for Jaguar, much as XJ40 had done two years before. The unveiling of XJ220 was propitiously timed, coming as it did on the heels of Jaguar's second World Championship and the Le Mans victory. A first glance at the sleek silver car might suggest that this was a road-going version of the TWR-Jaguar XJR-9. In fact, the truth was much more interesting.

The concept and birth of XJ220 was owed to the dream of one man, Jaguar's chief engineer Jim Randle. He had begun to consider the ultimate Jaguar sports car back in December 1984, at a time when Tom Walkinshaw was still testing the borrowed Group 44 XJR-5, and XJR-6 was only a gleam in Tony Southgate's eye. And while Walkinshaw and Southgate set out to create the most efficient Group C racing car, Jim Randle's line of thought led him towards a fully-equipped road-going car. While not intended as a racing car as such, Randle's dream car was conceived as a potential Group B car – a limited production supercar to match the Ferrari F40 and Porsche 959. Work on XJ220 began in early 1985, in both the styling studio and the engineering department. As Jaguar's resources were fully committed to XJ40 and other projects, it was understood that XJ220 could not take up company time or money. Nevertheless, a small band of enthusiastic volunteers emerged, each of whom was prepared to work on the car in his

*Opposite page:*
The 1988 Jaguar XJ220
prototype – a glimpse of the
Jaguar future.

spare time. A dozen or so Jaguar engineers and stylists became involved, and because of the nature of the project they became known as the 'Saturday Club'.

During 1985, two different styling proposals emerged. The decision was finally made in favour of Keith Helfet's design which was felt to be more in keeping with Jaguar's traditions. The South African-born Helfet had studied engineering in his native country before coming to England in 1975 to study automotive design at the Royal College of Art in London. He joined Jaguar soon after graduating in 1977, and seven years later had become one of the company's senior designers. He now became a key member of Randle's team.

Randle's concept called for a mid-engined car, using the 48-valve version of Jaguar's V12 engine that Walkinshaw had briefly tested in 1986, and with four-wheel drive. The team of engineers approached the well-known four-wheel drive specialists, FF Developments, to assist with planning the drivetrain of the car. Eventually, more than 40 of Jaguar's suppliers were persuaded into helping out with the project. The chassis, fabricated from sheet alloy, and the hand-rolled alloy body panels were made by Park Sheet Metal where the final assembly of the car was also carried out.

The four overhead cam 48-valve 6,222cc engine was said to develop over 500bhp, with Zytek electronic fuel injection. The five-speed gearbox, using Hewland gears, drove a centre epicyclic differential, mounted above the rear final drive, in unit with engine and gearbox; 69 per cent of

*Right:*
XJ220 – a magnificent
showpiece which
demonstrates highly
sophisticated technology and
design.

the torque was taken to the rear wheels, 31 per
cent to the front wheels which were driven by a
two-part quill shaft which passed through the V
of the engine. The centre, rear and front
differentials all incorporated viscous couplings.
The suspension was by double wishbones front
and rear, with single Koni units at the front and
two on each side at the back.

Any car using the Jaguar V12 engine is likely
to end up being pretty big. XJ220 was no
exception – with a 112in wheelbase and an
overall length of 202in, and a weight of around
3,500lb. Despite this, with some 500bhp it was
estimated that XJ220 would easily top 200mph
and might even get close to the 220mph suggested
by its designation. Acceleration should be pretty
dramatic too, with 60mph coming up in 3.5
seconds, and 100mph in 8 seconds.

Work on XJ220 progressed fairly slowly during
1986 and 1987. Randle continued to oversee the
project but chassis designer Frank Marsden was
appointed as project manager. Clive Lindsey who
had designed the air conditioning installation
was put in charge of chasing suppliers, to make
sure that things happened in the correct order.
Keith Helfet was being assisted by Mark Lloyd
who looked after aerodynamics and Nick Hull
who developed the interior styling, while their
boss, Geoff Lawson (Jaguar's chief stylist since
1984) kept a benevolent eye on the project
throughout.

After some three years of low-key preparation,
XJ220 finally came together in the six months
from March to October 1988. This was an
increasingly hectic time as the team worked
tirelessly to meet the self-imposed deadline of
having the car finished and ready for the Motor
Show. The ultimate decision of whether to show
the car or not lay with one man, Sir John Egan,
and he had not even seen the car yet, although
he was obviously being kept fully briefed about
its development and had even hinted at its
existence in public. But Sir John only saw the
almost finished car just a week before the Motor
Show press day. It did not take him long to make
up his mind – the car would be unveiled at the
Jaguar stand in the show.

XJ220 was a magnificent showpiece, demon-
strating the capabilities and talent of Jaguar's
engineers and designers. The flowing lines of the
body work were evocative of Jaguar sports cars
of the past – above all, the XJ13 – but with the
traditional themes brought fully up to date. The
oval shape of the front air intake echoed those of
the classic Jaguars of the past. Both the front chin

spoiler and the rear aerofoil were adjustable, and with an undertray to smooth the airflow underneath the car, XJ220 was designed to produce downforce increasing with speed.

As shown at the NEC in October 1988, XJ220 was almost ready for the road. After the show, the car was handed over to Tom Walkinshaw and Jaguar Sport, the newly-created joint venture between Jaguar and TWR, for assessment. For over a year, little was heard of the project, but in December 1989 it was finally announced that a developed version of XJ220 would go on sale in 1992, at a price of £361,000. The production XJ220 would be fitted with TWR's new V6 racing engine, a 3.5 litre twin-turbo unit developing 500 bhp, but with rear wheel drive only. Shorter by almost a foot, the proportions of the production XJ220 were even more beautiful than the original show car. Possibly as many as 350 examples of the car would be built in a new factory at Banbury by Project XJ220 Limited. Within days, the waiting list was over-subscribed!

But XJ220, or its descendant, can only be a limited production flagship at the top of a future Jaguar range. More important for the immediate future is the development of the XJ40 saloon car range. In the Frankfurt Motor Show in September 1989, Jaguar launched the 4-litre version of this car. The bigger engine had much improved power and torque compared to the 3.6-litre model which it replaced. Also at this time, Jaguar took the opportunity to alter other aspects of the car. The controversial instrument display was replaced by a set of classic dials, and there were slight retouches to the exterior styling. The 2.9-litre engine was not changed, although it was expected that a 3.2-litre version would eventually replace it. Looking further ahead, a long-wheelbase version of XJ40 was in the planning stages, and a V12-engined version was expected by the early 1990s.

When a V12-engined XJ40 appears, it will mean the end of the road for the timeless Series 3 body, over 20 years after the introduction of that original masterpiece, the first XJ6. The XJ40 shape is unlikely to last as long as that. There will probably be a new Jaguar saloon before the end of the century. Competition at the top end of the luxury market is increasing. BMW and Mercedes-Benz have followed Jaguar with V12 engines of their own, while Cadillac and several Japanese manufacturers may take the same path. Despite its relative age, the Jaguar V12 is still a worthy contender, with potential for further development, as has been shown by the racing cars.

*Left:*
The oval motif and the lavish use of glass are featured strikingly here.

The XJ-S is more successful than ever. The convertible model is by far the best-looking version of the car. But obviously, Jaguar are watching the German rivals closely. The appearance of the BMW850 and the new Mercedes-Benz SL may be a spur to looking closely at developing a successor to the 15-year-old XJ-S. The oldest model in the company's range is the Daimler limousine, first introduced in 1968 and now the only model still using the XK engine. It is now expected that the limousine will survive in its present form into the early 1990s, and it must be questionable whether Jaguar will develop a successor to cater for this very limited market.

It is virtually an open secret that Jaguar are working on a new sports car which will emerge, in typical Jaguar fashion, when it is ready. This probably means 1992 or 1993. The car is frequently referred to as the 'F-type' but it remains to be seen whether the production version will carry this designation. It is certainly an appropriate and handy title! The F-type will not be such a technological *tour-de-force* as the XJ220. It will be a conventional front-engined car, using the 4-litre AJ6 engine, possibly in turbocharged form. Likely to be a two-seater only, there will be open and closed versions. Spy photographs of early prototypes published in 1989 clearly showed that, in terms of styling, the F-type inclined towards Jaguar's sports car traditions, but was also both modern and elegant. One speculates that Keith Helfet, the XJ220 designer, has also been involved with this eagerly-awaited car.

As far as motor racing was concerned, the two TWR-Jaguar teams continued to operate for the 1989 racing season, with additional sponsorship from Dunlop. In the World Sports Car Championship series, the main competition was now from the Swiss-German Sauber-Mercedes team, while the toughest nut to crack in the American IMSA series was the Electramotive-Nissan team. Development of the XJR-9 continued, although the disappointing race results in the early part of 1989 seemed to suggest that the car was no longer so competitive, and that the basic four-year old design was becoming outdated.

In any case, the writing was on the wall. The present Group C formula comes to an end with the 1990 racing season. For 1991, the sports car championship will be contested by 3.5 litre cars without turbochargers, with engine specifications very similar to those of the new Formula 1 Grand Prix cars. If TWR-Jaguar want to remain in motor racing in 1991 and later, they will need a new engine. Actually, a new car was under develop-

ment. TWR had acquired the rights to the never fully developed V6-4V engine from Austin Rover's MG Metro 6R4 rally car, and used this as inspiration for their own turbocharged 3-litre V6 engine. It was suggested that this new engine might also have a part to play in future Jaguar road cars.

The V6 engine was installed in the new XJR-10 race car which made its debut in the American Lime Rock race on 29 May. Driven by Jan Lammers, the new car finished second after a Nissan. Jaguar stuck to the proven V12-engined XJR-9 for the Le Mans entries. However, there was not to be a repeat win. The best Jaguar finished fourth, driven by Jan Lammers, Patrick Tambay and Andrew Gilbert-Scott. A sister car was eighth, while the two other Jaguars both retired with mechanical failures. The Le Mans winners were the Sauber-Mercedes team. The World Championship version of the V6-engined car, known as the XJR-11, made its debut at Brands Hatch at the end of July 1989. Jan Lammers and Patrick Tambay finished fifth, but a sister car retired as did the single XJR-9. A month later at the Nürburgring, the XJR-11s finished fifth and tenth. At Donington and Spa the Jaguars retired, and while two Jaguars finished fifth and sixth in the last championship race of the season, at Mexico City on 29 October, these were the old XJR-9 V12-engined cars. The new World Champions were the Sauber-Mercedes team which won seven out of the eight races in the calendar.

The American Jaguar team had been slightly more successful. The race at Portland on 30 July was surrounded by controversy and protest, but eventually Jan Lammers and Price Cobb in the Jaguar XJR-10 were declared winners. A less problematical victory fell to Price Cobb at Tampa two months later, but this time the car was the XJR-9. Only in the last race of the IMSA season at Del Mar on 22 October did Jan Lammers score an undisputed victory in the Jaguar XJR-10, but when the results were totted up, Jaguar was still in second place for the manufacturers' championship in the IMSA series.

Meanwhile, TWR and Jaguar had set up the jointly-owned Jaguar Sport operation which, in 1988, launched a 5.3 litre specially-modified version of the XJ-S — at first a limited edition to mark the Le Mans victory, later as a production model. In the 1988 Motor Show this was followed by a sporting version of the XJ6 saloon, the XJR 3.6, later superseded by the XJR 4.0. Initially these had unmodified power units, but in 1989

Jaguar Sport introduced a 6-litre version of the XJ-S, called the XJR-S. There was undoubtedly more to come from the workshops at Kidlington.

In other areas, the company had made excellent progress in the five years since independence. Behind the scenes in the factories, much investment had been made in improved production facilities aimed at increasing capacity and efficiency. The most visible development was the £50 million programme to create the new engineering and design centre at Whitley, on the south-eastern outskirts of Coventry. Originally the engineering and design centre for Chrysler UK, Whitley has been extensively remodelled and improved by Jaguar and was officially opened in 1988 by Lord Young, the Secretary of State for Trade and Industry at that time. By then parts of the centre had been operational for well over a year. Whitley is the British equivalent of Porsche's research centre at Weissach.

The dealer network at home and abroad has been reorganized. In Britain there are now little more than 100 Jaguar dealerships, an increasing number of which are solus dealers, handling only Jaguar products. In many export markets Jaguar have set up subsidiary companies or joint ventures to handle only the Jaguar range, following the established pattern from the USA. The net result is to create a total Jaguar corporate image around the world. There will be a perceivable quality of ambience in Jaguar show-

rooms, commensurate with the quality of the product which is on sale.

The company's relationship with suppliers has been enormously improved. Using a mixture of the stick and the carrot, Jaguar have converted their suppliers to the Jaguar ideals of quality. This has been of enormous benefit and has helped the company to overcome the image of unreliability which dogged Jaguar in the bad days of the 1970s. The role of the suppliers is, and will remain, crucial to the company. For instance, Jaguar buy in all of their gearboxes, both manual and automatic. But there are two major areas where a car manufacturer needs to be self-sufficient in order to preserve an independent identity. These are the manufacture of engines and of bodyshells. It is here that Jaguar have

*Above:*
The XJ-S V-12 Convertible.

*Left:*
The XJR 4.0.

concentrated efforts in the 1980s, with the new AJ6 engine production line at Radford, and the Castle Bromwich body plant. Further to this, Jaguar have now set up a joint venture with motor components giant GKN Sankey to establish a new body pressings plant near Telford in Shropshire. Appropriately called Venture Pressings Limited, it is expected that this plant will begin to supply Jaguar's needs in 1991.

But the Jaguar board were in a Catch-22 situation. The more they did to improve the business, the more tempting a target their company became for a take-over bid. Largely because of the weak US dollar and the still-depressed North American market, Jaguar's profits continued to decline. Indeed, it became questionable whether the company could afford the development of the range of new models that was necessary for the future. In May 1989, the chairman of Ford in the USA, Donald Petersen, for the first time made a public declaration of his company's interest in Jaguar, which immediately sent the Jaguar share price upwards. When the first half-year figures for 1989 were published in September, Jaguar's pre-tax profit had slumped to £1.4 million, and there was actually a loss of £1.1 million after tax.

Within a matter of days, Ford played its hand. It was formally announced that Ford intended to acquire a stake of 15 per cent in Jaguar, the maximum permitted until the expiry of the government's golden share at the end of 1990. Ford at this time also indicated that their future goal was a 100 per cent acquisition of Jaguar. This was precisely the situation which Jaguar had wished to avoid. It appeared to be the hostile take-over that Sir John Egan had feared, and the Jaguar board now began to explore various possibilities that might permit the company to remain independent, even if this involved co-operation with another car manufacturer. The favoured scheme appeared to involve a deal with General Motors, under which GM would take an agreed stake in the Jaguar business, at first 15 per cent, doubling this after the expiry of the golden share. GM would also be prepared to inject further capital into Jaguar to finance the new model programme.

As it now seemed that Jaguar's future was going to be decided in a ferocious battle between the two multi-national automotive giants, the share price spiralled almost out of sight. Throughout October negotiations continued, and the shares went up and up, easily exceeding their previous best value reached in 1987. On 31 October, the time-bomb under Jaguar was exploded prematurely by Nicholas Ridley, Secretary of State for Trade and Industry, who announced he was prepared to waive the golden share. This left Sir John Egan with virtually no alternatives. After intense and protracted negotiations, Sir John announced jointly with Lindsey Halstead, chairman of Ford of Europe, on 2 November, that the Jaguar board was recommending the Ford bid to shareholders. The agreed bid was for £8.50 per share, putting a total value on Jaguar of £1.6 billion. Those investors who had held out ever since privatization would have their investment returned five-fold.

An extraordinary general meeting of Jaguar was called for 1 December but it was virtually a foregone conclusion that the board would get the 75 per cent majority it needed to alter the Articles of Association to allow any one shareholder to hold more than a 15 per cent stake in the company. So ended the year 1989, as dramatic a year as any in the history of the Jaguar company. It was also almost the end of the independent British motor industry. As well as Jaguar, Ford had taken over Aston Martin and AC, while GM now had control of Lotus. British Aerospace had sold a 20 per cent stake in the Rover Group to their Japanese partner, Honda. Of the established British car makers, this left only the small companies of Rolls-Royce, Reliant, Morgan and Bristol.

Why did Ford buy Jaguar? Despite their runaway success in the family car market, and despite an enviable record in motor sport, Ford of Europe had failed to conquer the luxury end of the market (in much the same way that Ford's Lincoln had failed to topple GM's Cadillac in the USA). It has been predicted that there will be considerable growth in the luxury sector both in Europe and in the USA over the next decade. Ford's attempts at buying into other European specialist manufacturers — Rover, Alfa Romeo and Saab — had all failed. Jaguar was a plum that was ripe for picking. At least the government's withdrawal of the golden share a year early has meant that Jaguar's future has now been settled, and there will not be a possibly damaging fight for the company in 1991.

Ford have been quick to make assurances that they respect Jaguar's heritage, that the company's headquarters will remain in the Midlands, and that they expect to make substantial investment in Jaguar. Ford fully realize the value of Jaguar's prestige and heritage — this is exactly why they bought the company in the first place — so there is no reason to fear that the Jaguar name will be diluted by badge-engineering. As long as these parameters are respected, there is no doubt that, with Ford backing, Jaguar can really begin to go places. The only question mark left hanging in the air after the first announcement of the deal was that of Sir John Egan's future: he himself was quick to point out that he might not make a good subordinate!

It is almost certain that following the take-over, we shall see Jaguar develop a new, smaller saloon car – to take on the likes of the BMW 5-series and effectively fill the gap between the top-of-the-line Ford Scorpio and the XJ40. Plans for this modern successor to the Mark II had already been considered by Jaguar before the merger, but had been shelved, primarily because the company on its own could not afford the investment to develop the new car, and the new production facilities it would require. So the future range of Jaguars emerges – XJ40 in various forms, the coming F-type, the new smaller saloon which may be code-named XJ80, and the XJ-S or its successor. There is a possibility of a new Jaguar factory built on a green field site in the West Midlands. As far as

marketing and selling Jaguar cars was concerned, no change was proposed to existing arrangements – there would not be any showrooms shared between Jaguars and Fords.

Even the Jaguar motor sport programme could be expected to benefit from Ford ownership. Ford themselves are very much aware of the prestige which success in motor sport can bring to a car manufacturer – and of course, Ford cars have won at Le Mans a few times in the past! All in all, although one must register disappointment that Jaguar could not stay independent, there is no doubt that the future under new ownership could be a bright one. Whatever happens, there is little doubt that the company will remain one of the most interesting car manufacturers to watch, of equal interest to the car enthusiast and to the student of business. The past, present and future of the company are closely linked. There have been ups and downs in the history of Jaguar, but it is possible to sort out the tangled web and uncover the strong thread of tradition, running through from the beginning in 1921 until today, and on to the future.

*Left:*
The XJR-S 6.0.

# APPENDIX I
# TECHNICAL SPECIFICATIONS

Technical specifications for all SS, Jaguar and Jaguar-type Daimler production models from 1931 to 1989.

General note: Specifications are for home market standard models, unless otherwise indicated. Until approximately 1970, Jaguar quoted power and torque as gross figures, from then on net figures were quoted, and this applies to the following specifications; but for consistency, bhp and lb ft have been used throughout, rather than kW and Nm. Power and torque figures are quoted for standard compression ratio engines throughout.

### SS1, 16 or 20hp – production period: 1932–36 (model years)

**Engine configuration**: 6 cylinders in line, side valves.

**Engine details**: 16hp 1932–33: *Bore*: 65.5mm. *Stroke*: 101.6mm. *Capacity*: 2,054cc. *Compression ratio*: 1932: 5.8:1; 1933: 6.0:1. *Carburation*: 1932: 1 Solex; 1933: 1 RAG. *Bhp/rpm*: 1932: 45/3800; 1933: 48/3600. – 20hp 1932–33: *Bore*: 73mm. *Stroke*: 101.6mm. *Capacity*: 2,552cc. *Compression ratio*: As 16hp. *Carburation*: As 16hp. *Bhp/rpm*: 1932: 55/3800; 1933: 62/3600. – 16hp 1934–36: *Bore*: 65.5mm. *Stroke*: 106mm. *Capacity*: 2,143cc. *Compression ratio*: 1934: 6.2:1; 1935–36: 7.0:1. *Carburation*: 1934: 1 RAG; 1935–36: 2 RAG. *Bhp/rpm*: 1934: 53/3600; 1935–36: 62/4000. – 20hp 1934–36: *Bore*: 73mm. *Stroke*: 106mm. *Capacity*: 2,664cc. *Compression ratio*: As 16hp. *Carburation*: As 16hp. *Bhp/rpm*: 1934: 68/3600; 1935–36: 70/4000. *Transmission*: Single dry plate clutch, 4-speed gearbox (synchromesh from 1934), spiral bevel final drive.

**Chassis and body**: Separate chassis, coachbuilt bodies. *Body styles*: Coupé (1932–34) 2-door saloon (1934–36), tourer (1934–35), airline saloon (1935–36), drophead coupé (1935). *Suspension*: Semi-elliptic springs front and rear. *Steering*: Cam and lever. *Brakes*: Mechanical drum brakes with Bendix cable operation. *Wheels and tyres*: Centrelock wire wheels, tyre size 28×5.50 (1932), 5.50×18 (1933–36).

**Dimensions**: *Wheelbase*: 2,845mm (1932), 3,023mm (1933–36). *Track, front*: 1,245mm (1932), 1,295mm (1933), 1,346mm (1934–36). *Track, rear*: 1,245mm (1932), 1,295mm (1933), 1,359mm (1934–36). *Overall length*: 4,420mm (1932), 4,724mm (1933-36), *Overall width*: 1,524mm (1932), 1,613mm (1933), 1,664mm (1934–36). *Overall height*: 1,397mm. *Weight*: 1,081kg (1932), 1933–36 from 1,297kg to 1,386kg depending on body style.

### SS2, 9, 10 or 12hp – production period: 1932–36 (model years)

**Engine configuration**: 4 cylinders in line, side valves.

**Engine details**: 9hp 1932–33: *Bore*: 60.25mm. *Stroke*: 88mm. *Capacity*: 1,004cc. *Compression ratio*: 6:1. *Carburation*: 1 Stromberg. *Bhp/rpm*: 28/4,000. – 10hp 1934–36: *Bore*: 63.5mm. *Stroke*: 106mm. *Capacity*: 1,343cc. *Compression ratio*: 1934: 6:1; 1935–36: 7:1. *Carburation*: 1934: 1 RAG; 1935–36: 2 RAG. *Bhp/rpm*: 1934: 32/4,000; 1935–36: 34/4,000. – 12hp 1934–36: *Bore*: 69.5mm. *Stroke*: 106mm. *Capacity*: 1,608cc. *Compression ratio*: As 10hp. *Carburation*: As 10hp. *Bhp/rpm*: 1934: 38/4,000; 1935–36: 40/4,000. *Transmission*: Single dry plate clutch, 3-speed gearbox (1932 only) or 4-speed gearbox (1933–36; synchromesh from 1934), spiral bevel final drive.

**Chassis and body**: Separate chassis, coachbuilt bodies. *Body styles*: Coupé (1932–34), 2-door saloon (1934–36), tourer (1934–35). *Suspension*: Semi-elliptic springs front and rear. *Steering*: 1932–33: Worm and nut; 1934–36: Cam and lever. *Brakes*: Mechanical drum brakes with Bendix cable operation. *Wheels and tyres*: 1932–33: Bolt-on wire wheels, tyre size 27×4.75; 1934–36: Centrelock wire wheels, tyre size 4.75×18.

**Dimensions**: *Wheelbase*: 2,286mm (1932–33), 2,642mm (1934–36). *Track, front*: 1,124mm (1932–33), 1,181mm (1934–36). *Track, rear*: 1,124mm (1932–33), 1,181mm (1934–36). *Overall length*: 3,658mm (1932–33), 4,166mm (1934–36). *Overall width*: 1,372mm (1932–33), 1,422mm (1934–36). *Overall height*: 1,372mm. *Weight*: 788kg (1932–33); 1934–36 from 1,017kg to 1,030kg depending on body style.

### SS90 – production period: 1935 only

**Engine configuration**: 6 cylinders in line, side valves.

**Engine details**: *Bore*: 73mm. *Stroke*: 106mm. *Capacity*: 2,664cc. *Compression ratio*: 7:1. *Carburation*: 2 RAG. *Bhp/rpm*: 70/4,000. *Transmission*: Single dry plate clutch, 4-speed synchromesh gearbox, spiral bevel final drive.

**Chassis and body**: Separate chassis, coachbuilt body. *Body style*: Open two-seater. *Suspension*: Semi-elliptic springs front and rear. *Steering*: Cam and lever. *Brakes*: Mechanical drum brakes with Bendix cable operation. *Wheels and tyres*: Centrelock wire wheels, tyre size 5.50×18.

**Dimensions**: *Wheelbase*: 2,642mm. *Track, front*: 1,372mm. *Track, rear*: 1,372mm. *Overall length*: 3,810mm. *Overall width*: 1,600mm. *Overall height*: 1,372mm. *Weight*: 1,144kg.

### SS Jaguar or Jaguar 2½-litre – production period: 1936–40 (model years) and 1945–48

**Engine configuration**: 6 cylinders in line, pushrod operated overhead valves.

**Engine details**: *Bore*: 73mm. *Stroke*: 106mm. *Capacity*: 2,664cc. *Compression ratio*: 1936: 6.4:1; 1937: 6.8:1; 1938–40: 7.6:1; 1945–48: 6.9 or 7.6:1. *Carburation*: 2 SU. *Bhp/rpm*: 1936: 102/4,600; 1937: 104/4,500; 1938–48: 105/4,600. *Transmission*: Single dry plate clutch, 4-speed synchromesh gearbox, final drive by spiral bevel (1936–40) or hypoid bevel (1945–48).

**Chassis and body**: Separate chassis, coachbuilt or pressed steel bodies. *Body styles*: Coachbuilt saloon (1936–37), tourer (1936–37) all-steel saloon (1938–48), drophead coupé (1938–40 and 1947–48). *Suspension*: Semi-elliptic springs front and rear. *Steering*: Worm and nut. *Brakes*: Mechanical drum brakes with Girling rod operation. *Wheel and tyres*: Centrelock wire wheels, tyre size 5.50×18.

**Dimensions**: *Wheelbase*: 3,023mm (1936–37), 3,048mm (1938–48). *Track, front*: 1,372mm. *Track, rear*: 1,372mm (1936–37), 1,422mm (1938–48). *Overall length*: 4,521mm (1936–37), 4,724mm (1938–48). *Overall width*: 1,702mm (1936–37), 1,676mm (1938–48). *Overall height*: 1,549mm. *Weight*: 1936 saloon: 1,538kg; 1937 saloon: 1,602kg; tourer: 1,398kg; 1938–48 saloon: 1,627kg; drophead coupé: 1703kg.

### SS Jaguar 1½ litre – production period: 1936–37 (model years)

**Engine configuration**: 4 cylinders in line, side valves.

**Engine details**: *Bore*: 69.5mm. *Stroke*: 106mm. *Capacity*: 1608cc. *Compression ratio*: 6.1:1. *Carburation*: 1 Solex. *Bhp/rpm*: 52/4,300. *Transmission*: Single dry plate clutch, 4-speed gearbox, spiral bevel final drive.

**Chassis and body**: Separate chassis, coachbuilt body. *Body style*: Saloon. *Suspension*: Semi-elliptic springs front and rear. *Steering*: Worm and nut. *Brakes*: Mechanical drum brakes with Girling rod operation. *Wheels and tyres*: Centrelock wire wheels, tyre size 4.75×18.

**Dimensions**: *Wheelbase*: 2,743mm. *Track, front*: 1,219mm. *Track, rear*: 1,219mm. *Overall length*: 4,242mm. *Overall width*: 1,562mm. *Overall height*: 1,524mm. *Weight*: 1,068kg.

### SS Jaguar or Jaguar 1½ litre – production period: 1938–40 (model years) and 1945–49

**Engine configuration**: 4 cylinders in line, pushrod operated overhead valves.

**Engine details**: *Bore*: 78mm. *Stroke*: 106mm. *Capacity*: 1776cc. *Compression ratio*: 1938–39: 7.2:1; 1940: 7.6:1; 1945–49: 6.8 or 7.6:1. *Carburation*: 1 SU. *Bhp/rpm*. 65/4,600. *Transmission*: Single dry plate clutch, 4-speed synchromesh gearbox, final drive by spiral bevel (1938–39) or hypoid bevel (1940 and 1945–49).

**Chassis and body**: Separate chassis, pressed steel bodies. *Body styles*: Saloon; drophead coupé (1938–40 only). *Suspension*: Semi-elliptic springs front and rear. *Steering*: Worm and nut. *Brakes*: Mechanical drum brakes with Girling rod operation. *Wheels and tyres*: Centrelock wire wheels, tyre size 5.25×18.

Dimensions: *Wheelbase*: 2,858mm. *Track, front*: 1,321mm. *Track, rear*: 1,397mm. *Overall length*: 4,394mm. *Overall width*: 1,664mm. *Overall height*: 1,524mm. *Weight*: Saloon: 1,347kg; drophead coupé: 1,398kg.

### SS Jaguar 100 2½ litre or 3½ litre – production period: 1936–40 (3½ litre 1938–40) (model years)

**Engine configuration**: 6 cylinders in line, pushrod operated overhead valves.

**Engine details**: 2½ litre: *Bore*: 73mm. *Stroke*: 106mm. *Capacity*: 2,664cc. *Compression ratio*: 7:1. *Carburation*: 2 SU. *Bhp/rpm*: 102/4,600. – 3½ litre: *Bore*: 82mm. *Stroke*: 110mm. *Capacity*: 3,485cc. *Compression ratio*: 7:1. *Carburation*: 2 SU. *Bhp/rpm*: 125/4,250. *Transmission*: Single dry plate clutch, 4-speed synchromesh gearbox, final drive by spiral bevel.

**Chassis and body**: Separate chassis, coachbuilt body. *Body styles*: Open two-seater; fixed-head coupé (one-off for 1938 Motor Show). *Suspension*: Semi-elliptic springs front and rear. *Steering*: Worm and nut. *Brakes*: Mechanical drum brakes with Girling rod operation. *Wheels and tyres*: Centrelock wire wheels, tyre size 5.50×18.

**Dimensions**: *Wheelbase*: 2,642mm. *Track, front*: 1,372mm (2½ litre), 1,334mm (3½ litre). *Track, rear*: 1,372mm. *Overall length*: 3,810mm (2½ litre), 3,886mm (3½ litre). *Overall width*: 1,600mm. *Overall height*: 1,372mm. *Weight*: 1,170kg (2½ litre), 1,208kg (3½ litre).

### SS Jaguar or Jaguar 3½ litre – production period: 1938–40 (model years) and 1945–48

**Engine configuration**: 6 cylinders in line, pushrod operated overhead valves.

**Engine details**: *Bore*: 82mm. *Stroke*: 110mm. *Capacity*: 3,485cc. *Compression ratio*: 7.2:1; 1945–48 alternatively 6.6:1. *Carburation*: 2 SU. *Bhp/rpm*: 125/4,500. *Transmission*: Single dry plate clutch, 4-speed synchromesh gearbox, final drive by spiral bevel (1938–40) or hypoid bevel (1945–48).

**Chassis and body**: Separate chassis, pressed steel bodies. *Body styles*: Saloon; drophead coupé (1938–40 and 1947–48). *Suspension*: Semi-elliptic springs front and rear. *Steering*: Worm and nut. *Brakes*: Mechanical drum brakes with Girling rod operation. *Wheels and tyres*: Centrelock wire wheels, tyre size 5.50×18.

**Dimensions**: *Wheelbase*: 3,048mm. *Track, front*: 1,372mm. *Track, rear*: 1,422mm. *Overall length*: 4,724mm. *Overall width*: 1,676mm. *Overall height*: 1,549mm. *Weight*: Saloon: 1,665kg; drophead coupé: 1729kg.

### Jaguar Mark V 2½ litre and 3½ litre – production period: 1948–51

**Engine configuration**: 6 cylinders in line, pushrod operated overhead valves.

**Engine details**: 2½ litre: *Bore*: 73mm. *Stroke*: 106mm. *Capacity*: 2,664cc. *Compression ratio*: 7.3:1. *Carburation*: 2 SU. *Bhp/rpm*: 102/4,600. – 3½ litre: *Bore*: 82mm. *Stroke*: 110mm. *Capacity*: 3,485cc. *Compression ratio*: 6.75:1. *Carburation*: 2 SU. *Bhp/rpm*: 125/4,250. *Transmission*: Single dry plate clutch, 4-speed synchromesh gearbox, hypoid bevel final drive.

**Chassis and body**: Separate chassis, pressed steel bodies. *Body styles*: Saloon, drophead coupé. *Suspension*: Independent front suspension with torsion bars; semi-elliptic rear springs. *Steering*: Recirculating ball. *Brakes*: Girling hydraulic drum brakes. *Wheels and tyres*: Pressed steel disc wheels, tyre size 6.70×16.

**Dimensions**: *Wheelbase*: 3,048mm. *Track, front*: 1,422mm. *Track, rear*: 1,461mm. *Overall length*: 4,750mm. *Overall width*: 1,753mm. *Overall height*: 1,588mm. *Weight*: 2½ litre saloon: 1,653kg; 2½ litre drophead coupé: 1,729kg; 3½ litre saloon: 1,678kg; 3½ litre drophead coupé: 1,754kg.

### Jaguar XK120 – production period: 1948–54

**Engine configurations**: 6 cylinders in line, twin overhead camshafts.

**Engine details**: *Bore*: 83mm. *Stroke*: 106mm. *Capacity*: 3,442cc. *Compression ratio*: 8:1; 7 or 9:1 optional. *Carburation*: 2 SU. *Bhp/rpm*: 160/5,000; 180/5,300 on Special Equipment model. *Torque, lb ft/rpm*: 195/2,500; 203/4,000 on Special Equipment model. *Transmission*: Single dry plate clutch, 4-speed synchromesh gearbox, hypoid bevel final drive.

**Chassis and body**: Separate chassis, aluminium body on 1948–50 cars, steel body 1950–54. *Body styles*: Open two-seater 1948–54; fixed head coupé from 1951; drophead coupé from 1953. *Suspension*: Independent front suspension with torsion bars; semi-elliptic rear springs. *Steering*: Recirculating ball. *Brakes*: Lockheed hydraulic drum brakes. *Wheels and tyres*: Pressed steel disc wheels, centre-lock wire wheels optional from 1951, tyre size 6.00×16.

**Dimensions**: *Wheelbase*: 2,591mm. *Track, front*: 1,295mm. *Track, rear*: 1,270mm. *Overall length*: 4,420mm. *Overall width*: 1,574mm. *Overall height*: 1,332mm (open two-seater), 1,359mm (coupé models). *Weight*: Aluminium-bodied open two-seater: 1,297kg; steel-bodied open two-seater: 1,322kg; fixed-head coupé: 1,373kg; drophead coupé: 1,398kg.

### Jaguar Mark VII, Mark VIIM and Mark VIII – production period: 1950–54, 1954–57 and 1956–59

**Engine configurations**: 6 cylinders in line, twin overhead camshafts.

**Engine details**: *Bore*: 83mm. *Stroke*: 106mm. *Capacity*: 3,442cc. *Compression ratio*: 8:1; 7:1 optional, on Mark VIII 9:1 also optional. *Carburation*: 2 SU. *Bhp/rpm*: Mark VII: 160/5,200; Mark VIIM: 190/5,500; Mark VIII: 210/5,500. *Torque, lb ft/rpm*: Mark VII: 195/2,500; Mark VIIM: 203/3,000; Mark VIII: 216/3,000. *Transmission*: Single dry plate clutch, 4-speed synchromesh gearbox, hypoid bevel final drive. Automatic transmission optional from 1953, overdrive optional from 1954.

**Chassis and body**: Separate chassis, pressed steel body. *Body style*: Saloon. *Suspension*: Independent front suspension with torsion bars; semi-elliptic rear springs. *Steering*: Re-circulating ball. *Brakes*: Girling hydraulic drum brakes, with servo assistance. *Wheels and tyres*: Pressed steel disc wheels, tyre size 6.70×16.

**Dimensions**: *Wheelbase*: 3,048mm. *Track, front*: 1,422mm (1950–52); 1,435mm (1952–59). *Track, rear*: 1,461mm (1950–52); 1,473mm (1952–59). *Overall length*: 4,991mm. *Overall width*: 1,854mm. *Overall height*: 1,600mm. *Weight*: Mark VII: 1,754kg; Mark VIIM: 1,767kg; Mark VIII: 1,831kg (with automatic transmission).

### Jaguar C-type – production period: 1952–53

**Engine configuration**: 6 cylinders in line, twin overhead camshafts.

**Engine details**: *Bore*: 83mm. *Stroke*: 106mm. *Capacity*: 3,442cc. *Compression ratio*: 8:1. *Carburation*: 2 SU. *Bhp/rpm*: 200/5,800. *Torque, lb ft/rpm*: 220/3,900. *Transmission*: Single dry plate clutch, 4-speed synchromesh gearbox, hypoid bevel final drive.

**Chassis and body**: Tubular space frame, aluminium body. *Body style*: Open two-seater. *Suspension*: Independent front suspension with torsion bars; transverse torsion bars and trailing arms at rear. *Steering*: Rack and pinion. *Brakes*: Lockheed hydraulic drum brakes. *Wheels and tyres*: Centrelock wire wheels with light alloy rims, tyre size 6.00×16 (front) and 6.50×16 (rear).

**Dimensions**: *Wheelbase*: 2,438mm. *Track, front*: 1,295mm. *Track, rear*: 1,295mm. *Overall length*: 3,988mm. *Overall width*: 1,638mm. *Overall height*: 1,080mm. *Weight*: 1,017kg.

*Note*: Works racing cars first seen in 1951. Later works cars differed considerably in specification, having among other features triple Weber carburettors and Dunlop disc brakes.

### Jaguar D-type and XK-SS – production period: 1955–57

**Engine configuration**: 6 cylinders in line, twin overhead camshafts, dry-sump lubrication.

**Engine details**: *Bore*: 83mm. *Stroke*: 106mm. *Capacity*: 3,442cc. *Compression ratio*: 9:1. *Carburation*: 3 Weber. *Bhp/rpm*: 250/6,000. *Torque, lb ft/rpm*: 248/4,500. *Transmission*: Triple dry plate clutch, 4-speed all-synchromesh gearbox, hypoid bevel final drive.

**Chassis and body**: Aluminium monocoque with front subframe. *Body style*: Open two-seater; *Suspension*: Independent front suspension with torsion bars; transverse torsion bars and trailing arms at rear. *Steering*: Rack and pinion. *Brakes*: Dunlop disc brakes, with hydraulic servo assistance. *Wheels and tyres*: Centrelock light alloy/steel disc wheels, tyre size 6.50×16 or 6.50×17.

**Dimensions**: *Wheelbase*: 2,301mm. *Track, front*: 1,270mm. *Track, rear*: 1,219mm. *Overall length*: 3,912mm; XK-SS: 3,988mm. *Overall width*: 1,661mm. *Overall height*: 800mm (to scuttle), 1,118mm (to top of optional tail fin). *Weight*: 876kg; XK-SS: 915kg.

*Note*: Works racing cars were first seen in 1954. Some racing D-types had fuel injection; engine capacities for racing included 2.4 litres, 3.8 litres and 3.0 litres. All XK-SS cars were modified from existing D-types and had full road equipment (windscreen, hood, bumpers, luggage rack, etc).

### Jaguar XK 140 – production period: 1954–57

**Engine configuration**: 6 cylinders in line, twin overhead camshafts.

**Engine details**: *Bore*: 83mm. *Stroke*: 106mm. *Capacity*: 3,442cc. *Compression ratio*: 8:1; 7 or 9:1 optional. *Carburation*: 2 SU. *Bhp/rpm*: 190/5,500; 210/5,750 on Special Equipment model. *Torque, lb ft/rpm*: 210/2,500; 213/4,000 on Special Equipment model. *Transmission*: Single dry plate clutch, 4-speed synchromesh gearbox, hypoid bevel final drive. Overdrive optional; automatic transmission optional 1956–57.

**Chassis and body**: Separate chassis, pressed steel body. *Body styles*: Open two-seater, fixed-head coupé, drophead coupé. *Suspension*: Independent front suspension with torsion bars; semi-elliptic rear springs. *Steering*: Rack and pinion. *Brakes*: Lockheed hydraulic drum brakes. *Wheels and tyres*: Pressed steel disc wheels, centrelock wire wheels optional, tyre size 6.00×16.

**Dimensions**: *Wheelbase*: 2,591mm. *Track, front*: 1,308mm. *Track, rear*: 1,305mm. *Overall length*: 4,470mm. *Overall width*: 1,638mm. *Overall height*: 1,358mm. (open two-seater), 1,397mm (coupé models). *Weight*: Open two-seater: 1,345kg; fixed-head coupé: 1,425kg; drophead coupé: 1,475kg.

### Jaguar 2.4 litre and 3.4 litre – production period: 1955–59 and 1957–59

**Engine configuration**: 6 cylinders in line, twin overhead camshafts.

**Engine details**: 2.4 litre. *Bore*: 83mm. *Stroke*: 76.5mm. *Capacity*: 2,483cc. *Compression ratio*: 8:1; 7:1 optional. *Carburation*: 2 Solex. *Bhp/rpm*: 112/5,750. *Torque, lb ft/rpm*: 140/2,000. – 3.4 litre. *Bore*: 83mm. *Stroke*: 106mm. *Capacity*: 3,442cc. *Compression ratio*: 8:1; 7 or 9:1 optional. *Carburation*: 2 SU. *Bhp/rpm*: 210/5,500. *Torque, lb ft/rpm*: 216/3,000. *Transmission*: Single dry plate clutch, 4-speed synchromesh gearbox, hypoid bevel final drive. Overdrive optional, automatic transmission optional from 1957.

**Chassis and body**: Unitary construction. *Body style*: Saloon. *Suspension*: Independent front suspension with coil springs; cantilevered semi-elliptic rear springs. *Steering*: Recirculating ball. *Brakes*: Lockheed hydraulic drum brakes, with servo assistance; Dunlop disc brakes optional from 1957. *Wheels and tyres*: Pressed steel disc wheels, centrelock wire wheels optional, tyre size 6.40×15.

**Dimensions**: *Wheelbase*: 2,727mm. *Track, front*: 1,387mm. *Track, rear*: 1,273mm. *Overall length*: 4,591mm. *Overall width*: 1,695mm. *Overall height*: 1,461mm. *Weight*: 2.4 litre: 1,373kg; 3.4 litre: 1,449kg.

### Jaguar XK150 3.4 litre and 3.8 litre – production period: 1957–61

**Engine configuration**: 6 cylinders in line, twin overhead camshafts.

**Engine details**: 3.4 litre: *Bore*: 83mm. *Stroke*: 106mm. *Capacity*: 3,442cc. *Compression ratio*: 8:1; 7 or 9:1 optional; 9:1 standard on S model. *Carburation*: 2 SU; 3 SU on S model. *Bhp/rpm*: 190/5,500; 210/5,500 on Special Equipment model; 250/5,500 on S model. *Torque, lb ft/rpm*: 210/2,500; 216/3,000 on Special Equipment model; 240/4,500 on S model. – 3.8 litre: *Bore*: 87mm. *Stroke*: 106mm. *Capacity*: 3,781cc. *Compression ratio*: 9:1; 8:1 optional. *Carburation*: As 3.4 litre. *Bhp/rpm*: 220/5,500; 265/5,500 on S model. *Torque, lb ft/rpm*: 240/3,000; 260/4,000 on S model. *Transmission*: Single dry plate clutch, 4-speed synchromesh gearbox, hypoid bevel final drive, limited slip differential on S models. Overdrive optional, standard on S models. Automatic transmission optional, not on S models.

**Chassis and body**: Separate chassis, pressed steel body. *Body styles*: Fixed-head coupé (1957–60), drophead coupé (1957–60), open two-seater (1958–61). *Suspension*: Independent front suspension with torsion bars; semi-elliptic rear springs. *Steering*: Rack and pinion. *Brakes*: Lockheed hydraulic drum brakes (few cars, if any, built with these), or Dunlop disc brakes with servo assistance. *Wheels and tyres*: Centrelock wire wheels (a few cars had pressed steel disc wheels), tyre size 6.00×16.

**Dimensions**: *Wheelbase*: 2.591mm. *Track, front*: 1,302mm. *Track, rear*: 1,302mm. *Overall length*: 4,496mm. *Overall width*: 1,638mm. *Overall height*: 1,372mm (open two-seater), 1,397mm (coupé models). *Weight*: 1,434 to 1,500kg, depending on model.

*Note*: 3.4S model introduced in early 1959, 3.8 and 3.8S models in late 1959.

### Jaguar Mark IX – production period: 1958–61

**Engine configuration**: 6 cylinders in line, twin overhead camshafts.

**Engine details**: *Bore*: 87mm. *Stroke*: 106mm. *Capacity*: 3,781cc. *Compression ratio*: 8:1; 7:1 optional. *Carburation*: 2 SU. *Bhp/rpm*: 220/5,500. *Torque, lb ft/rpm*: 240/3,000. *Transmission*: Single dry plate clutch, 4-speed synchromesh gearbox, hypoid bevel final drive. Overdrive or automatic transmission optional.

**Chassis and body**: Separate chassis, pressed steel body. *Body style*: Saloon. *Suspension*: Independent front suspension with torsion bars, semi-elliptic rear springs. *Steering*: Recirculating ball, with power assistance. *Brakes*: Dunlop disc brakes, with servo assistance. *Wheels and tyres*: Pressed steel disc wheels, tyre size 6.70×16.

**Dimensions**: *Wheelbase*: 3,048mm. *Track, front*: 1,435mm. *Track, rear*: 1,473mm. *Overall length*: 4,991mm. *Overall width*: 1,854mm. *Overall height*: 1,600mm. *Weight*: 1,805kg.

### Jaguar Mark II 2.4 litre, 3.4 litre and 3.8 litre – production period: 1959–67

**Engine configuration**: 6 cylinders in line, twin overhead camshafts.

**Engine details**: 2.4 litre: *Bore*: 83mm. *Stroke*: 76.5mm. *Capacity*: 2,483cc. *Compression ratio*: 8:1; 7:1 optional. *Carburation*: 2 Solex. *Bhp/rpm*: 120/5,750. *Torque, lb ft/rpm*: 144/2,000. – 3.4 litre: *Bore*: 83mm. *Stroke*: 106mm. *Capacity*: 3,442cc. *Compression ratio*: As 2.4 litre but 9:1 also optional. *Carburation*: 2 SU. *Bhp/rpm*: 210/5,500. *Torque, lb ft/rpm*: 216/3,000. – 3.8 litre: *Bore*: 87mm. *Stroke*: 106mm. *Capacity*: 3,781cc. *Compression ratio*: As 3.4 litre. *Carburation*: As 3.4 litre. *Bhp/rpm*: 220/5,500. *Torque, lb ft/rpm*: 240/3,000. *Transmission*: Single dry plate clutch, 4-speed synchromesh gearbox (first gear synchronized from 1965), hypoid bevel final drive. Overdrive or automatic transmission optional.

**Chassis and body**: Unitary construction. *Body style*: Saloon. *Suspension*: Independent front suspension with coil springs; cantilevered semi-elliptic rear springs. *Steering*: Recirculating ball, power assistance optional. *Brakes*: Dunlop disc brakes, with servo assistance. *Wheels and tyres*: Pressed steel disc wheels, centrelock wire wheels optional, tyre size 6.40×15.

**Dimensions**: *Wheelbase*: 2,727mm. *Track, front*: 1,397mm. *Track, rear*: 1,356mm. *Overall length*: 4,591mm. *Overall width*: 1,695mm. *Overall height*: 1,467mm. *Weight*: 2.4 litre: 1,449kg; 3.4 litre: 1,500kg; 3.8 litre: 1,525kg.

**Jaguar E-type 3.8 litre Series 1 — production period: 1961—64**

**Engine configuration**: 6 cylinders in line, twin overhead camshafts.

**Engine details**: *Bore*: 87mm. *Stroke*: 106mm. *Capacity*: 3,781cc. *Compression ratio*: 9:1; 8:1 optional. *Carburation*: 3 SU. *Bhp/rpm*: 265/5,500. *Torque, lb ft/rpm*: 260/4,000. *Transmission*: Single dry plate clutch, 4-speed synchromesh gearbox, hypoid bevel final drive, limited slip differential.

**Chassis and body**: Steel monocoque with front subframe. *Body styles*: Open two-seater (hardtop optional), fixed-head coupé. *Suspension*: Independent, with torsion bars at front and coil springs at rear. *Steering*: Rack and pinion. *Brakes*: Dunlop disc brakes with dual hydraulic circuits and servo assistance. *Wheels and tyres*: Centrelock wire wheels, tyre size 6.40×15.

**Dimensions**: *Wheelbase*: 2,438mm. *Track, front*: 1,270mm, *Track, rear*: 1,270mm. *Overall length*: 4,458mm. *Overall width*: 1,657mm. *Overall height*: 1,194mm (open two-seater), 1,219mm (coupé). *Weight*: 1,220kg (open two-seater), 1,233kg (coupé).

**Jaguar Mark X 3.8 litre, Mark X 4.2 litre and 420 G — production period: 1961—64, 1964—66 and 1966—70**

**Engine configuration**: 6 cylinders in line, twin overhead camshafts.

**Engine details**: 3.8 litre: *Bore*: 87mm. *Stroke*: 106mm. *Capacity*: 3,781cc. *Compression ratio*: 8:1; 7 or 9:1 optional. *Carburation*: 3 SU. *Bhp/rpm*: 265/5,500. *Torque, lb ft/rpm*: 260/4,000. — 4.2 litre and 420G: *Bore*: 92mm. *Stroke*: 106mm. *Capacity*: 4,235cc. *Compression ratio*: As 3.8 litre. *Carburation*: 3 SU. *Bhp/rpm*: 265/5,400. *Torque, lb ft/rpm*: 283/4,000. *Transmission*: Single dry plate clutch, 4-speed synchromesh gearbox (first gear synchronized from 1964), hypoid bevel final drive. Overdrive or automatic transmission optional.

**Chassis and body**: Unitary construction. *Body styles*: Saloon, limousine. *Suspension*: Independent front and rear with coil springs. *Steering*: Recirculating ball with power assistance. *Brakes*: Dunlop disc brakes with dual hydraulic circuits and servo assistance. *Wheels and tyres*: Pressed steel disc wheels, tyre size 7.50×14 or 205—14.

**Dimensions**: *Wheelbase*: 3,048mm. *Track, front*: 1,473mm. *Track, rear*: 1,473mm. *Overall length*: 5,131mm. *Overall width*: 1,930mm. *Overall height*: 1,391mm. *Weight*: 1,894kg.

**Daimler 2½ litre V8 and V8-250 — production period: 1962—67 and 1967—69**

**Engine configuration**: 8 cylinders in 90 deg V, pushrod operated overhead valves.

**Engine details**: *Bore*: 76.2mm. *Stroke*: 69.85mm. *Capacity*: 2,548cc. *Compression ratio*: 8.2:1. *Carburation*: 2 SU. *Bhp/rpm*: 142/5,800. *Torque, lb ft/rpm*: 155/3,600. *Transmission*: Automatic transmission standard. Optional on V8-250: Single dry plate clutch, 4-speed all-synchromesh gearbox, overdrive optional. Hypoid bevel final drive.

**Chassis and body**: Unitary construction. *Body style*: Saloon. *Suspension*: Independent front suspension with coil springs; cantilevered semi-elliptic rear springs. *Steering*: Recirculating ball, power assistance optional. *Brakes*: Dunlop disc brakes with servo assistance. *Wheels and tyres*: Pressed steel disc wheels, tyre size 6.40×15 or 185—15.

**Dimensions**: *Wheelbase*: 2,727mm. *Track, front*: 1,397mm. *Track, rear*: 1,356mm. *Overall length*: 4,591mm. *Overall width*: 1,695mm. *Overall height*: 1,467mm. *Weight*: 1,424kg.

**Jaguar S-type 3.4 litre and 3.8 litre — production period: 1963—68**

**Engine configuration**: 6 cylinders in line, twin overhead camshafts.

**Engine details**: 3.4 litre: *Bore*: 83mm. *Stroke*: 106mm. *Capacity*: 3,442cc. *Compression ratio*: 8:1; 7 or 9:1 optional. *Carburation*: 2 SU. *Bhp/rpm*: 210/5,500. *Torque, lb ft/rpm*: 216/3,000. — 3.8 litre: *Bore*: 87mm. *Stroke*: 106mm. *Capacity*: 3,781cc. *Compression ratio*: As 3.4 litre. *Carburation*: 2 SU. *Bhp/rpm*: 220/5,500. *Torque, lb ft/rpm*: 240/3000. *Transmission*: Single dry plate clutch, 4-speed synchromesh gearbox (first gear synchronized from 1964), hypoid bevel final drive. Overdrive or automatic transmission optional.

**Chassis and body**: Unitary construction. *Body style*: Saloon. *Suspension*: Independent front and rear with coil springs. *Steering*: Recirculating ball, power assistance optional. *Brakes*: Dunlop disc brakes with dual hydraulic circuits and servo assistance. *Wheels and tyres*: Pressed steel disc wheels, centrelock wire wheels optional, tyre size 6.40×15 or 185—15.

**Dimensions**: *Wheelbase*: 2,731mm. *Track, front*: 1,403mm. *Track, rear*: 1,378mm. *Overall length*: 4,750mm. *Overall width*: 1,683mm. *Overall height*: 1,416mm. *Weight*: 3.4 litre: 1,627kg; 3.8 litre: 1,678kg.

**Jaguar E-type 4.2 litre Series 1 and Series 2 — production period: 1964—68 (two-plus-two from 1965) and 1968—70**

**Engine configuration**: 6 cylinders in line, twin overhead camshafts.

**Engine details**: *Bore*: 92mm. *Stroke*: 106mm. *Capacity*: 4,235cc. *Compression ratio*: 9:1; 8:1 optional. *Carburation*: 3 SU. *Bhp/rpm*: 265/5,400. *Torque, lb ft/rpm*: 283/4,000. *Transmission*: Single dry plate clutch, 4-speed all-synchromesh gearbox, hypoid bevel final drive, limited slip differential. Automatic transmission optional on two-plus-two model.

**Chassis and body**: Steel monocoque with front subframe. *Body styles*: Open two-seater (hardtop optional), fixed-head coupé, two-plus-two coupé. *Suspension*: Independent, with torsion bars at front and coil springs at rear. *Steering*: Rack and pinion, power assistance optional on Series 2. *Brakes*: Dunlop disc brakes with dual hydraulic circuits and servo assistance. *Wheels and tyres*: Centrelock wire wheels, tyre size 6.40×15 or 185—15.

**Dimensions**: Open two-seater and fixed-head coupé: *Wheelbase*: 2,438mm. *Track, front*: 1,270mm. *Track, rear*: 1,270mm. *Overall length*: 4,445mm. *Overall width*: 1,676mm (Series 2: 1,683mm). *Overall height*: 1,194mm (open two-seater), 1,226mm (fixed-head coupé). *Weight*: 1,246kg (open two-seater), 1,271kg (fixed-head coupé) — add approximately 25kg for Series 2 models. Two-plus-two coupé: *Wheelbase*: 2,667mm. *Track, front*: 1,276mm. *Track, rear*: 1,276mm. *Overall length*: 4,686mm. *Overall width*: 1,676mm (Series 2: 1,683mm). *Overall height*: 1,283mm. *Weight*: 1,398kg (Series 2: 1,436kg).

**Jaguar 420 and Daimler Sovereign — production period: 1966—68, Daimler 1966—69**

**Engine configuration**: 6 cylinders in line, twin overhead camshafts.

**Engine details**: *Bore*: 92mm. *Stroke*: 106mm. *Capacity*: 4,235cc. *Compression ratio*: 8:1; 7 or 9:1 optional. *Carburation*: 2 SU. *Bhp/rpm*: 245/5,500. *Torque, lb ft/rpm*: 283/3,750. *Transmission*: Single dry plate clutch, 4-speed all-synchromesh gearbox, hypoid bevel final drive. Overdrive or automatic transmission optional; overdrive standard on Daimler.

**Chassis and body**: Unitary construction *Body style*: Saloon. *Suspension*: Independent front and rear with coil springs. *Steering*: Recirculating ball, power assistance optional (standard on Daimler). *Brakes*: Girling disc brakes with dual hydraulic circuits and servo assistance. *Wheels and tyres*: Pressed steel disc wheels, centrelock wire wheels optional, tyre size 6.40×15 or 185—15.

**Dimensions**: *Wheelbase*: 2,737mm. *Track, front*: 1,410mm. *Track, rear*: 1,384mm. *Overall length*: 4,763mm. *Overall width*: 1,702mm. *Overall height*: 1,429mm. *Weight*: 1,678kg.

**Jaguar 240 and 340 – production period: 1967–69 and 1967–68**

**Engine configuration**: 6 cylinders in line, twin overhead camshafts.

**Engine details**: 240: *Bore*: 83mm. *Stroke*: 76.5mm. *Capacity*: 2,483cc. *Compression ratio*: 8:1; 7:1 optional. *Carburation*: 2 SU. *Bhp/rpm*: 133/5,500. *Torque, lb ft/rpm*: 146/3,700. – 340: *Bore*: 83mm. *Stroke*: 106mm. *Capacity*: 3,442cc. *Compression ratio*: As 240. *Carburation*: 2 SU. *Bhp/rpm*: 210/5,500. *Torque, lb ft/rpm*: 216/3,000 *Transmission*: Single dry plate clutch, 4-speed all-synchromesh gearbox, hypoid bevel final drive. Overdrive or automatic transmission optional.

**Chassis and body**: Unitary construction. *Body style*: Saloon. *Suspension*: Independent front suspension with coil springs; cantilevered semi-elliptic rear springs. *Steering*: Recirculating ball, power assistance optional (on 340 only). *Brakes*: Dunlop disc brakes with servo assistance. *Wheels and tyres*: Pressed steel disc wheels, tyre size 6.40×15 or 185–15.

**Dimensions**: *Wheelbase*: 2,727mm. *Track, front*: 1,397mm. *Track, rear*: 1,356mm. *Overall length*: 4,547mm. *Overall width*: 1,695mm. *Overall height*: 1,467mm. *Weight*: 240: 1,449kg; 340: 1,525kg.

---

**Daimler DS420 – production period: 1968 to date**

**Engine configuration**: 6 cylinders in line, twin overhead camshafts.

**Engine details**: *Bore*: 92mm. *Stroke*: 106mm. *Capacity*: 4,235cc. *Compression ratio*: 8:1; later models 7.5:1. *Carburation*: 2 SU. *Bhp/rpm*: 248/5,500; later models 164(net)/4,500. *Torque, lb ft/rpm*: 283/3,750; later models 222(net)/2,500. *Transmission*: Automatic transmission, hypoid bevel final drive, limited slip differential.

**Chassis and body**: Unitary construction. *Body styles*: 8/9 seater limousine; landaulette (from 1974; to special order only); available in 'chassis' form for specialist coachwork. *Suspension*: Independent front and rear with coil springs. *Steering*: Recirculating ball with power assistance. *Brakes*: Girling disc brakes, on later models ventilated at front, with dual hydraulic circuits and servo assistance. *Wheels and tyres*: Pressed steel disc wheels, tyre size 225–15, on later models 205/70 HR15 or 235/70HR-15.

**Dimensions**: *Wheelbase*: 3,581mm. *Track, front*: 1,473mm. *Track, rear*: 1,473mm. *Overall length*: 5,740mm. *Overall width*: 1,969mm. *Overall height*: 1,619mm. *Weight*: 2,174kg.

---

**Jaguar XJ6 and Daimler Sovereign Series 1, 2.8 and 4.2 litre – production period: 1968–73 (Daimler from 1969, lwb from 1972)**

**Engine configuration**: 6 cylinders in line, twin overhead camshafts.

**Engine details**: 2.8 litre. *Bore*: 83mm. *Stroke*: 86mm. *Capacity*: 2,791cc. *Compression ratio*: 9:1; 7 or 8:1 optional. *Carburation*: 2 SU. *Bhp/rpm*: 180/6,000. *Torque, lb ft/rpm*: 182/3,750. – 4.2 litre: *Bore*: 92mm. *Stroke*: 106mm. *Capacity*: 4,235cc. *Compression ratio*: As 2.8 litre. *Carburation*: 2 SU. *Bhp/rpm*: 245/5,500. *Torque, lb ft/rpm*: 283/3,750. *Transmission*: Single dry plate clutch, 4-speed all-synchromesh gearbox, hypoid bevel final drive. Overdrive optional on Jaguar, standard on Daimler. Automatic transmission optional.

**Chassis and body**: Unitary construction. *Body styles*: Saloon, long wheelbase saloon (4.2 litre only). *Suspension*: Independent front and rear with coil springs. *Steering*: Rack and pinion; power assistance optional on Jaguar 2.8 litre, standard on other models. *Brakes*: Girling disc brakes with dual hydraulic circuits and servo assistance. *Wheels and tyres*: Pressed steel disc wheels, tyre size E70VR-15 SP.

**Dimensions**: *Wheelbase*: 2,762mm; 2,864mm (lwb). *Track, front*: 1,473mm. *Track, rear*: 1,486mm. *Overall length*: 4,813mm; 4,947mm (lwb). *Overall width*: 1,759mm. *Overall height*: 1,372mm. *Weight*: 1,665kg (2.8 litre); 1,691kg (4.2 litre).

---

**Jaguar E-type V12 Series 3 – production period: 1971–75 (two-plus-two 1970–73)**

**Engine configuration**: 12 cylinders in 60 deg V, all-alloy construction, one overhead camshaft per bank.

**Engine details**: *Bore*: 90mm. *Stroke*: 70mm. *Capacity*: 5,343cc. *Compression ratio*: 9:1. *Carburation*: 4 Zenith-Stromberg. *Bhp/rpm*: 272/5,850. *Torque, lb ft/rpm*: 304/3,600. *Transmission*: Single dry plate clutch, 4-speed all-synchromesh gearbox, hypoid bevel final drive, limited slip differential. Automatic transmission optional.

**Chassis and body**: Steel monocoque with front sub-frame. *Body styles*: Open two-seater (hard top optional), two-plus-two coupé. *Suspension*: Independent, with torsion bars at front and coil springs at rear. *Steering*: Rack and pinion, power assistance optional. *Brakes*: Girling disc brakes, ventilated at front, with dual hydraulic circuits and servo assistance. *Wheels and tyres*: Pressed steel disc wheels, centrelock wire wheels optional, tyre size E70VR-15.

**Dimensions**: *Wheelbase*: 2,667mm. *Track, front*: 1,384mm. *Track, rear*: 1,346mm. *Overall length*: 4,674mm. *Overall width*: 1,683mm. *Overall height*: 1,245mm (open two-seater), 1,295mm (coupé). *Weight*: 1,462kg (open two-seater), 1,500kg (coupé).

---

**Jaguar XJ12 and Daimler Double-Six Series 1 – production period: 1972–73**

**Engine configuration**: 12 cylinders in 60 deg V, all-alloy construction, one overhead camshaft per bank.

**Engine details**: *Bore*: 90mm. *Stroke*: 70mm. *Capacity*: 5,343cc. *Compression ratio*: 9:1; 8:1 optional. *Carburation*: 4 Zenith-Stromberg. *Bhp/rpm*: 253/6,000. *Torque, lb ft/rpm*: 302/3,500. *Transmission*: Automatic transmission, hypoid bevel final drive, limited slip differential.

**Chassis and body**: Unitary construction. *Body styles*: Saloon, long wheelbase saloon (Jaguar), Vanden Plas saloon (Daimler). *Suspension*: Independent front and rear with coil springs. *Steering*: Rack and pinion, with power assistance. *Brakes*: Girling disc brakes, ventilated at front, with dual hydraulic circuits and servo assistance. *Wheels and tyres*: Pressed steel disc wheels, tyre size E70VR-15 SP.

**Dimensions**: *Wheelbase*: 2,762mm; 2,864mm (lwb and VdP). *Track, front*: 1,473mm. *Track, rear*: 1,486mm. *Overall length*: 4,813mm; 4,947mm (lwb and VdP), *Overall width*: 1,759mm. *Overall height*: 1,372mm. *Weight*: 1,780kg.

---

**Jaguar XJ6 and Daimler Sovereign Series 2, 3.4 and 4.2 litre – production period: 1973–79 (3.4 litre from 1975, Daimler 3.4 litre to 1978 only)**

**Engine configuration**: 6 cylinders in line, twin overhead camshafts.

**Engine details**: 3.4 litre: *Bore*: 83mm. *Stroke*: 106mm. *Capacity*: 3,442cc. *Compression ratio*: 8.8:1. *Carburation*: 2 SU. *Bhp/rpm*: 163/5,000. *Torque, lb ft/rpm*: 188/3,500. – 4.2-litre: *Bore*: 92mm. *Stroke*: 106mm. *Capacity*: 4,235cc. *Compression ratio*: 8.5:1; 7.8:1 optional. *Carburation*: 2 SU; on US specification cars, replaced by electronic fuel injection in 1978. *Bhp/rpm*: 183/4,500. *Torque, lb ft/rpm*: 230/3,000. *Transmission*: Single dry plate clutch. To 1978, 4-speed all-synchromesh gearbox with optional overdrive (overdrive standard on Daimler). 1978–79, 5-speed all-synchromesh gearbox, overdrive discontinued. Hypoid bevel final drive. Automatic transmission optional.

**Chassis and body**: Unitary construction. *Body styles*: Saloon, Vanden Plas saloon (Daimler 4.2 litre only, from 1975), coupé (not 3.4 litre; 1975–78 only). *Suspension*: Independent front and rear with coil springs. *Steering*: Rack and pinion with power assistance. *Brakes*: Girling disc brakes, ventilated at front, with dual hydraulic circuits and servo assistance. *Wheels and tyres*: Pressed steel disc wheels, cast alloy wheels optional from 1977, tyre size E70VR-15.

**Dimensions**: *Wheelbase*: 2,864mm (saloon), 2,762mm (coupé). *Track, front*: 1,473mm. *Track, rear*: 1,486mm. *Overall length*: 4,947mm (saloon), 4,813mm (coupé). *Overall width*: 1,759mm. *Overall height*: 1,372mm. *Weight*: 1,730kg (saloon), 1,691kg (coupé).

*Note*: A short wheelbase saloon, and a Jaguar 2.8 litre engined export-only model were made in 1973–74.

### Jaguar XJ12 and Daimler Double-Six Series 2 – production period: 1973–79

**Engine configuration**: 12 cylinders in 60 deg V, all-alloy construction, one overhead camshaft per bank.

**Engine details**: *Bore*: 90mm. *Stroke*: 70mm. *Capacity*: 5,343cc. *Compression ratio*: 9:1. *Carburation*: 4 Zenith-Stromberg; replaced by electronic fuel injection in 1975. *Bhp/rpm*: 253/6,000 (carburettor model), 285/5,750 (fuel injection model). *Torque, lb ft/rpm*: 302/3,500 (carb model), 294/3,500 (f.i. model). *Transmission*: Automatic transmission; GM 400 gearbox replaced Borg-Warner gearbox in 1977. Hypoid bevel final drive, limited slip differential.

**Chassis and body**: Unitary construction. *Body styles*: Saloon, Vanden Plas saloon (Daimler only), coupé (1975–78 only). *Suspension*: Independent front and rear with coil springs. *Steering*: Rack and pinion with power assistance. *Brakes*: Girling disc brakes, ventilated at front, with dual hydraulic circuits and servo assistance. *Wheels and tyres*: Pressed steel disc wheels, cast alloy wheels optional from 1975, tyre size 205/70VR-15 SP.

**Dimensions**: *Wheelbase*: 2,864mm (saloon), 2,762mm (coupé). *Track, front*: 1,473mm. *Track, rear*: 1,486mm. *Overall length*: 4,947mm (saloon), 4,813mm (coupé). *Overall width*: 1,759mm. *Overall height*: 1,372mm. *Weight*: 1,820kg (saloon), 1,785kg (coupé).

---

### Jaguar XJ-S and XJ-S HE – production period: 1975–81 and 1981 to date

**Engine configuration**: 12 cylinders in 60 deg V, all-alloy construction, one overhead camshaft per bank.

**Engine details**: *Bore*: 90mm. *Stroke*: 70mm. *Capacity*: 5,343cc. *Compression ratio*: 9:1; HE model: 12.5:1. *Fuel system*: Electronic fuel injection. *Bhp/rpm*: 285/5,500; HE model: 295/5,500. *Torque, lb ft/rpm*: 294/3,500; HE model 320/3,250. *Transmission*: Automatic transmission, torque converter and 3-speed gearbox; Borg-Warner to 1977, GM 400 from 1977. Manual option to 1979: Single dry plate clutch and 4-speed all-synchromesh gearbox. Hypoid bevel final drive, limited slip differential.

**Chassis and body**: Unitary construction. *Body styles*: Two-plus-two coupé, two-seater cabriolet (1985–1988), convertible from 1988. *Suspension*: Independent front and rear with coil springs. *Steering*: Rack and pinion with power assistance. *Brakes*: Girling disc brakes, ventilated at front, with dual hydraulic circuits and servo assistance. – Anti-lock braking on later models. *Wheels and tyres*: Cast alloy wheels, 6K×15, 6.5J×15 on HE; tyre size: 205/70VR-15, 215/70VR-15 on HE.

**Dimensions**: *Wheelbase*: 2,591mm. *Track, front*: 1,473mm: HE: 1,488mm. *Track, rear*: 1,486mm; HE: 1,504mm. *Overall length*: 4,864mm; HE: 4,765mm. *Overall width*: 1,793mm. *Overall height*: 1,262mm. *Weight*: 1,683kg; HE: 1,755kg; convertible: 1,902kg.

---

### Jaguar XJ6/Sovereign and Daimler Sovereign/4.2 Series 3, 3.4 and 4.2 litre – production period: 1979 to 1987

**Engine configuration**: 6 cylinders in line, twin overhead camshafts.

**Engine details**: 3.4 litre (Jaguar only): *Bore*: 83mm. *Stroke*: 106mm. *Capacity*: 3,442cc. *Compression ratio*: 8.4:1. *Carburation*: 2 SU. *Bhp/rpm*: 162/5,250. *Torque, lb ft/rpm*: 188/3,500. – 4.2 litre: *Bore*: 92mm. *Stroke*: 106mm. *Capacity*: 4,235cc. *Compression ratio*: 8.7:1. *Fuel system*: Electronic fuel injection. *Bhp/rpm*: 205/5,000. *Torque, lb ft/rpm*: 231/3,500. *Transmission*: Single dry plate clutch and 5-speed all-synchromesh gearbox; or automatic transmission, torque converter and 3-speed Borg-Warner or GM gearbox. Hypoid bevel final drive.

**Chassis and body**: Unitary construction. *Body styles*: Saloon, Vanden Plas saloon (Daimler, to 1983 only). *Suspension*: Independent front and rear with coil springs. *Steering*: Rack and pinion with power assistance. *Brakes*: Girling disc brakes, ventilated at front, with dual hydraulic circuits and servo assistance. *Wheels and tyres*: Pressed steel disc wheels, cast alloy wheels optional (standard on Jaguar Sovereign and Daimler 4.2), tyre size 205/70VR-15.

**Dimensions**: *Wheelbase*: 2,864mm. *Track, front*: 1,473mm. *Track, rear*: 1,486mm. *Overall length*: 4,958mm. *Overall width*: 1,771mm. *Overall height*: 1,372mm. *Weight*: 1,767kg (3.4 litre), 1,800kg (4.2 litre), 1,832kg (Sovereign).

*Note*: A Jaguar 4.2 litre Vanden Plas saloon was made for export from 1981.

---

### Jaguar XJ12/HE/Sovereign HE/V12 and Daimler Double-Six/HE Series 3 – production period: 1979 to date (HE models: From 1981)

**Engine configurations**: 12 cylinders in 60 deg V, all-alloy construction, one overhead camshaft per bank.

**Engine details**: *Bore*: 90mm. *Stroke*: 70mm. *Capacity*: 5,343cc. *Compression ratio*: 9:1; HE model: 12.5:1. *Fuel system*: Electronic fuel injection. *Bhp/rpm*: 289/5,750; HE model: 295/5,500. *Torque, lb ft/rpm*: 294/3,500; HE model: 320/3,250. *Transmission*: Automatic transmission, torque converter and GM 400 3-speed gearbox. Hypoid bevel final drive, limited slip differential.

**Chassis and body**: Unitary construction. *Body styles*: Saloon, Vanden Plas saloon (Daimler, to 1983 only). *Suspension*: Independent front and rear with coil springs. *Steering*: Rack and pinion with power assistance. *Brakes*: Girling disc brakes, ventilated at front, with dual hydraulic circuits and servo assistance. *Wheels and tyres*: Pressed steel disc, cast alloy optional (standard on Jaguar from 1981 and Daimler from 1983), tyre size 205/70VR-15; 215/70VR-15 on HE models.

**Dimensions**: *Wheelbase*: 2,865mm. *Track, front*: 1,481mm. *Track, rear*: 1,496mm. *Overall length*: 4,958mm. *Overall width*: 1,770mm. *Overall height*: 1,372mm. *Weight*: 1,932kg.

*Note*: A Jaguar Vanden Plas saloon was made for export from 1981.

---

### Jaguar XJ-S 3.6 – production period: 1983 to date

**Engine configuration**: 6 cylinders in line, inclined at 15 deg, all-alloy construction, two overhead camshafts, four valves per cylinder.

**Engine details**: *Bore*: 91mm. *Stroke*: 92mm. *Capacity*: 3,590cc. *Compression ratio*: 9.6:1. *Fuel system*: Electronic fuel injection. *Bhp/rpm*: 221/5,000. *Torque, lb ft/rpm*: 249/4,000. *Transmission*: Single dry plate clutch, 5-speed all-synchromesh Getrag gearbox, hypoid bevel final drive, limited slip differential. Automatic transmission optional from 1987, 4-speed ZF gearbox.

**Chassis and body**: Unitary construction. *Body styles*: Two-plus-two coupé, two-seater cabriolet (to 1987). *Suspension*: Independent front and rear with coil springs. *Steering*: Rack and pinion with power assistance. *Brakes*: Girling disc brakes, ventilated at front, with dual hydraulic circuits and servo assistance. Anti-lock braking system on later models. *Wheels and tyres*: Cast alloy wheels, 6JK×15 on early coupé, 6.5J×15 on cabriolet and later coupé models. Tyre size 215/70VR-15 or 235/60VR-15.

**Dimensions**: *Wheelbase*: 2,591mm. *Track, front*: 1,480 or 1,488mm. *Track, rear*: 1,495 or 1,504mm (depending on wheel size). *Overall length*: 4,765mm. *Overall width*: 1,793mm. *Overall height*: 1,262mm. *Weight*: 1,660kg.

---

### Jaguar XJ40 XJ6, Sovereign and Daimler 3.6 – production period: 1986 to date

**Engine configuration**: 6 cylinders in line, inclined at 15 deg, all-alloy construction, one overhead camshaft and two valves per cylinder (2.9 litre), or two overhead camshafts and four valves per cylinder (3.6 litre).

**Engine details**: 2.9 litre: *Bore*: 91mm. *Stroke*: 74.8mm. *Capacity*: 2,919cc. *Compression ratio*: 12.6:1. *Fuel system*: Bosch electronic fuel injection. *Bhp/rpm*: 165/5,000. *Torque, lb ft/rpm*: 176/4,000. – 3.6 litre: *Bore*: 91mm. *Stroke*: 92mm. *Capacity*: 3,590cc. *Compression ratio*: 9.6:1. *Fuel system*: Lucas electronic fuel injection. *Bhp/rpm*: 221/5,000. *Torque, lb ft/rpm*: 249/4,000. *Transmission*: Single dry plate clutch, 5-speed all-synchromesh Getrag gearbox, hypoid bevel final drive, limited slip differential optional on Jaguar models, standard on Daimler. Alternatively 4-speed automatic ZF gearbox (standard on Sovereign and Daimler models).

**Chassis and body**: Unitary construction. *Body style*: Saloon. *Suspension*: Independent front and rear with coil springs. Ride levelling standard on Daimler, optional on other models. *Steering*: Rack and pinion with power assistance. *Brakes*: Girling disc brakes, ventilated at front, with dual hydraulic circuits and power assistance. Anti-lock braking standard on Sovereign and Daimler, optional on XJ6. *Wheels and tyres*: Steel wheels standard on XJ6, cast alloy wheels standard on Sovereign and Daimler, optional on XJ6. Dunlop-Michelin TD wheel system, wheel size 390×180mm TD, tyre size 220/65VR-390 TD.

**Dimensions**: *Wheelbase*: 2,870mm. *Track, front*: 1,500mm. *Track, rear*: 1,498mm. *Overall length*: 4,988mm. *Overall width*: 2,005mm. *Overall height*: 1,380mm (XJ6), 1,358mm (Sovereign and Daimler). *Weight*: 1,720kg (2.9 litre models), 1,770kg (3.6 litre models).

*Note*: In the USA, two models are sold, Jaguar XJ6 and Jaguar Vanden Plas. They are equipped to levels comparable to the Sovereign and Daimler models respectively. Both have the 3.6 litre engine, to a slightly different specification, and are offered with automatic transmission only.

# APPENDIX II
# PRODUCTION FIGURES

The tables which follow contain what it is hoped are the most comprehensive and detailed production figures which have yet been compiled and published. They give details of all SS, SS Jaguar, Jaguar and Jaguar-built Daimlers from 1931 to the end of 1988.

The figures have been compiled using Jaguar's own records. From 1 August 1951, approximately when production began in the present-day factory at Browns Lane, Jaguar's production control department compiled weekly statistics of cars produced, and these records form the basis of the figures from 1951 to 1988. Until 1967, annual figures were compiled on 1 August, and from 1968 to 1976 on 1 October, as these dates marked the start of the new financial year. From 1977, Jaguar's financial year has followed the calendar year. For ease of reference, all post-World War Two figures have been re-calculated so that in the following tables all figures from 1945 onwards are given by calendar year. The pre-war figures by contrast are compiled by 'model year' which typically means the 12-month period from 1 August in one year, to 31 July in the following year.

For the period from 1931 to 1 August 1951, the production figures have been based on the known chassis number sequences used for the different models, but with constant reference to the actual production records which are happily preserved all the way back to 1931. However the 'caveat' must be added that, as far as the SS1, SS2 and SS90 models are concerned, Jaguar's records are not in chassis number order. Indeed, the SS2 models of 1931–33 did not even have their own chassis number series as they used what is believed to be the numbers of the Standard 'Little Nine' chassis on which they were based. Figures for these models may therefore be slightly inaccurate. Ideally, the SS1 and SS2 records should be subject to more intensive research which might also yield separate figures for the different styles of bodywork which are absent from the tables that follow.

Inevitably some cars have not been included – typically cars which were not built as part of the normal production run, or were not given ordinary chassis numbers. Prototypes are therefore excluded; except the XJ40 prototypes and pre-production cars of 1983–86 which are included. All known C-types and D-types – which were given straight-forward chassis numbers, even if many of them were not 'production cars' – have been included. Incidentally, for those who argue that there were only 53 C-types, the 54th is XKC-054, thought to be the experimental so-called C/D type of 1953. And of the 87 D-types, 16 were converted to XK-SS specification.

As far as it is possible to be certain, all export cars supplied in CKD or SKD form (Completely Knocked Down, or Semi-Knocked Down) for assembly abroad have been included. Most Jaguar saloon models, from the Mark VII to the XJ Series 2 (until 1979), were exported in this form, perhaps the best known example being the XJ6 4.2 litre Series 2 'Executive' assembled in South Africa in the 1970s. Cars supplied in chassis form only, whether pre-war or post-war, have been included and are usually counted as part of the 'saloon' figures or in whichever series they belong by virtue of their chassis numbers. In case of the Daimler Majestic Major they are counted together with the limousines. The only exception to the rule is the present-day Daimler DS 420 where 'chassis only' figures are available for the entire production run and have been quoted separately.

A few models have not been listed separately. The most glaring omission is the absence of a breakdown between the various XK150 models, ie 3.4 litre, 3.4 litre 'S', 3.8 litre and 3.8 litre 'S'. However to get such figures accurately would involve counting the 9,385 XK150s separately . . . Nor do the various 'Special Equipment' models feature separately. Such versions were made of the 1½ litre (1937–49), of the various XK models, and of the 2.4-litre saloon (1955–59) – in the case of the latter far outnumbering the standard model. The Mark X and 420G limousines are included in the saloon figures. It should be pointed out that none of these sub-variants had its own chassis number series. No distinction has been made between the E-type Series 1 4.2 litre and the so-called 'Series 1½' model of 1967–68, and in later years the HE-engined V12 models (XJ12, XJ-S and Daimler Double-Six from 1981 onwards) have been counted with their predecessors.

Pre-war, SS and Jaguar cars were only available with right-hand drive, but from 1945 onwards most models were offered with left-hand drive as well. It would be possible to give RHD/LHD breakdowns but only until 1978 when Jaguar's classic chassis numbering system was replaced by the VIN (Vehicle Identification Number) system, but I have felt it less important to provide such figures. I also feel it is of relatively little interest to provide breakdown figures between models with different transmission systems (manual, manual with overdrive, and automatic) which in any case it would be almost impossible to compile for all models.

As far as Daimler are concerned, although Jaguar only took over this company in 1960, figures have been quoted from the start of production of the SP-250 model in 1959, but other pre-Jaguar Daimlers – notably the 3.8 litre six-cylinder Majestic which was discontinued in 1960 – have been excluded.

Strangely enough, one of the worst headaches has been to assess the proportions of Jaguar versus Daimler in the company's 1983 statistics which (perhaps uncritically!) lump all 'Sovereign' models together, this being the year when this model name passed from Daimler to Jaguar. In the same year a similar problem exists in trying to sort out the Daimler Vanden Plas models (which were being phased out) from the ordinary Daimlers. It should perhaps be pointed out that the Jaguar Vanden Plas models from 1981 onwards were for export only, primarily to the USA, or in the case of the XJ12 Vanden Plas, to Canada. In 1986 and 1987, some Daimler models were counted by Jaguar together with the North American Vanden Plas cars (XJ6 and XJ12 models) so the splits quoted in the following tables are approximate, as are the overall figures for each of the models concerned, but the individual annual totals are not affected.

Armed with a pocket calculator (a most necessary implement for the motoring historian!) the reader may find amusement by working out the total production figure of Jaguar and associated marques which will be found to stand at almost 954,000 cars to the end of 1988. At the current rate of production it may therefore be estimated that Jaguar's millionth car will roll off the assembly line towards the end of 1989. Doubtless this will be occasion for some celebration at Browns Lane . . .

My thanks are due to Ian Luckett and Richard Chillingsworth of Jaguar Cars Limited who gave me the run of their records, patiently put up with my research for days on end and diligently answered my queries on the most obscure minutiae. It may be added that in this day and age it is heartening to find a motor car manufacturer which still believes in keeping *proper* records: every Jaguar car is recorded with a hand-written entry in a large leather-bound ledger, giving the full production history and specification of the car, in much the same way that they began doing it in 1931!

*Right:*
The AJ6 engine.

| SS and SS Jaguar 1931–1940 | 1931–32 | 1932–33 | 1933–34 | 1934–35 | 1935–36 | 1936–37 | 1937–38 | 1938–39 | 1939–40 | Total per model |
|---|---|---|---|---|---|---|---|---|---|---|
| SS 1 (various bodies) | 502 | 1,250 | 1,166 | 1,164 | 146 | | | | | 4,228 |
| SS 2 (various bodies) | 275 | 276 | 625 | 537 | 88 | | | | | 1,801 |
| SS 90 (o2s) | | | | 23 | 1 | | | | | 24 |
| SS Jaguar (1½-l. sal. sv) | | | | | 700 | 1,494 | 56 | | | 2,250 |
| SS Jaguar (2½-l. sal. cb) | | | | | 1,448 | 1,996 | | | | 3,444 |
| SS Jaguar (2½-l. tourer) | | | | | 53 | 52 | | | | 105 |
| SS Jaguar 100 (2½-l. o2s) | | | | | 31 | 95 | 50 | 14 | 1 | 191 |
| SS Jaguar 100 (3½-l. o2s) | | | | | | | 82 | 35 | 1 | 118 |
| SS Jaguar (1½-l. sal. ohv) | | | | | | | 602 | 3,152 | 654 | 4,408 |
| SS Jaguar (1½-l. dhc) | | | | | | | 78 | 565 | 34 | 677 |
| SS Jaguar (2½-l. sal. as) | | | | | | | 669 | 781 | 129 | 1,579 |
| SS Jaguar (2½-l. dhc) | | | | | | | 93 | 180 | 6 | 279 |
| SS Jaguar (3½-l. sal) | | | | | | | 545 | 457 | 65 | 1,067 |
| SS Jaguar (3½-l. dhc) | | | | | | | 102 | 136 | 3 | 241 |
| Total SS/SS Jaguar per year | 777 | 1,526 | 1,791 | 1,724 | 2,467 | 3,637 | 2,277 | 5,320 | 893 | Grand total for 1931–1940 20,412 |

| Jaguar 1945–1954 | 1945 | 1946 | 1947 | 1948 | 1949 | 1950 | 1951 | 1952 | 1953 | 1954 | Total per model |
|---|---|---|---|---|---|---|---|---|---|---|---|
| 1½-litre (sal) | 141 | 1,765 | 2,151 | 1,670 | 34 | | | | | | 5,761 |
| 2½-litre (sal) | | 426 | 604 | 679 | 40 | | | | | | 1,749 |
| 3½-litre (sal) | | 737 | 1,591 | 1,295 | 237 | | | | | | 3,860 |
| 2½-litre (dhc) | | | | 101 | | | | | | | 101 |
| 3½-litre (dhc) | | | | 498 | | | | | | | 498 |
| Mark V (2½l. sal) | | | | | 760 | 906 | 5 | | | | 1,671 |
| Mark V (3½l. sal) | | | | 7 | 3,013 | 4,077 | 731 | | | | 7,828 |
| Mark V (2½l. dhc.) | | | | | 29 | | | | | | 29 |
| Mark V (3½l. dhc) | | | | 1 | 9 | 667 | 294 | | | | 971 |
| XK120 (o2s) | | | | | 97 | 1,519 | 1,114 | 1,658 | 1,260 | 1,966 | 7,614 |
| XK120 (fhc) | | | | | | | 212 | 1,318 | 868 | 282 | 2,680 |
| XK120 (dhc) | | | | | | | | 1 | 1,251 | 515 | 1,767 |
| C-type | | | | | | | 3 | 25 | 26 | | 54 |
| Mark VII (sal) | | | | | | 8 | 4,137 | 5,966 | 6,694 | 4,132 | 20,937 |
| Mark VII M (sal) | | | | | | | | | | 2,322 | (see next table) |
| D-type | | | | | | | | | | 6 | (see next table) |
| XK140 (o2s) | | | | | | | | | | 575 | (see next table) |
| XK140 (fhc) | | | | | | | | | | 4 | (see next table) |
| XK140 (dhc) | | | | | | | | | | 92 | (see next table) |
| Total Jaguar per year | 141 | 2,928 | 4,346 | 4,251 | 4,190 | 7,206 | 6,496 | 8,968 | 10,099 | 9,894 | |

| Jaguar 1955–1964 Daimler 1959–1964 | 1955 | 1956 | 1957 | 1958 | 1959 | 1960 | 1961 | 1962 | 1963 | 1964 | Total per model |
|---|---|---|---|---|---|---|---|---|---|---|---|
| Mark VII M (sal) | 6,087 | 1,598 | 53 | | | | | | | | **10,060** |
| D-type/XK-SS | 34 | 27 | 4/16 | | | | | | | | **87** |
| XK140 (o2s) | 1,451 | 1,130 | 191 | | | | | | | | **3,347** |
| XK140 (fhc) | 1,809 | 961 | 24 | | | | | | | | **2,798** |
| XK140 (dhc) | 1,455 | 1,199 | 44 | | | | | | | | **2,790** |
| 2.4-litre (sal.) | 32 | 8,029 | 3,984 | 4,441 | 3,219 | | | | | | **19,705** |
| 3.4-litre (sal.) | | | 4,536 | 7,164 | 5,580 | | | | | | **17,280** |
| Mark VIII (sal.) | | 261 | 3,600 | 2,324 | 62 | | | | | | **6,247** |
| Mark IX (sal) | | | | 928 | 4,915 | 3,555 | 603 | 1 | | | **10,002** |
| XK150 (o2s) | | | | 1,916 | 260 | 86 | 2 | | | | **2,264** |
| XK150 (fhc) | | | 1,053 | 1,633 | 1,070 | 692 | | | | | **4,448** |
| XK150 (dhc) | | | 171 | 1,050 | 871 | 581 | | | | | **2,673** |
| E-type 3.8 (o2s) | | | | | | | 1,729 | 2,726 | 2,023 | 1,340 | **7,818** |
| E-type 3.8 (fhc) | | | | | | | 453 | 3,540 | 2,042 | 1,628 | **7,663** |
| Mark X (3.8-l. sal) | | | | | | | 4 | 4,312 | 6,572 | 2,073 | **12,961** |
| Mark II (2.4-l. sal) | | | | | 1,119 | 6,717 | 6,459 | 3,358 | 2,857 | 1,904 | (see next table) |
| Mark II (3.4-l. sal) | | | | | 748 | 5,284 | 6,050 | 4,660 | 4,155 | 3,539 | (see next table) |
| Mark II (3.8-l. sal) | | | | | 665 | 5,534 | 8,727 | 4,725 | 3,241 | 2,631 | (see next table) |
| S-type (3.4-l. sal) | | | | | | | | | 1 | 2,169 | (see next table) |
| S-type (3.8-l. sal) | | | | | | | | | 42 | 4,863 | (see next table) |
| Mark X (4.2-l. sal) | | | | | | | | | | 385 | (see next table) |
| E-type 4.2 (o2s) | | | | | | | | | | 461 | (see next table) |
| E-type 4.2 (fhc) | | | | | | | | | | 513 | (see next table) |
| **Total Jaguar per year** | 10,868 | 13,205 | 13,676 | 19,456 | 18,509 | 22,449 | 24,027 | 23,322 | 20,933 | 21,506 | |
| Daimler SP-250 | | | | | 110 | 893 | 730 | 564 | 229 | 128 | **2,654** |
| Majestic Major (sal) | | | | | | 8 | 429 | 116 | 179 | 142 | (see next table) |
| Majestic Major (lim) | | | | | | 2 | 38 | 171 | 138 | 117 | (see next table) |
| 2½-litre V-8 (sal) | | | | | | | | 8 | 2,444 | 3,969 | (see next table) |
| **Total Daimler per year** | | | | | 110 | 903 | 1,197 | 859 | 2,990 | 4,356 | |
| **Jaguar/Daimler yearly totals** | | | | | 18,619 | 23,352 | 25,224 | 24,181 | 23,923 | 25,862 | |

| Jaguar 1965–1974 | 1965 | 1966 | 1967 | 1968 | 1969 | 1970 | 1971 | 1972 | 1973 | 1974 | Total per model |
|---|---|---|---|---|---|---|---|---|---|---|---|
| Mark II (2.4-l. sal) | 1,355 | 1,592 | 961 | | | | | | | | **26,322** |
| Mark II (3.4-l. sal) | 2,091 | 1,454 | 1,550 | | | | | | | | **29,531** |
| Mark II (3.8-l. sal) | 1,401 | 689 | 235 | | | | | | | | **27,848** |
| S-type (3.4-l. sal) | 3,825 | 2,575 | 646 | 712 | | | | | | | **9,928** |
| S-type (3.8-l. sal) | 5,916 | 3,685 | 362 | 197 | | | | | | | **15,065** |
| Mark X (4.2-l. sal) | 3,296 | 1,991 | | | | | | | | | **5,672** |
| E-type 4.2 (o2s) | 2,237 | 2,349 | 2,500 | 2,004 | | | | | | | **9,551** |
| E-type 4.2 (fhc) | 3,056 | 1,904 | 1,205 | 1,093 | | | | | | | **7,771** |
| E-type 4.2 (2 + 2) | 1 | 2,627 | 1,284 | 1,674 | | | | | | | **5,586** |
| 420 (sal) | | 1,350 | 5,512 | 3,374 | | | | | | | **10,236** |
| 420G (sal) | | 32 | 1,640 | 1,653 | 1,617 | 600 | | | | | **5,542** |
| 240 (sal) | | | 911 | 2,827 | 692 | | | | | | **4,430** |
| 340 (sal) | | | 1,005 | 1,799 | | | | | | | **2,804** |
| E-type S.2 (o2s) | | | | 984 | 4,287 | 3,370 | | | | | **8,641** |
| E-type S.2 (fhc) | | | | 615 | 2,397 | 1,866 | | | | | **4,878** |
| E-type S.2 (2 + 2) | | | | 702 | 3,264 | 1,363 | | | | | **5,329** |
| XJ6 S.1 (2.8 sal. swb) | | | | 143 | 5,372 | 6,242 | 4,450 | 2,308 | 807 | | **19,322** |
| XJ6 S.1 (4.2 sal. swb) | | | | 496 | 7,800 | 11,876 | 18,173 | 12,432 | 8,300 | | **59,077** |
| XJ6 S.1 (4.2 sal. lwb) | | | | | | | | 232 | 642 | | **874** |
| E-type S.3 (V-12. o2s) | | | | | | | 340 | 1,718 | 3,165 | 2,759 | **7,982** |
| E-type S.3 (V-12. 2 + 2) | | | | | | 87 | 3,406 | 2,296 | 1,521 | | **7,310** |
| XJ12 S.1 (sal. swb) | | | | | | | | 669 | 1,805 | | **2,474** |
| XJ12 S.1 (sal. lwb) | | | | | | | | 254 | 500 | | **754** |
| XJ6 S.2 (2.8 sal. swb) | | | | | | | | | 3 | 167 | **170** |
| XJ6 S.2 (4.2 sal. swb) | | | | | | | | | 5,521 | 6,626 | **12,147** |
| XJ6 S.2 (4.2 sal. lwb) | | | | | | | | | 370 | 14,012 | (see next table) |
| XJ6 S.2 (4.2 coupé) | | | | | | | | | 2 | 1 | (see next table) |
| XJ12 S.2 (sal. lwb) | | | | | | | | | 985 | 5,479 | (see next table) |
| XJ12 S.2 (coupé) | | | | | | | | | | 11 | (see next table) |
| **Total Jaguar per year** | 23,178 | 20,248 | 17,811 | 18,273 | 25,429 | 25,404 | 26,369 | 19,909 | 23,621 | 29,055 | |

| Daimler 1965–1974 | 1965 | 1966 | 1967 | 1968 | 1969 | 1970 | 1971 | 1972 | 1973 | 1974 | Total per model |
|---|---|---|---|---|---|---|---|---|---|---|---|
| Majestic Major (sal) | 153 | 81 | 62 | 14 | | | | | | | **1,184** |
| Majestic Major (lim) | 144 | 131 | 108 | 18 | | | | | | | **867** |
| 2½-litre V8 (sal) | 3,430 | 2,200 | 967 | | | | | | | | **13,018** |
| Sovereign (sal) | | 422 | 2,210 | 2,151 | 1,041 | | | | | | **5,824** |
| V8-250 (sal) | | | 803 | 2,871 | 1,223 | | | | | | **4,897** |
| DS420 (lim) | | | | 18 | 291 | 428 | 236 | 244 | 263 | 243 | (see next table) |
| DS420 (chassis) | | | | 6 | 33 | 61 | 50 | 43 | 31 | 46 | (see next table) |
| Sovereign S1 (2.8 sal. swb) | | | | | 208 | 1,383 | 806 | 621 | 215 | | **3,233** |
| Sovereign S1 (4.2 sal. swb) | | | | | 389 | 2,332 | 4,088 | 3,390 | 1,323 | | **11,522** |
| Sovereign S1 (4.2 sal. lwb) | | | | | | | | | 386 | | **386** |
| Double-Six S1 (sal. swb) | | | | | | | | 237 | 297 | | **534** |
| Double-Six S1 (sal. VdP) | | | | | | | | 97 | 254 | | **351** |
| Sovereign S2 (4.2 sal. swb) | | | | | | | | | 1,027 | 1,408 | **2,435** |
| Sovereign S2 (4.2 sal. lwb) | | | | | | | | | 156 | 3,357 | (see next table) |
| Double-Six S2 (sal. lwb) | | | | | | | | | 120 | 1,111 | (see next table) |
| Double-Six S2 (sal. VdP) | | | | | | | | | 200 | 661 | (see next table) |
| Double-Six S2 (coupé) | | | | | | | | | | 1 | (see next table) |
| **Total Daimler per year** | **3,727** | **2,834** | **4,150** | **5,078** | **3,185** | **4,204** | **5,180** | **4,632** | **4,272** | **6,827** | |
| **Total Jaguar per year** | **23,178** | **20,248** | **17,811** | **18,273** | **25,429** | **25,404** | **26,369** | **19,909** | **23,621** | **29,055** | |
| **Grand total: Jaguar and Daimler per year** | **26,905** | **23,082** | **21,961** | **23,351** | **28,614** | **29,608** | **31,549** | **24,541** | **27,893** | **35,882** | |

| Jaguar and Daimler 1975–1981 | 1975 | 1976 | 1977 | 1978 | 1979 | 1980 | 1981 | Total per model |
|---|---|---|---|---|---|---|---|---|
| XJ6 S2 (4.2 sal. lwb) | 8,597 | 10,125 | 9,241 | 14,684 | 775 | | | **57,804** |
| XJ6 S2 (4.2 coupé) | 2,925 | 1,746 | 1,776 | 37 | | | | **6,487** |
| XJ12 S2 (sal. lwb) | 1,303 | 2,737 | 1,904 | 3,337 | 265 | | | **16,010** |
| XJ12 S2 (coupé) | 821 | 663 | 329 | 31 | | | | **1,855** |
| XJ6 S2 (3.4 sal. lwb) | 2,570 | 1,660 | 1,569 | 1,072 | 9 | | | **6,880** |
| XJ-S (V-12 coupé) | 1,245 | 3,082 | 3,890 | 3,121 | 2,405 | 1,057 | 1,292 | (see next table) |
| XJ6 S3 (3.4 sal) | | | | 1 | 625 | 553 | 892 | (see next table) |
| XJ6 S3 (4.2 sal) | | | | 7 | 5,864 | 9,026 | 9,447 | (see next table) |
| XJ6 S3 (4.2 sal. VdP) | | | | | | | 120 | (see next table) |
| XJ12 S3 (sal) | | | | 6 | 970 | 789 | 462 | (see next table) |
| XJ12 S3 (sal. VdP) | | | | | | | 12 | (see next table) |
| **Total Jaguar per year** | **17,461** | **20,013** | **18,709** | **22,296** | **10,913** | **11,425** | **12,225** | |
| Daimler DS 420 (lim) | 235 | 145 | 123 | 139 | 129 | 103 | 169 | (see next table) |
| DS 420 (chassis) | 64 | 40 | 51 | 48 | 44 | 40 | 22 | (see next table) |
| Sovereign S2 (3.4 sal. lwb) | 892 | 707 | 728 | 14 | | | | **2,341** |
| Sovereign S2 (4.2 sal. lwb) | 2,044 | 2,320 | 2,467 | 3,971 | 216 | | | **14,531** |
| Sovereign S2 (4.2 sal. VdP) | 199 | 319 | 219 | 146 | | | | **883** |
| Sovereign S2 (4.2 coupé) | 471 | 587 | 613 | 6 | | | | **1,677** |
| Double-Six S2 (sal. lwb) | 129 | 287 | 230 | 688 | 43 | | | **2,608** |
| Double-Six S2 (sal. VdP) | 181 | 192 | 208 | 274 | 10 | | | **1,726** |
| Double-Six S2 (coupé) | 76 | 149 | 159 | 22 | | | | **407** |
| Sovereign S3 (4.2 sal) | | | | | 2,347 | 2,444 | 1,214 | (see next table) |
| Sovereign S3 (4.2 sal. VdP) | | | | | 43 | 240 | 77 | (see next table) |
| Double-Six S3 (sal) | | | | | 513 | 349 | 227 | (see next table) |
| Double-Six S.3 (sal. VdP) | | | | 1 | 25 | 261 | 171 | (see next table) |
| **Total Daimler per year** | **4,291** | **4,746** | **4,798** | **5,309** | **3,370** | **3,437** | **1,880** | |
| **Grand total: Jaguar and Daimler per year** | **21,752** | **24,759** | **23,507** | **27,605** | **14,283** | **14,862** | **14,105** | |

| Jaguar and Daimler 1982–1988 | 1982 | 1983 | 1984 | 1985 | 1986 | 1987 | 1988 | Total per model (to end of 1988) |
|---|---|---|---|---|---|---|---|---|
| XJ-S (3.6 coupé) | 18 | 131 | 539 | 810 | 645 | 1,260 | 2,021 | **5,424** |
| XJ-S (3.6 cabr) | 5 | 22 | 256 | 459 | 201 | 207 | | **1,150** |
| XJ-S (V-12 coupé) | 3,455 | 4,402 | 5,814 | 6,040 | 6,703 | 6,791 | 4,974 | **54,271** |
| XJ-S (V-12 cabr) | | | | 4 | 690 | 1,455 | 1,581 | 132 | **3,862** |
| XJ-S (V-12 conv) | | | | | | 59 | 2,803 | **2,862** |
| XJ6 S3 (3.4 sal) | 824 | 826 | 860 | 778 | 408 | | | **5,767** |
| XJ6 S3 (4.2 sal) | 12,199 | 14,231 | 13,594 | 14,625 | 15,541 | 3,031 | | **97,565** |
| XJ6 S3 (4.2 sal. VdP) | 1,438 | 2,639 | 4,092 | 4,490 | 5,491* | 567 | | **18,837** |
| Sovereign (4.2 sal) | | 971* | 5,047 | 6,821 | 4,057 | 159 | | **17,055** |
| XJ12 S3 (sal) | 424 | 210 | | | | | | **2,861** |
| XJ12 S3 (sal. VdP) | 76 | 159 | 254 | 364 | 624* | 613* | 451 | **2,553** |
| Sovereign (V-12 sal) | | 421* | 1,489 | 1,695 | 1,443 | 596 | 794 | **6,438** |
| XJ6 (2.9 sal) | | 16 | 37 | 42 | 640 | 2,620 | 3,019 | **6,374** |
| Sovereign (2.9 sal) | | | 1 | 3 | 430 | 823 | 834 | **2,091** |
| XJ6 (3.6 sal) | | 8 | 19 | 26 | 715 | 2,228 | 3,986 | **6,982** |
| Sovereign (3.6 sal) | | | 4 | 13 | 1,439 | 18,782 | 20,331 | **40,569** |
| Vanden Plas (3.6 sal) | | | | | | 3,881* | 5,767 | **9,648** |
| **Total Jaguar per year** | **18,439** | **24,036** | **32,010** | **36,856** | **39,792** | **43,198** | **45,112** | |
| Daimler DS 420 (lim) | 102 | 141 | 143 | 168 | 131 | 145 | 121 | **3,717** |
| DS 420 (chassis) | 16 | 25 | 25 | 45 | 41 | 39 | 32 | **802** |
| Sovereign S3 (4.2 sal) | 2,502 | 2,142* | 486 | 546 | 149* | | | **11,830** |
| Sovereign S3 (4.2 sal. VdP) | 188 | 150* | | | | | | **698** |
| Double-Six S3 (sal) | 581 | 911* | 770 | 853 | 768* | 472* | 911 | **6,355** |
| Double-Six S3 (sal. VdP) | 334 | 367* | | | | | | **1,159** |
| Daimler (3.6 sal) | | 14 | 20 | 40 | 379 | 4,108* | 4772 | **9,333** |
| **Total Daimler per year** | **3,723** | **3,750** | **1,444** | **1,652** | **1,468** | **4,764** | **5,836** | |
| **Grand total: Jaguar and Daimler per year** | **22,162** | **27,786** | **33,454** | **38,508** | **41,260** | **47,962** | **50,948** | |

Note: These figures are approximate. It is difficult to distinguish between Daimler Sovereign and Jaguar Sovereign, and between Daimler and Daimler Vanden Plas Models, in Jaguar's production statistic for 1983. Similarly, in 1986 and 1987 it is difficult to distinguish between the North American export only Jaguar Vanden Plas models, and the Daimler-badged models to similar specifications for the rest of the world. The relevant model totals are also affected, but the annual totals quoted above should be correct.

# INDEX